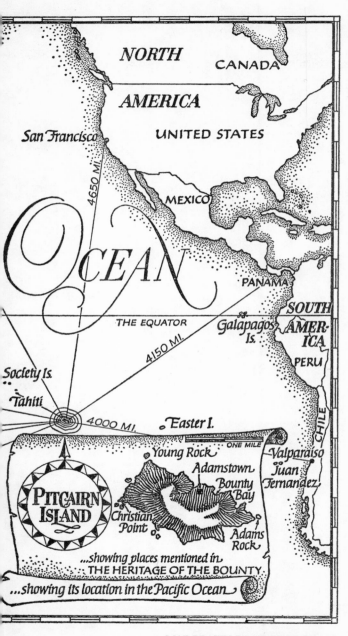

PITCAIRN ISLAND

...showing places mentioned in
THE HERITAGE OF THE BOUNTY

...showing its location in the Pacific Ocean

MAP DRAWN BY STEPHEN KRAFT

THE PITCAIRN ISLANDERS

HARRY L. SHAPIRO

[Formerly *The Heritage of the Bounty*]

REVISED WITH A NEW POSTSCRIPT

ILLUSTRATED WITH PHOTOGRAPHS

A CLARION BOOK
PUBLISHED BY SIMON AND SCHUSTER

A Clarion Book
Published by Simon and Schuster
Rockefeller Center, 630 Fifth Avenue
New York, New York 10020
All rights reserved
including the right of reproduction
in whole or in part in any form
Copyright © 1936, 1962 by Harry L. Shapiro

First Clarion printing 1968

Manufactured in the United States of America
Printed by Murray Printing Company, Forge Village, Mass.
Bound by Electronic Perfect Binders, Inc., Brooklyn, N.Y.

ACKNOWLEDGMENTS

Chiefly I am indebted to Mr. Templeton Crocker not only for my visit to Pitcairn but also for his invaluable aid in recording island documents.

To all the Pitcairn Islanders I owe my best thanks for their patience and coöperation. It would be impossible, where everyone was so uniformly kind, to distinguish one above another.

To Mr. Cooze I am obliged for many hours of tedious clerical assistance.

To my colleagues, Dr. James Chapin, Mr. Lee Jaques, and Dr. George Lyman, I am grateful for many kindnesses.

TABLE OF CONTENTS

VI. POSTSCRIPT

EPISTLE DEDICATORY

[*To Professor E. A. Hooton*]

DEAR EARNEST:

This book on the Pitcairn Islanders has every right to claim you as its godfather. Because it all started, you may remember, one winter morning back in 1922 in the classroom on the second floor of the Peabody Museum. On that occasion you happened to relate the story of Pitcairn Island. I don't know how many times you had told that yarn before, or have told it since, but for me it was marvelously new and exciting.

I had been lolling on one of those hard, wooden benches gnawed with the graffiti of generations of anonymous Harvard undergraduates; my attention was about equally divided between the intricate pattern of bare winter branches against the warm, red brick of the Agassiz and the tedious business of recording in grotesque, lecture-note English your erudite remarks on race mixture. If I remember correctly, the Rehobother Bastards had been occupying our attention for the past several lectures. We had, following your lead, delved into the genetics of those Hottentot-Boer hybrids, drab offspring of dull unions. Then with all the magic of the movies the scene shifted, and we were in the warm, vibrant Pacific, on the Cytherean shores of Tahiti, amidst the turmoil of a mutiny on board the *Bounty* and stranded on a forgotten speck of land called Pitcairn, where human folly was succeeded by inhuman virtue.

That unique narrative of an eighteenth-century bread-fruit expedition resolving itself into mutiny, court-martial, hanging, crime, murder, and, finally, a new population of mixed bloods made a glorious text, and no one realized it better than you.

The traceries of the old trees were forgotten, and my notebook still shows a lacuna for that day. Who could dream of arboreal designs, and what memory needed jogging for such events? I distinctly recall that you paused, after the narrative, and commented that you would rather go to Pitcairn than anywhere else in the world. I was impressed. But you were, to use an inelegant analogy, like a hen who, on finding a particularly juicy morsel, was calling on her little chicks to come and get it. I was one of those chicks and, with the selfishness of the very young, grabbed at it while you complacently looked on, quietly pleased. After all, what could have made a more absorbing subject for research than the heredity of the hybrid Anglo-Polynesian children of the *Bounty?*

When the arrangements to go to Pitcairn were finally made possible in the following spring by a Bishop Museum Fellowship from Yale, I was scarcely more elated than you, and when I started out on my journey in July, 1923, your benediction made the task seem lighter. You know most of what happened on that trip: the negotiations for a means of reaching inaccessible Pitcairn, the voyage to Panama where the best I could do was to take passage on the ill-fated *Paparoa* (she was later burned at sea) on the chance that she might break the long, slow voyage to New Zealand by a brief call at Pitcairn. But I don't know whether I ever told you that the captain, a tough, old, red-faced Englishman, refused point-blank to drop me at the island. I didn't have the proper papers. His reason was that since Pitcairn was not an official point of call, he had no authority to discharge passengers there, and under the circumstances would have to present a full passenger list at his destination in

Auckland. Nor have I ever revealed that in desperation I had plotted to jump ship when we reached the island. One of the passengers was in my confidence and ready to aid my plans. The day before we were due to arrive at Pitcairn I secretly packed, and we hoped that I and my belongings might be surreptitiously lowered into one of the island boats and taken ashore without the captain's knowledge. I hadn't come all those thousands of miles to be cheated of my goal when it was almost within my grasp.

Then fate or "something" intervened. Just before we were scheduled to sight Pitcairn, a brief but severe tropical storm descended on us. The sun vanished behind clouds as thick and gloomy as any Ryder ever painted, the glass fell alarmingly, and the aged joints of the *Paparoa* began to groan. The captain, fearful of the dangers of approaching Pitcairn in a storm, altered his course, and I passed the island without even a glimpse of what I had come to see.

A couple of weeks later I found myself at Auckland, New Zealand, facing a choice. I could return to Panama and try again to reach Pitcairn (at that time only outward-bound ships, I was informed, ever stopped there). Or I could go on to Norfolk Island, where the larger part of the descendants of the mutineers of the *Bounty* now live. The lack of time and money, principally the latter, forced me to choose Norfolk. From Sydney, Australia, I made the six-day trip in a small Burns-Philp steamer to Norfolk where I remained about five months gathering material for a study of the descendants of the mutineers of the *Bounty* and their Tahitian wives.

The kindliness of the Norfolk Islanders, their hospitality, their affection indeed gratified me, beset as I was with the weighty responsibilities of my first independent piece of research. But they were not Pitcairn Islanders. And my desire to visit Pitcairn, though thwarted, did not die. It certainly received little encouragement. After each of my successive trips to Polynesia, I sighed regretfully that I was still unable to voyage to that isolated rock in the middle of the south Pacific. Pitcairn seemed like an unrealizable dream.

When, therefore, Templeton Crocker invited me in the spring of 1934 to join his expedition to the eastern Pacific for the American Museum of Natural History, I was naturally delighted to accept. And when he generously asked me where I wished in particular to go, I promptly answered Pitcairn.

We left San Francisco September 13, 1934, on board the *Zaca*, veteran of a world cruise and a number of scientific voyages. This time I was duly armed with official documents from the High Commissioner of the Western Pacific, in whose jurisdiction Pitcairn lies. I was informed that it was necessary to receive the unanimous consent of the islanders before anyone could land on Pitcairn. Since we encountered no opposition to our sojourn I assume that we had been thoroughly approved of before our arrival.

The *Zaca*, as you have seen from her photographs, is a handsome, two-masted gaff-rigged schooner built on the lines of a Newfoundland Bank fisherman. She is 118 feet long over all, is 96 feet at the water line, and has a 23-foot beam and a draft of 14 feet. The gross tonnage is 84. Power is furnished by two Diesel engines of about 120 H.P. each. She is beautifully equipped and very comfortable.

The first leg of our itinerary landed us, after twenty-one perfect days such as only the Pacific can provide, in the Marquesas. From these islands we proceeded to the brimming coral atolls called the Tuamotus, to Tahiti, to the Austral Islands, to Rapa famous for its Polynesian Amazons, to Mangareva, once the scene of an amazing hierarchy, and then to Pitcairn which we reached December 23, 1934. That day was the one hundred and forty-seventh anniversary of the sailing of the *Bounty* from Spithead, England. For ten days the *Zaca* lay off the rocky coast of Pitcairn while I lived ashore. The story of that visit and the account of my researches are contained in the following pages which are, as I started by saying in the beginning, dedicated to you. Rarely is a duty so felicitously contained in a pleasure or a debt so blessed to a debtor as mine are to you.

Affectionately,

H.L.S.

New York City
October, 1935

I. PERSONAL

1

MY FIRST DAY ON PITCAIRN

It was curious not feeling elated, not even feeling a trace of exaltation. Yet here, at last, was Pitcairn, the island where a part of the mutinous crew of H.M.S. *Bounty* sought refuge and found death. The fabulous island which had nurtured the children of these mutineers and their children's children. It was, at first, a mere smudge, scarcely more perceptible than a cloud on the horizon, too mirage-like to be the goal at the end of 9000 miles, the attainment of a passionate desire nursed for twelve years. As I contemplated this shadow of an island I wondered at my strange anesthesia where there should have been a wild, leaping excitement. I supposed, now that the moment I had anticipated so long was here, that the increasing tension of the past three months had created its own antidote, that my reactions, like those of an over-trained athlete, had gone stale. Besides, I was really terrified that I might be disappointed. The numerous books I had read, the many pictures I had created from this reading, had shaped in my mind a Pitcairn that I couldn't bear to have altered by the inexorable impact of reality. But there it was at last before me, ready for me, with unguessed impressions and experiences to be added to my store.

As I watched the dim gray shadow my solid resistance melted in proportion as Pitcairn slowly thickened into a deeper gray, then to purple and green, and a more natural excitement succeeded my lethargy.

That silhouette, remembered from ancient woodcuts, inky plates, and blurred photographs, was familiar. But, despite its familiarity, it had a character that no representation had ever conveyed. It was chunky, solid, and massive as I had anticipated. But from a distance its cliffs did not appear as impregnable as the Gibraltar I had imagined. Later I was to discover that I was mistaken. From the angle of our approach it looked like an inverted canoe, and strangely un-Polynesian. To me a Polynesian island is either a lofty volcanic pile, eroded into deep mysterious valleys and unscalable pinnacles, or else it is next to nothing—the merest coral reef rising just enough above the level of the sea to support its comb of cocoanut trees. But Pitcairn had neither the wild picturesque quality of a Mooréa nor the ineffable sadness of a coral atoll.

Pitcairn is situated in the south Pacific in latitude 25° 4′ S and longitude 130° 19′ W. It is roughly about 4000 miles west of Valparaiso, Chile, and about 2500 miles southeast of Tahiti. Only slightly more than two miles in length, it seemed lilliputian on the vast plain of the Pacific. No wonder the mutineers of the *Bounty* who landed here in 1790 had been lost to the world. It was a lump of an island, but its associations cast a glamour about it that made me forget its insignificance in a rapidly increasing anxiety to reach the shore, to make the famed and perilous landing, and to see the children of Christian, Adams, and Young—the progeny of the mutineers of the *Bounty*.

I had ample time from 7 a.m., when I first saw Pitcairn, until 10 a.m., when we dropped anchor off Bounty Bay, to review the story of this extraordinary island or, more exactly, of these extraordinary islanders, whom we saw coming out to us in two huge dories built on the lines of a whale boat. But their history and their significance to my scientific mission faded before the prospect of actually seeing them, which became more and more imminent as their boats rapidly devoured the half mile or so which separated the *Zaca* and the shore. The boats were full of men, two or three to a seat with the rest standing between. Twenty-eight oars, fourteen to each boat, rose and dipped with a steady rhythm, an obvious power, and the efficiency if not the grace of a racing crew. Then suddenly and swiftly they were alongside, shouting hearty greetings in a strange intonation, and, like a horde of invaders, some forty men swarmed onto the deck of the *Zaca*. Without waiting for a ladder they eagerly clambered aboard. They filled the decks. In their pleasure to see us they grasped every hand: sailors', cook's, captain's, and guests'. The social distinctions of a yacht vanished without a trace, and the *Zaca* succumbed to a wave of simple and hearty good-fellowship.

I found myself, with the others in the *Zaca's* party, besieged by a seemingly interminable succession of hands. One after another each of the islanders pressed forward, extended a hand, gave a hearty shake, uttered a pleasant greeting, and was pushed aside by another eager applicant. The confusion gradually subsided, and soon every member of our party was surrounded by a group of island men, each of us answering almost identical questions.

"Where do you come from?"

"Are you staying long?"

"When are you coming ashore?"

Then followed numerous queries about the *Zaca*, her size, engines, and speed.

With somewhat more leisure, after the confusion of the first greeting, I began consciously to inspect our visitors. My first impression was slightly disappointing. I had expected to see definite indications of the Tahitian contribution to their mixed Anglo-Polynesian origin. Instead, the men, *en masse*, were more like a group of Englishmen—dock workers—with ugly, knobby hands and feet, roughened and calloused by labor. They wore nondescript garments, the gifts of passing vessels or bartered from the crew of the New Zealand Shipping Company steamers. Battered officers' caps were clapped on mops of shaggy hair. Blue sea-jackets rubbed shoulders with ancient tweed coats. And hardly a pair of trousers matched its companion jacket. Shirts, open at the throat, revealed strong muscular necks and hairy chests. A glance at their bare feet explained why shoes were unnecessary. To rough, callous, padded feet like these, shoes could only be an encumbrance, at best an adornment, never a protection where nature had so amply fulfilled her function.

But I was not interested in their clothes. I was more concerned with their faces and their physical structure. I was examining them with a professional eye, picking out traits reminiscent of their English and Tahitian ancestors. What I saw seemed at once heterogeneous and curiously repetitious. On the whole, as I had remarked, they were rather English-looking, though varied in type. But in all of them a similar pattern was discernible—large prominent noses slightly beaked, heavy brows defined by bony bars above the eyes, giving the forehead a pronounced slope in profile. The complexion was ruddy and weather-beaten and the hair dark, although with a suggestion of fairer color here and there. The almost universal loss of teeth had produced a curious sucking-in of the cheeks and a collapse of the mouth. Several in my rapid survey reminded me of the bird man in Barnum and Bailey's circus—thin prominent nose, retreating brow, and atrophied, edentulous jaws.

In my examination of these faces I was suddenly arrested by one that was strangely familiar, then by another. For a moment I had difficulty in associating them with a persistent memory. Then I had it. They were the two Young brothers Sir Arthur Keith had photographed twenty years before on their visit to London as sailors on the *Mana*. I spoke to Edward Young.

"Aren't you the man that Sir Arthur Keith examined in London?"

"Why yes," he replied. "How did you know?"

"I recognized you from the photograph he published," I replied.

After about an hour spent in becoming acquainted with our visitors, I prepared to go ashore. I had elected to live with one of the islanders, Burley Warren. He had pressed his hospitality so warmly that despite the disappointment of others who had also put forth claims, I had arranged to stay at his house. With my bags and instruments in Burley's safe custody, I dropped into the island boat as it rose in the swell. It was a stout, heavy boat and very roomy. As soon as it was packed, we pushed off and started for shore.

Everything was at once so strange and fascinating that I found myself consciously watching every gesture and every item of behavior. I noticed that these men were so accustomed to their duties that, without a word of command or a show of authority, oars were promptly taken up and a man sprang to the guiding stern-sweep. As we rowed to shore they kept up a chatter of conversation, frequently lapsing into a dialect unintelligible to me.

Although the weather was exceptionally calm, I became apprehensive as we neared the shore. Former callers had described so vividly the hazards of landing at Bounty Bay that despite the universal praise of the islanders' skill in maneuvering their boats I could not but feel somewhat uneasy. Instruments immersed in the sea might rust or even be lost, and cameras bathed in brine suffered no improvement. Besides, I did not relish getting wet myself. Experience on other islands had led me to expect someone to assume command as we reached the danger point, but even though we were now close in shore, the men seemed almost phlegmatic, even disorganized, to my apprehensive frame of mind. Ahead of us were rocks and more rocks, then the narrow shingle at the base of a steep cliff. This so-called Bounty Bay was no bay to me. It was not even a cove. Nothing protected it from the swelling pulsations of the Pacific, as they rhythmically threw masses of surf and spray against the rocks. At last, as I had finally decided that these were not superskilled boatmen but foolhardy idiots, the rowing ceased without a spoken command. We paused. Wave after wave came up, lifted our boat high on its crest, passed on again as we dropped down into the trough. Once or twice a voice cried, "Now." But apparently the men recognized it as premature, or else they waited for the command of a more trusted voice, for suddenly someone yelled, "Now," and eagerly the word was taken up. "Now, now," "pull, pull," came from all parts of the boat. In response to the exhortations, oars were dug into the sea, and the boat gathered a momentum to match the oncoming swell. With a turn and a skilful pointing of the boat we had rounded the huge boulders into a narrow channel hardly visible to an inexperienced eye, and carried by the force of the awaited swell we were thrown straight and true down the short, narrow channel and hard onto the pebbly shingle.

The force of the impact of the boat on the shore threw me forward and onto my feet. Briskly the men began leaping into the shallow water. Scorning to use the arms lifted up to bear me dry-shod to the beach, I leaped for a point beyond the edge of the nibbling waves. To my chagrin I fell flat on my face. But no one laughed at the ridiculous figure I must have cut. Instead, several rushed up to assist me. Recovering my dignity and nursing a wrenched ankle, I took a position well up on the sharply sloping beach. From there I could examine the landing place and watch the activities of the men.

The beach itself is but a very narrow pebbly ramp. On one side stretches a rock-strewn shore impossible for launching or beaching any craft; on the other a shoulder of the cliff juts forward and drops its bulk directly into the sea. From below the level of the tide up to the boat-houses a fan-shaped runway of logs—like a corduroy road—has been laid down. On this the heavy dories are pulled up or lowered by main force. Its convenience is obvious to anyone who has tried to drag a heavy boat

through sand and gravel. A cluster of about a dozen
open-ended, thatched roofed sheds serve as boat-houses.
I saw housed within their narrow confines only two kinds
of craft—a heavy dory and a small dugout used for
fishing.

Back of the boat-houses loomed the cliff. It rose sheer
from the narrow beach on which I stood to a height of
several hundred feet. Across its face of reddish-black volcanic rock a broad smear of an alien white stone stood
out sharply. And high above I could see the green of a
foliage securely rooted on the plateau. I scanned the
precipice for a possible ascent, but although I knew from
the published accounts of its difficulty that a trail existed, I could see none. I turned to watch the islanders.
The scene, flanked by huge spray-wet rocks, was a very
active one. Pitcairn urchins, boys and girls, in wet clothes
which clung to their firm and supple little bodies were
splashing in the water and clambering over boulders
fallen from the cliff. The men, having deposited their
cargo on the shore, were hauling the boat up the way.
All muscles were enlisted and taxed to their utmost to
budge the heavy bulk. At first it did not move, but by
repeated efforts and by pulling in rhythm, they started
it on its progress to the boat-house. Watching the effort
necessary to beach their boats, I decided that only pressing need would persuade me to call on the islanders for
transportation to the yacht.

As I stood entranced by the scene, Burley, the well-
named, came up to where I stood and in a gentle, shy,
and somewhat deprecatory voice that I came to recognize as characteristic of this stout, simple-hearted man,
asked me if I were ready to go home. Assenting, I
turned to follow my guide and host. Walking to the rear
of the boat-houses we came upon the path which had
been hidden from my view. About as wide as a narrow
lane and rutted by the wear of innumerable bare feet
and by rivulets of rain water, it now, during a dry spell,
was hard and gravelly. We followed this path as it

sharply climbed the narrow talus to the point where it reached the sheer face of the rocky precipice. Turning, the path now hugged the wall-like side of the cliff. Like a fire escape on a New York tenement house it mounted sharply and flat against the precipice. Breathless but less exhausted than I had anticipated, I gained the midway point which was rather more horizontal and permitted me to catch my second wind for the final and steepest climb. I noted with satisfaction that some of the natives also had found this a taxing ascent, for rough stone steps were crudely let into the grade. Observing the ease with which Burley and the others climbed, I secretly exonerated my own red-faced, blown, and puffy condition on the ground that months on a yacht had unfitted me for so sudden and strenuous an exertion.

In no condition to exchange graceful amenities after this climb, I came face to face with the female and the senile sections of the colony. There in front of us and above us, seated on rocks and standing in groups, were the women and the old folks. Several came forward, the older ones with considerable poise, the younger ones rather shyly, to shake my hand and offer a hearty or mumbled greeting, depending on their age. The women, barefooted like their husbands and brothers, were clad in simple cotton dresses. Most of them were bareheaded, although one or two, either more fortunate or vainer than the others, wore hats—toques—of an outmoded fashion. Like the men, they had lost many of their teeth, and so at first sight they were by no means prepossessing.

Pausing here at the top of the ascent, we could enjoy the cool breezes which swept in off the Pacific and contemplate the climb we had just accomplished. Several hundred feet below, in open view, lay the waters on which the *Zaca* had been rolling and plunging for days and weeks. Even now with my feet firmly planted on the earth the sight of the long, fascinating undulations of the sea brought sharply back to some sympathetic nerve

the rhythm of its measured beat. The deep pure blue
faded into the hazy horizon, and an overpowering feeling of constriction and isolation welled up from its
sparkling, impersonal surface. Directly below, the rocky
coast of the island caught the sea in a firm white line of
broken surf. I could see the minute figures of men at
the landing and watch some of them making the ascent.

I now turned to see the island itself. The clear, cloud-
less sky poured down a bath of brilliant sunlight that
caused every blade and every leaf to reflect its radiance.
At my feet the red-brown road open to the sky wound
its sinuous course, making a narrow terrace along the side
of a slope. Above, as well as below the lane, the slope
was steep. On a ridge, cocoanut palms wove their fragile
tracery against the sky. Closer at hand was a rich and
varied growth of green, though unfortunately in my
botanical ignorance I could recognize only a few species. Among them I did notice the close, umbrageous
orange, the lemon, the stiff-armed breadfruit, and the
miro. In effect, however, the thick growth that covered
the slopes and softened the angles of the hills endowed
the island with an appearance of rank fertility.

Burley, to whom these sights were as natural as breath-
ing and as little thought-provoking, stood waiting for me
to tear myself away. We now struck off down the main
road which was more like a curving swath through the
green foliage than a tunneled avenue, and soon espied
the outlying houses of the village which is about a quarter of a mile distant from the cliff overlooking the landing at Bounty Bay. These structures were simple, unpainted dwellings, one story high, with walls of roughly
cut, horizontal planks overlapping like clapboards. The
roofs were covered by corrugated iron which though
aesthetically inferior to thatch is more durable and col-
lects rain water more effectively.

Finally the road made a turn and led downward to
the village itself. About fifty houses were clustered in a
compact group, only their roofs and walls showing

through the masses of green trees and shrubbery. My notions of Adamstown, as the settlement is sometimes called, were definite. From early descriptions I had expected to see the houses neatly arranged about a village green. Beechey in 1825 had so described it. Nothing could have been more different. There was no trace of arrangement or order of any kind. Branching off from the main road were a succession of smaller paths, and from these stemmed others, no one of which kept to a straight line. Curving, twisting, crossing back and forth, these lanes, determined by convenience, formed a veritable maze in which I later often found myself wandering helplessly. Along these lanes, so close to the roadway that a passerby could peep through the window or door, the sprawling houses of the islanders were scattered, according to no regular pattern that I could detect. We followed one of these paths downward into a thicket of dwellings. A mere footpath, its narrow, hard surface pounded firm by the patter of countless feet, it was edged by miniature gullies cut into the unprotected earth by the run-off of rain storms. Where its course met the dry and shallow bed of some rain-born stream a neat bridge of a couple of logs spanned the break. Rounding the corners of houses and cutting across back yards we followed the trail to the third or fourth house—the last on that bypath. This was the home of Burley Warren.

Not knowing our destination, I had no time to scrutinize the house, before we arrived at the door. Standing on the threshold was Eleanor, Burley's wife, daughter of David Young and great-great-granddaughter of Edward Young of the *Bounty*. Above medium height, with a well-built upstanding body, she made a pleasant figure. Her masses of almost black hair, caught simply in a knot at the back of her head, her rather wide brow and face shaded and relieved by a natural sweep of hair, and her dark brown eyes, wide set and full, added a definite charm to her habitual expression of pleasant simplicity. Shyly, with a suspicion of embarrassed awkwardness,

Eleanor made me welcome and ushered me into her home. Crossing a threshold, two low steps above the ground, I entered the family living room. Wide, roughly-cut, but smooth boards covered the floor. The walls and ceiling were hung with wall paper which needed replacing. But so hard is wall paper to come by that no doubt Burley preferred retaining his tattered paper to having none at all, even though torn spots revealed the burlap beneath on which it was hung. A homemade, slat-bottomed, cushionless couch occupied one corner. A table was set between two windows on the side wall, and an old and elaborate bureau shared another wall with a harmonium of the same vintage. Besides crippled kitchen chairs, the only other furniture was a stout chest whose nicked and battered condition lent a nautical air to the room.

The hospitality of Burley and Eleanor was so warm-hearted, so generous, that I immediately felt at home, and I knew that I should like them. In their unpretentious way, with the native good manners of unpremeditated simplicity, they had the art of welcoming a stranger. Although the morning was practically gone and it was an hour when, under ordinary circumstances, I would be thinking of lunch, Eleanor asked me if I wanted "breakfast."

Preferring to put my things in order, I was shown to a narrow room which led directly from the living room. It was just wide enough for the length of a bed set against a single window. At the other end of the room were two more sea chests. A few hang-headed nails, which needed readjustment each time I ventured to trust my garments to them, sufficed for a closet. I took this to be the room of one or two of the three sons of the family, since it was the only other bedroom besides Burley's and Eleanor's. Theirs was a much larger one opening off mine and contained two beds. I must have dispossessed the boys who retired to their parents' room to make way for the guest. But since they never seemed to display any resentment, I concluded that the shift was accepted with the resignation children sometimes accord to their parents' arrangements.

The islanders were too excited and disorganized by the unaccustomed visit of a yacht for me to begin my investigations on the day of arrival, even had my own state of mind permitted. Consequently, I felt that I was not losing precious time when I decided to accept Burley's invitation to accompany him to the plantation where he wished to gather a basket of pineapples. The *Ruahine*, a New Zealand Shipping Company steamer on her way to Panama, was expected soon, and during her brief stay the men were accustomed to board her in order to sell curios to the passengers or to barter fruits and vegetables for clothing or foreign foodstuffs.

Burley and I set out once more, accompanied this time by his eight-year-old son, named (like an echo) Curley. Weaving our way around the neighboring houses, we were stopped frequently by islanders who shook my hand and passed a pleasant welcoming word. One elderly lady reminded me so forcefully of my own New England that it was with difficulty that I recollected her origin. Tall and flat-chested, with a high curved beak of a nose, she enhanced her similarity to a well-known type of New England spinsterhood almost to caricature by keeping up a steady and voluble chatter of unsolicited reminiscences and genealogical lore. Burley finally saved me from the burden of my politeness, and we continued to climb the footpath up the slope to the main village road. Just above the spot where this path abutted onto the road, I caught a glimpse of the only place that might be called a community center—a flat open area about one hundred feet square and about six to ten feet directly above the road. Here were a two-storied, many-windowed church, like a New England meeting house without a steeple, the courthouse, and the signal bell suspended on a crossbar. Not stopping to examine these buildings we proceeded on our way. The road led down into a slight hollow and then climbed again steadily until it reached the plateau which forms the top of the island. Part way up we met some men descending with an underslung wheelbarrow full of gnarled and knotted lumps of wood. We all stopped to rest and sinking down onto the grass alongside the narrow road, I lit my pipe.

Since the history of the Pitcairn Islanders was uppermost in my mind and since I had been, as I walked with Burley, silently checking my illusions acquired from reading against what I was actually seeing, I fell to questioning these roadside companions on the events of the first years on Pitcairn. It was natural to expect that John Adams, last survivor on Pitcairn of the *Bounty* mutineers, and the ten surviving Tahitian women of those who had accompanied them would have frequently retold their exploits to an eager audience of children, and those listeners would transmit the story in turn to a newer crop of ears—and so on unto the present. But expectation overran the facts. I was told almost to the very phrases the accounts I had read for myself, and I discovered that these modern islanders learned their yarn not from some rich local tradition handed down inviolate through generations, but from the very books I had myself consulted. In fact, my own information proved to be wider than theirs, since their sources were derived from only two or three accounts while mine included every item that twelve years of search had revealed.

When I reflected later on this strange absence of a contemporary tradition, the reason suddenly seemed clear to me. The situation here bore no analogy to our own conditions. Tradition is born of reminiscence, and reminiscence generally flourishes where there are at least two companions both of whom have taken a part in its making, for otherwise one would inevitably become a bore. The Civil War veterans around the village stove, each enjoying the yarn for his own contribution's sake, must have repeated their story so often that the younger generation could not escape its memory. On Pitcairn,

Adams had no companion with whom to warm over ancient grudges or lament the turn of events. Certainly, the women who spoke an aborted English and Adams who spoke a similar Tahitian could hardly have settled down to a comfortable chat about old times. And during the long years before the growing infants were old enough to constitute an audience, Adams must have learned the peace of silence. But whatever the cause of this poverty of historical detail, the comfort of my resting place was delightful and compensation enough for loitering. The tall grass on the bank was soft, and above my head lofty, full-leaved trees, leaning down from the slope above the road, spread a pleasant shade against the sun. In front of me I could see over the descending curve of the hill and spy the tin roofs of the village glistening in the sun. Not far away, a mountain spring trickled through a greener, richer foliage than that around us.

Fragrant both of nature and of romance as our station was, Burley had still his pineapples to gather, and regretfully I tore myself away to continue the laborious climb. With each advancing step more and more of the island presented itself, and the temptation to stop was strong. Finally we attained a bluff which offered an incomparable view. To our right and below us lay the tree-tufted carpet of the precipitous valley in which the village snuggled. From this distance only the roofs of the houses were visible, and each one made a spangle of light in the thick green.

To the left, a tower of rock lifted its solid mass against the heavens. Facing us and the sea, one side of the escarpment formed a wall-like precipice. As I stood gazing at it Burley said,

"See that cave."

Now that it was pointed out to me, I did see a darker patch on the wall of rock and studying it more closely I discerned its character.

"That," said Burley, "is Christian's cave."

My merely mild interest in caves in general was replaced instantly by a vivid interest in this particular one.

"Sixty or seventy people can live in that comfortably," Burley added, for my information. As he was not one of those who are historically or antiquarianly-minded, I did not tax his anxiety to please by asking for information concerning Christian's use of this retreat. I already knew the tradition that here Fletcher Christian, the leader of the mutiny on the *Bounty,* retired alone and, from that niche high above the sea, often sat and pondered over the same waters that had borne him here, far from his native Isle of Man. It took no great flight of the imagination to reconstruct that scene nor did I find it difficult to guess the gnawing thoughts, the resignation, the wild revolt the sea must have induced in turn in the mind of that unfortunate man. Here he sat, no doubt, rehearsing his grievances against Bligh, his captain, whipping himself anew to a fury against the insults endured on the *Bounty,* and justifying his actions as natural to any man in similar circumstances. But he must have had moments when a bitter regret seized him that he had ever led the mutiny which ended with an honorable career in the Royal Navy snuffed out like a candle, and himself yoked forever to a crew of tough sailors and a band of alien women and, worst of all, severed eternally from family and friends. The time had not yet come when a South Sea island was automatically regarded as a romantic retreat, for Rousseau's association of the Savage Man with the ideal life had not affected the philosophy of the sailor. To Christian his fate must have been awful to contemplate, and relief must have come to him in the form of a vain hope that some day a chance sail would release him from his prison.

And there before me were perhaps the only things that had remained unchanged for one hundred forty-five years, since the days when Fletcher Christian seated in his cave had dreamed over them and hated them—the sea and the sky.

But again pineapples, like a persistent theme song,

once more banished other melodies. Dogging after Burley, I continued to climb. Soon we came upon a group of little cabins. These, explained Burley, were the "camps," and I discovered that several weeks a year many of the families take a vacation by moving into these camps on the plateau. They were empty now, and I did not hesitate to peek into their interiors. They consisted mainly of one or two rooms, fitted with roughly constructed beds and similarly made tables and chairs. Cooking appeared to be carried on either at outdoor fireplaces or in sheds. Passing these dwellings we finally reached some of the plantations. We went through patches of Irish potatoes, pineapples, and *kumara,* a kind of sweet potato. Burley's destination was a fair-sized patch, about an acre in extent, entirely devoted to pineapples, and there he rapidly selected enough ripe fruits to fill his basket. He cut an extra one for us, and never did pineapple taste sweeter or pour more juice from its flesh than this one. Warm with the sun it gave off a delicious fragrance, but its juices drying on my hands left them uncomfortably sticky until I washed them on our return.

The descent was rapid and uninterrupted, the steep decline lending speed to our legs. Again I was entering the village, somewhat more familiar this time. We went straight to Burley's house. On our arrival Eleanor began preparing a meal. This time I did not refuse. We sat down to a long table, I on a chair at the head, the rest on benches. On my left were Burley and Eleanor and opposite were Lyndon, Curley, and Douglas, the three Warren lads, silent, shy, and watchful. The youngest, Douglas, had, in addition to his shyness, an ingratiatingly pert expression.

I remembered at least one custom of the Pitcairn Islanders. I therefore waited. When we were all seated, Burley in a low voice said a simple grace. That devout act was as effective as anything I had seen in symbolizing Pitcairn. Indeed, each visitor to Pitcairn in turn had recorded the solemn effect of this simple and invariably

observed act of piety. It was, in effect, a link with home
—and with the customs of an innocent youth. To one of
my generation, saying grace belongs to a remembered
past, and so this act, aside from its peculiarly Pitcairn
flavor, was poignantly nostalgic.

But the smell of wholesome, simple food stimulating
an already hungry digestive system did not permit me
to linger long over these musings. As the Pitcairn Islanders would say, I fell to and tucked away a fair share
of the grub. There were soup, boiled potatoes, Irish and
sweet, chicken, bread, jam, and a drink brewed from
bran husks. The service was of the simplest character:
thick unmatched plates stamped with the insignia of
the New Zealand Shipping Company, blackened metal
knives, forks, and spoons, for which one reached to an
old jam jar in which they were arranged business end up
like a murderous bouquet.

After lunch, I sought out Parkins Christian, the chief
magistrate, to ask him to call a general meeting that evening at which I intended to explain the purpose of my
visit as tactfully as possible. I found Parkins at home surrounded by his family. I had already met him on board
the *Zaca*, but that did not prevent my being impressed
again by his truly extraordinary personality. Tall, lean,
and muscular, his mere physical presence was enough to
dominate a crowd. But in addition, his rather handsome
face, distinctly Polynesian in its brown swarthiness, and
his deep brown eyes, set off by graying hair, had an alert
repose that inspired confidence and respect. Spoken
rather slowly and in a vibrant drawl, his words had humor and pertinence. It was remarkable to see this man,
raised on a remote island, far from contact with the
world, and lettered only to the extent provided by an inadequate island school, conduct himself with poise and
dignity. Parkins agreed to assemble the island population
at the courthouse where I could address them after
supper.

Retiring once more to Burley's house which I had

come by now to regard as home, I spent the afternoon greeting callers and arranging my paraphernalia. I found myself repeating so often the same admiring phrases about Pitcairn that I came to mistrust the sincerity of my emotions. But the visitors so obviously expected the praise that I could not bring myself to refuse it, nor did I wish to. As my acquaintance with the islanders widened I suddenly remembered Mary Ann McCoy. Norman Hall had met her and he had reported in his *Tale of a Shipwreck* her hope that I might visit Pitcairn and complete a study of the descendants of the mutineers of the *Bounty* that I had commenced twelve years before on Norfolk Island. In fact, Hall had entrusted to my care the delivery of a book and a letter to Miss McCoy. With the double purpose, therefore, of discharging my duty and of making the acquaintance of Mary Ann McCoy, I prepared to call on her. I found her living in a little three-room house whose interior was scrupulously neat and clean. She had been expecting my visit, and, as she rose to greet me, I realized that she was blind. Her blindness was provocative of an overwhelming tenderness. She moved with such care and gentle confidence, her aged and wrinkled face was brushed with so tender a smile, and her appearance of fragility was so poignant that I felt that she was as delicate and precious as an ancient porcelain. I wish I could convey the feeling she invoked. She was a small woman, shortened further by a stoop, with soft hands twisted by age. Her face was rather large, with prominent cheek bones and with a nose somewhat wide at the nostrils but saved from coarseness by a high curving bridge. Her forehead was heavy and had a pronounced slope, but the rugged character of the brow was softened by delicate white hair. I couldn't see her eyes which were concealed by a pair of blue spectacles, but her voice and her smile of chastened patience compensated for the veiling of those features.

I was particularly eager to meet "Aunt" Ann, as I called her, following the universal island custom, because

she was one of the very few survivors of the third generation born on Pitcairn. Born in 1851, her eighty-four
years represented more than half the history of the colony, and I hoped to receive information from her that
otherwise would die with her.

"I've heard of you," she said, "from Mr. Hall."

"And I have come to talk to you about the old folks,"
I answered.

"I am so glad," she continued. "For after I am gone,
no one will remember. It is such a pity that none of the
young people take an interest."

Aunt Ann was the only islander who had ever visited
the other branch of the colony at Norfolk, and her eagerness to hear from me some word about her relatives
there led us into conversation along that channel. When
the afternoon had almost gone, I left Aunt Ann with a
promise to return soon and set to work on genealogies.

On my return to Burley's I did what was to happen
frequently for the next day or two—I became lost in the
tangled skein of paths. One of the children, quickly observing my bewilderment, came and guided me to the
door. Supper was ready on my arrival, and again I sat
down to food substantially like that at luncheon.

We had just finished supper, and the twilight was rapidly deepening, when I heard the sharp stroke of a bell.
Associations were so strong that I turned to Burley and
stated more than asked, "Church?" "No," he responded.
"Your meetin'."

Taking an electric torch to light our homeward path,
we picked our way along shadowy lanes towards the
courthouse. We were among the first arrivals at the meeting place. Someone unrecognizable in the waning light
hailed me and invited me to a seat. Along the road side
of the square was a long narrow bench on the very edge
of a ten-foot bank which dropped vertically to the road
below it. Here sat the slowly assembling islanders, awaiting the opening of the meeting. Parkins soon appeared
and, after a wait of about fifteen minutes, he sang out in

his rich drawl, "All in, everybody," and led the way to
the courthouse. This was a single large room, one end of
which was partitioned off as a post office. The remainder
of the room contained about fifteen long benches. Over
one hundred men and women crowded into the room
until every bench was full and every chair occupied. A
single kerosene lamp on the speaker's table threw an uncertain light which left the further corners of the room
in darkness. I could see directly in front of me a glowing
mass of faces with intent eyes and—back of these—only
eyes. Suddenly and unbidden the thought came to me
that the success of my work depended on the coöperation
of these people, and immediately fear seized me that they
might not understand, might even be hostile and resent
strangers, however scientific in aim, prying into their intimate lives. For a moment I longed for the godlike
power of the entomologist or the zoölogist who had no
need to placate his subjects or to consult their convenience. To my mind these eyes had taken on a hostile look.
And I had to tell them that I had come from America
to study their heredity, probe into their genealogies, and
determine the results of race mixture between English
and Polynesian.

I hardly heard Parkins' introduction. Something about
"come from far away" and "hospitality." And then I was
on my feet and speaking. Without plan, I began telling
these unblinking eyes that I was quite nervous and
deeply moved to be here at last, addressing Pitcairn Islanders. That confession seemed to break the fixity of
those eyes, for I noticed some smiles and a general relaxation. I proceeded to tell of my visit to Norfolk Island
among their cousins twelve years ago and to recall
names familiar to them. I lingered on the hospitality I
had received from the Norfolk Islanders. Introducing the
purpose of my visit I was relieved to detect an alert interest in my plans to study among them the consequences of race mixture, and when I illustrated my
points by the studies I had made in Norfolk I knew I

had won their approval. Their assent was definitely clinched when I promised that medical assistance would be given to all those in need of it by the *Zaca's* physician, Dr. George Lyman.

Immediately after I concluded, a number of men and women rose to ask questions. In clear, unembarrassed voices and with the manners of people accustomed to speaking their minds in public meetings, they framed their queries with skill. Having answered these questions, I was then surrounded by a number of the men who displayed a keen interest in the genealogical charts collected on Norfolk. I very soon discovered, however, that their interest centered on whether or not their own lines were represented. Before closing the meeting, someone suggested a rising vote of thanks, for what I couldn't fathom, and I knew that the first encounter had been won. But taught by experience in these matters, I was not yet counting chickens. The laborious work of catching every islander on the wing and examining physically each in turn would be no easy task.

I was glad to start for home at last, and the thought of the bed awaiting me there occupied my mind. But I did not earn my rest so soon, for a number of men and women followed me right into Burley's house. Passersby, seeing the light and hearing the voices, joined the party, and thus we conversed until ten o'clock. When our guests saw that I could scarcely keep my eyes open, they laughingly rose and departed. Needless to say, I did not linger in preparing for sleep, and even the springless bed and grass-stuffed mattress offered no hindrance to the almost immediate oblivion that rounded off my first day on Pitcairn.

II. HISTORICAL

2

MUTINY ON THE *BOUNTY*

The story of the mutiny on the *Bounty* and of the subsequent settlement on Pitcairn is a perennial in an old-
fashioned garden of favorite yarns. But even standard
perennials undergo successive waves of popular approval
and comparative neglect. Although the Pitcairn adventure has never been completely forgotten, it has suffered
periods of obscurity only to be revived by its mere telling. Sir John Barrow's *Mutiny and Piratical Seizure of
H.M.S. Bounty,* published in 1831, was one of the first
narratives to create a wide interest in Pitcairn. About
twenty years later, the Rev. Thomas Boyles Murray issued *Pitcairn* of which, by 1860, 30,000 copies had been
sold. At this time Sunday schools throughout the United
States were glutted with tracts in which the lesson of
Pitcairn was neatly pointed. Murderers and cutthroats
might found a modern Eden, ran the parable, evil might
produce good, and the simple and primitive might har-
bor the true righteousness, if the voice of God were
heeded as on Pitcairn.

Again another burst of general interest in Pitcairn was
started in the seventies by Lady Belcher's account. And
at the turn of the century the *Story of Pitcairn by a Native Daughter,* ran through a number of editions. But it
remained for that admirable combination of Nordhoff
and Hall to capture the virility and romance of this
unique story. The appeal of their narratives has secured

them a very large audience, and already they have taken their place as classics in the literature of romantic adventure.

The story of Pitcairn properly begins with the breadfruit tree. Fabulous, if not miraculous, to the eighteenth-century Englishman, that tree started the chain of events to be recounted here. The explorers of the Pacific had carried back to the civilized world many a tale of the wonders they witnessed: islands devoted to Venus, savage man in the lap of a bountiful nature, giant statues on Easter Island, and a godlike race descended from Homeric heroes. But it was the breadfruit which stimulated most the practical imagination; at least it caused a group of Englishmen, interested in the West Indian plantations, to petition their sovereign, George III, patron of geographical exploration, to dispatch an expedition to Tahiti in the South Seas and to bring back specimens of this extraordinary tree. The breadfruit is a tropical plant, large-leaved and stately, and bears abundantly round green fruit about the size of a large grapefruit. When baked in a native underground oven it tastes like hot bread, or perhaps more like a cross between hot bread and potatoes. In Polynesia where it is indigenous, it is a staple food, since it requires little attention, bears the year round, and has a large crop. For plantation slaves, thought British planters, the fruit of such a tree would be nutritious, and for British pockets decidedly advantageous. Therefore, the petition begged that these plants be transplanted to the West Indies. The proposal had the weighty support of Sir Joseph Banks, president of the Royal Society.

In due course, Lieutenant William Bligh of His Majesty's Navy was assigned in August, 1787, to this task. Bligh was selected because he had an excellent reputation as a seaman and because of his experience in the South Seas, acquired as one of Captain James Cook's officers on the ill-fated third voyage. Although only about thirty-three years old, Bligh had already had a long and hard experience in that brutal school—the British Navy in the eighteenth century. Contemporary portraits picture a small-featured gentleman of pleasant mien, not the fierce-browed, heavy-featured sea dog carelessly associated with the sailor of those times.

Already the fame of Otaheite, as the English then spelt Tahiti, or of la Nouvelle Cythère, as the more romantic French called it, was widespread. Wallis in 1767, and Bougainville in 1768, had reported its discovery. Cook had contributed to its glamour by returning with Omai, a native of the island, who created a sensation in London's drawing rooms, sang Tahitian love songs at the Burneys', and charmed sophisticated ladies. Even the great Johnson met Omai, and Boswell has recorded the master's apt comment, fitting for more than one Tahitian.

"Sir," said Johnson, "he had passed his time, while in England, only in the best company; so that all that he had acquired of our manners was genteel. As a proof of this, Sir, Lord Mulgrave and he dined one day at Streatham. They sat with their backs to the light fronting me, so that I could not see distinctly; and there was so little of the savage in Omai, that I was afraid to speak to either, lest I should mistake one for the other."

Gouty gentlemen at the Crown and Anchor roared, no doubt, at the frank stories of love in the islands, and over coffee cups and between puffs at their pipes must have envied Bligh, the lucky dog, his opportunities. But no record remains of what Bligh himself thought as he unknowingly faced the supreme adventure of his life.

The *Bounty* had been designated for the voyage. She was of 215 tons burden, 90 feet in length, and with a beam of 24 feet 3 inches. Refitted at Deptford, the great cabin was converted into a conservatory to house the plants that were to be gathered at Tahiti. A false floor was laid down, with holes designed to secure the pots from shifting. The ship's complement consisted of Captain Bligh, one master, three warrant officers, one surgeon, two master's mates, two midshipmen, thirty-four

petty officers and seamen, one botanist, and one gardener, making in all forty-six. Of the officers Fletcher
Christian, the master's mate, was an old shipmate of
Bligh who had personally selected him for the post. Peter
Heywood and George Stewart, midshipmen, were appointed through family influences. The sailors were all
carefully chosen for the mission.

By December of the same year, the *Bounty* was finally ready for her journey. Her holds were filled with
provisions for eighteen months, and, in addition, articles
for trade with the Tahitians were taken aboard. Bligh
knew the eagerness with which the natives sought, and
when occasion offered stole, iron nails, mirrors, and axes.

The sailing directions recommended the passage
around the Horn. Therefore after laying on wine and
other provisions at the Canaries, Bligh, setting his course
for South America, sailed from Spithead, December 23,
1787. The voyage proceeded with the usual encounters
of weather. Periods of rain and storm were succeeded
by calm and relaxation during which the ship's stores
were aired, and the men repaired the damages suffered.

There are two accounts of the voyage. One is Bligh's
own which he published in his defense immediately on
his return to England. The other is by James Morrison,
boatswain's mate. Mr. Rawson casts doubt on the validity
of the latter as a contemporary report. He recalls that
Morrison not only went through a mutiny, lived on
Tahiti for months, was chained aboard the *Pandora*, was
wrecked on the Great Barrier Reef, but endured other
vicissitudes, a combination of events which makes it im-
probable that the author had either the writing materials
or the means to preserve a journal. Besides these docu-
mentary evidences, there are the testimony of the men
court-martialed in England, Adams' stories, and the bits
of tradition which have survived.

In all this contradictory body of evidence it is difficult
to ascertain the truth, and, undoubtedly, eye witnesses
might honestly record varying reactions according to

their points of view. There is no question, however, that on several occasions Bligh used blunt quarter-deck methods in handling his crew. Most of his difficulties with the crew were concerned with food, and the accusation has been made that his double function as master and purser encouraged him to shave the ship's victualing to his own advantage. In any event, except for some disciplinary measures that Bligh well knew how to administer, and with which the crew were familiar, nothing of obvious moment occurred during the voyage to Tahiti to disturb Bligh's peace of mind.

In April, 1789, after an unsuccessful attempt to round the Horn, Bligh was forced to change his plans. He had feared boisterous weather at the Horn and had been foresighted enough to secure discretional orders from the Admiralty. He now proceeded to the Cape of Good Hope on the other side of the Atlantic. In the bald way of the sailor, Bligh briefly touches on the remainder of the outward voyage. After departing from Africa, the *Bounty* touched at Van Diemen's Land (now Tasmania), black aborigines were observed and described, and once more the ship was on her way. Finally, ten months after leaving England, the *Bounty* found a resting place at Matavai Bay, Tahiti. It was then October 26, 1788.

Despite Bligh's traditional reputation, he was capable of actions of remarkable consideration. Before arriving at Tahiti he had had posted a list of instructions governing the behavior of the crew in their commerce with the natives. Among other provisions his experience at Tahiti had taught him to demand of each sailor a physical examination. At a time when most captains were criminally negligent of the havoc that their crews might cause among an unprotected people, Bligh thus attempted to forestall the spreading of venereal disease among the Tahitians.

The sailors were also enjoined from bartering independently lest it interfere with the procural of the ship's necessities—and no mention was to be made of Cook's death. Bligh knew the veneration with which the Tahitians regarded Cook, or "Toote" in the native tongue, and he wished to avail himself of whatever magic that name might invoke.

If the modern visitor to Tahiti is amazed to see the crowds of curious islanders throng the pier for the scheduled and long-established visits of a mail steamer, what must have been the reception the *Bounty* received? The dozen or so European vessels to reach these shores before the arrival of Bligh had not satiated the curiosity of a people always interested in nautical innovations, and fascinated, moreover, by white men who were regarded as of partly divine origin.

As for the *Bounty's* crew, their pleasure must have been unbounded. Ten months at sea! They were young and hungry for fresh food and the company of women. Barter was immediately commenced with the hordes of natives who surrounded the ship in their canoes. Some of them even swam out, too impatient to await a place in a canoe. It was not long before intimacies were established with the natives. It was customary to select some applicant as a special friend, or "tyo," from among the islanders who eagerly presented themselves for the honor. One's *tyo* brought fruits and presents of native manufacture and in return expected nails, mirrors, and bits of iron. Bligh recorded that scarcely one of his people was without his *tyo*. And so whole-heartedly were the demands of *tyo*ship and barter indulged that the *Bounty* was soon in danger of falling apart from the removal of her nails.

Scenes of festivity frequently occurred. The quick-witted Tahitians soon adjusted themselves to the social idiosyncrasies of their visitors and discovered that an infallible way to fill their beakers with wine was to rise and shout, "Te arii no Pretanie" (the King of England). Oberreah, a prominent chieftainess, came out to visit Bligh and unknown to him, native machinations were under way to utilize his prestige in island politics.

But Bligh had not forgotten his mission. Suspecting that the islanders might refuse an honest, frank request for breadfruit plants, he laid an indirect approach. Presenting gifts to Tinah, the chief of Matavai, from the King of England, Bligh asked him, "And will you send something to King George in return?" "Yes," replied Tinah, "I will send him anything I have." Whereupon Bligh immediately suggested breadfruit plants as an adequate gift to King George. Being thus under obligation according to his own code, Tinah had no alternative but to assent. It seems strange that it never occurred to Bligh that all this maneuvering might be unnecessary, and that breadfruit might be forthcoming for the mere asking.

At all events, the work of slipping, potting, and transferring the plants was soon under way. For the next six months gardening was the principal concern of Mr. Nelson, the botanist, and Mr. Brown, the gardener. It is needless to mention what occupied the attention of the ship's company.

During these months two episodes occurred which assume significance in the light of subsequent events, although they probably have no direct bearing on them. At four o'clock on the morning of January 5, 1789, a small cutter was found missing, together with three men. Bligh immediately dispatched a searching party, and the men were retaken at the island of Taha, one of the Society group. The deserters were punished by lashes and imprisonment. A month later, the ship's cable was found severed, except for one strand. Bligh, in retrospect, came to believe that this was an intentional act on the part of one of his own men who hoped thereby to put the ship ashore, thus prolonging a pleasant stay at Tahiti. But at the time he suspected the natives and made a strict search for the culprit among them. No one, however, was found guilty. It seems more likely that the cable was severed neither by natives nor crew, but was chafed by the coral heads which abounded in the lagoon.

By March 31, all the plants were aboard: 774 pots, 39 tubs, and 24 boxes, containing in all 1,015 breadfruit plants besides other specimens of Tahitian flora, filled the cabin prepared for their reception. Four days later, on April 4, the *Bounty* was ready to depart. The farewells were long and no doubt tearful. Six months are a long time. With banana stalks hanging from the yardarms, and with cocoanuts piled, and pigs squealing, on the decks, the *Bounty* spread her canvas and, passing through the opening in the reef, set sail on her homeward voyage. But before making for the West Indies and England, Bligh set his course for Endeavour Straits and Java where he had been directed to secure additional botanical specimens.

Twenty-three days later, on the night of April 27, the *Bounty* was standing between Tofoa and Kotoo in the Tonga group. The watch had been divided into three parts: the master, Mr. Fryer, having the first; the gunner, the middle; and Fletcher Christian, the master's mate, the morning watch. Captain Bligh had retired for the night with his "mind entirely free from suspicion." But he was not destined to awaken to the same state of mind. He was actually aroused by Fletcher Christian and Thomas Burkitt to find himself a prisoner. This day, April 28, saw a mutiny on the high seas, gave birth to a series of adventures of the most incredible character, and resulted in the establishment of a unique settlement that to this day remains its tangible result.

We shall never know the exact circumstances surrounding the birth of the mutiny. Many stories survive. Christian is represented as having carefully planned the *coup* and, on the other hand, as having acted on impulse. Uncle Cornish Quintal once related to me a story handed down in his family from his mutineer ancestor, Matthew Quintal. According to this account Fletcher Christian, during his watch, was gloomily leaning over the rail of the ship when Matthew Quintal approached him and asked him what was the matter. Christian declared vehemently that he was unable to bear Bligh's abuse any longer and was contemplating casting adrift in a cutter. Quintal then counseled that they take the ship, a suggestion that Christian was quick to adopt.

The following account in Bligh's own words may be accepted as substantially correct, although he probably erred in attaching blame to some of the men and may well have heightened the effect of his story by several judicious brush strokes.

"Just before sun-rising, Mr. Christian, with the Master-at-arms, gunner's mate, and Thomas Burkitt, seaman, came into my cabin while I was asleep, and seizing me, tied my hands with a cord behind my back, and threatened me with instant death, if I spoke or made the least noise. I, however, called so loud as to alarm everyone: but they had already secured the officers who were not of their party, by placing centinels at their doors. There were three men at my cabin door, besides the four within; Christian had only a cutlass in his hand, the others had muskets and bayonets. I was hauled out of bed, and forced on deck in my shirt, suffering great pains from the tightness with which they had tied my hands. I demanded the reason for such violence, but received no other answer than threats of instant death, if I did not hold my tongue. Mr. Elphinston, master's mate, was kept in his berth; Mr. Nelson, botanist, Mr. Peckover, gunner, Mr. Ledward, surgeon, and the master, were confined to their cabins; and also the clerk, Mr. Samuel, but he soon obtained leave to come on deck. The fore hatchway was guarded by centinels; the boatswain and the carpenter were, however, allowed to come on deck, where they saw me standing abaft the mizen-mast, with my hands tied behind my back, under a guard, with Christian at their head.

"The boatswain was now ordered to hoist the launch out, with a threat, if he did not do it instantly, to take care of himself.

"The boat being out, Mr. Hayward [not to be confused with Peter Heywood, who remained with Christian] and Mr. Hallet, midshipmen, and Mr. Samuel, were ordered into it; upon which I demanded the cause of such an order, and endeavoured to persuade someone to a sense of duty; but it was to no effect.

" 'Hold your tongue, Sir, or you are dead this instant,' was constantly repeated to me.

"The master, by this time, had sent to be allowed to come on deck, which was permitted; but he was soon ordered back again to his cabin.

"I continued my endeavours to turn the tide of affairs, when Christian changed the cutlass he had in his hand for a bayonet, that was brought to him, and, holding me with a strong grip by the cord that tied my hands, he, with many oaths, threatened to kill me immediately if I would not be quiet: the villains around me had their pieces cocked and bayonets fixed. Particular people were now called on to go into the boat, and were hurried over the side: whence I concluded that with these people I was to be set adrift.

"I, therefore, made another effort to bring about a change, but with no other effect than to be threatened with having my brains blown out.

"The boatswain and the seamen, who were to go in the boat, were allowed to collect twine, canvas, lines, sails, cordage, an eight and twenty gallon cask of water, and the carpenter to take his tool chest. Mr. Samuel got 150 pounds of bread, with a small quantity of rum and wine. He also got a quadrant and a compass into the boat; but he was forbidden, on pain of death, to touch either map, ephemeris, book of astronomical observations, sextant, time-keeper, or any other of my surveys or drawings.

"The mutineers now hurried those they meant to get rid of into the boat. When most of them were in, Christian directed a dram to be served to each of his own crew. I now unhappily saw that nothing could be done to effect the recovery of the ship: there was no one to

assist me, and every endeavour on my part was answered with threats of death.

"The officers were called, and forced over the side
into the boat, while I was kept apart from everyone,
abaft the mizen-mast; Christian, armed with a bayonet, holding me by the bandage that secured my hands.
The guard around me had their pieces cocked, but, on
my daring the ungrateful wretches to fire, they uncocked
them.

"Isaac Martin, one of the guards over me, I saw, had
an inclination to assist me, and, as he fed me a shaddock
(my lips being quite parched with my endeavours to
bring about a change), we explained our wishes to each
other by our looks; but this being observed, Martin was
instantly removed from me; his inclination then was to
leave the ship, for which purpose he got into the boat;
but with many threats they obliged him to return.

"The armourer, Joseph Coleman, and the two carpenters, McIntosh and Norman, were also kept contrary to
their inclination and they begged of me, after I was
astern in the boat, to remember that they declared that
they had no hand in the transaction. Michael Byrne, I
am told, likewise wanted to leave the ship.

"It is of no moment for me to recount my endeavours
to bring back the offenders to a sense of their duty: all
I could do was by speaking to them in general; but my
endeavours were to no avail, for I was kept securely
bound, and no one but the guard was suffered to come
near me.

"To Mr. Samuel I am indebted for securing my jour-
nals and commission, with some material ship papers.
Without these I had nothing to certify what I had done,
and my honour and character might have been suspected, without my possessing a proper document to
have defended them. All this he did with great resolution, though guarded and strictly watched. He attempted to save the time-keeper, and a box with all my
surveys, drawings, and remarks for fifteen years past,

which were very numerous, when he was hurried away, with 'Damn your eyes, you're well off to get what you have.'

"It appeared to me, that Christian was some time in doubt whether he should keep the carpenter or his mates; at length he determined on the latter, and the carpenter was ordered into the boat. He was permitted, but not without some opposition, to take his tool chest.

"Much altercation took place between the mutinous crew during the whole business; some swore, 'I'll be damned if he does not find his way home, if he gets anything with him' (meaning me); others, when the carpenter's chest was carried away, 'Damn my eyes, he will have a vessel built in a month.' While others laughed at the helpless situation of the boat, being very deep, and so little room for those who were in her. As for Christian, he seemed meditating instant destruction on himself and everyone.

"I asked for arms, but they laughed at me, and said that I was well acquainted with the people where I was going, and therefore did not want them; four cutlasses, however, were thrown into the boat, after we were veered astern.

"When the officers and men, with whom I was suffered to have no communication, were put into the boat, they only waited for me, and the master-at-arms informed Christian of it; who then said, 'Come, Captain Bligh, your officers and men are now in the boat, and you must go with them; if you attempt to make the least resistance you will instantly be put to death'; and, without any further ceremony, holding me by the cord that tied my hands, with a tribe of armed ruffians about me, I was forced over the side, where they untied my hands. Being in the boat we were veered astern by a rope. A few pieces of pork were then thrown to us, and some clothes, also the cutlasses I have already mentioned; and it was now that the armourer and carpenters called out to me to remember that they had no hand in the transaction. After having undergone a great deal of ridicule, and been kept some time to make sport for these unfeeling wretches, we were at length cast adrift in the open ocean.

"Notwithstanding the roughness with which I was treated, the remembrance of past kindnesses produced some signs of remorse in Christian. When they were forcing me out of the ship, I asked him if this treatment was a proper return of the many instances he had received of my friendship. He appeared disturbed at my question, and answered, with much emotion, 'That, Captain Bligh, that is the thing; I am in hell—I am in hell.'"

Morrison, however, reports this differently. According to him, Bligh begged of Christian to desist in his course, saying: "I'll pawn my honour, I'll give my bond, Mr. Christian, never to think of this, if you'll desist," urging, at the same time, consideration at least for his wife and family.

Christian replied, "No, Captain Bligh, if you had any honour, things would not have come to this; and if you had any regard for your wife and family, you should have thought of them before, and not behaved so much like a villain."

When the boatswain, Mr. Cole, also attempted to plead with Christian, he was told, "It is too late, I have been in hell for this fortnight past, and I am determined to bear it no longer, and you know, Mr. Cole, that I have been used like a dog all the voyage."

The motivation of Christian's leadership in the mutiny has been variously interpreted. Morrison's account, which vaguely resembles the Quintal tradition reported by Uncle Cornish, relates that Christian, being hurt by the insensitive treatment he had endured at Bligh's hand, had quietly determined to leave the ship. To this end he had arranged to be supplied with part of a roast pig, nails, beads, and other articles of trade, all of which he had stowed in a bag hidden in the clue of Midshipman Tinkler's hammock. His accomplices were the boatswain, the carpenter, and two midshipmen (Stewart and Hayward). As a means of navigation, Christian had constructed a rude raft of some staves and stout planks. When the opportunity of escaping did not present itself during the first and middle watch of the fateful day, he laid down at half past three in the morning to sleep until the time was propitious. Morrison continues his narrative by reporting that at four o'clock when Mr. Stewart came to relieve Christian, he found the latter asleep and urged him to abandon his plans. But Christian, anticipating no interference from Hayward, the mate of his watch, asleep on the arms chest, or from Hallet, the other midshipman, who was absent, suddenly conceived the idea of forcibly taking the ship. Christian first spoke of his intentions to Matthew Quintal and Isaac Martin, who had suffered floggings from Bligh. These men readily fell in with Christian's plan, and to them were added a number of other seamen who had no love for Bligh. The arms chest was then secured, and Christian and his mutineers proceeded to place Bligh under guard and to restrain all others not in his party.

Bligh's prompt defense published on his return to England presents a different picture. Unable to conceive his own actions as inspiring mutinous and bitter resentment, he deduces that the mutiny was a carefully laid conspiracy to enable the men to return to the licentious idleness of Tahiti. Moreover, he marvels at the diabolic secrecy which prevailed, since none of the sailors who accompanied him were cognizant of Christian's plans.

The truth is probably somewhere between these divergent views. Bligh's record is a black one. He was the victim of another mutiny years later at Botany Bay in New South Wales. His treatment of his crew was harsh, even though it can be justified as common enough in the period. He did publicly and repeatedly insult Christian, an officer. On the other hand, Tahiti must have been a sailor's dream of heaven. And among these rough sailors, there must have been some ready enough, with-

out special provocation, to exchange their lots for softer
berths ashore at Tahiti. To this tinder in the crew was
applied the fire of Christian. Geoffrey Rawson describes
him as an "unusual type of man." Of superior birth and
breed to the rough seamen of the forecastle, he was at
the same time of an ardent and passionate nature. He
was "a great man for the women, and Lamb, with whom
he sailed in the *Britannia,* said of him that 'he was then
one of the most foolish young men I ever knew in regard
to the sex.'"

There is nothing to show that Christian had cold-
bloodedly arranged a mutiny, except Bligh's deductions.
There is the entire circumstantial setting to convince us
that an accumulated bitterness and resentment on the
part of Christian against Bligh spontaneously meshed
into a natural regret among the men at leaving Tahiti.
Thus geared, these motives were sufficient and complementary.

In the voluminous discussion of the direct and indirect
circumstances leading to the mutiny on the *Bounty,* the
ages of the mutineers have been curiously neglected.
Christian was only twenty-four. The youngest was seventeen and the oldest forty. The average age of all twenty-
five mutineers was about twenty-six and a half years.
These figures are based on Admiralty records which were
perhaps entered at the outset of the voyage. But even
an allowance of a year and a half from the date of the
record to the time of the mutiny, still leaves the mutineers a youthful crew. Had the crew consisted of older
and less responsive men, perhaps no mutiny would have
occurred.

It is tempting to divert this narrative from the main
current of the history of Pitcairn and to pause for Bligh's
adventure in the *Bounty's* cutter. But that is a story in
itself. There were nineteen men, including Bligh, scantily
supplied with 150 pounds of bread, 32 pounds of pork,
6 quarts of rum, 6 bottles of wine, and 28 gallons of
water. They were crowded into an open boat and set

down in an uncharted sea. Despair and the courage born of extremity must have filled every heart as the men watched the *Bounty* sail away. And had they known the agony they were to endure, they might not have had the hardihood to face it. The true temper of Bligh appeared now and persisted through the next forty-one days. Through trackless seas, under broiling suns, with gnawing hunger in their bellies and with swollen tongues in hot, choking throats, these men, under the firm, watchful command of Bligh, made one of the most extraordinary voyages on record. They met hostile natives, they navigated dangerous waters, they sailed 3,618 miles to a haven in Timor. Of the nineteen men only twelve reached England and home.

The others, the mutineers, were twenty-five in number. Not one of the seamen elected to go with Bligh. In addition, three of the midshipmen and some of the petty officers remained on the *Bounty*. This is the full list of mutineers:

FLETCHER CHRISTIAN, *master's mate*
PETER HEYWOOD, *midshipman*
EDWARD YOUNG, *midshipman*
GEORGE STEWART, *midshipman*
CHARLES CHURCHILL, *master-at-arms*
JOHN MILLS, *gunner's mate*
JAMES MORRISON, *boatswain's mate*
THOMAS BURKITT, *able seaman*
MATTHEW QUINTAL, *able seaman*
JOHN SUMNER, *able seaman*
JOHN MILLWARD, *able seaman*
WILLIAM MCCOY, *able seaman*
HENRY HILLBRANT, *able seaman*
MICHAEL BYRNE, *able seaman*
WILLIAM MUSPRAT, *able seaman*
ALEXANDER SMITH, *able seaman*
JOHN WILLIAMS, *able seaman*
THOMAS ELLISON, *able seaman*

Isaac Martin, *able seaman*
Richard Skinner, *able seaman*
Matthew Thompson, *able seaman*
William Brown, *gardener*
Joseph Coleman, *armorer*
Charles Norman, *carpenter's mate*
Thomas McIntosh, *carpenter's crew*

With Fletcher Christian in command, the course of the *Bounty* was directed toward the island of Tubuai, about 300 miles south of Tahiti. This in itself might be taken to indicate that the lure of Tahiti was not the primary motivation of the mutiny. On May 25, 1789, they reached Tubuai. All the breadfruit plants laboriously collected and carefully nurtured for six months were now discarded, and the mutineers appropriated the property of the departed men.

The Tubuaians on close acquaintance proved less hospitable than the Tahitian experience had led the mutineers to expect. Unable to obtain from the suspicious natives the supplies necessary for a settlement, Christian was forced to make his way once more to Tahiti where he could anticipate a warmer reception.

An episode occurred at this stage which impressed on Christian the possibility that one mutiny might lead to another. A plot was hatched to relieve Christian of the command, but it was discovered in time. From then on the keys to the arms chest were carefully guarded. Morrison, to whom we owe a knowledge of this attempt, adds, however, that Christian never lost the respect of his men even though they might disagree with him.

When the *Bounty* arrived at Tahiti on June 6, Christian took a leaf from Bligh's book. He informed the natives that Bligh had met Cook and that the *Bounty* had been sent back to obtain additional supplies. The name of the heroic and already mythical Cook procured within a few days 312 hogs, 38 goats, and 8 dozen fowl in addition to the bull and cow deposited by Bligh. The livestock Bligh had taken such pains to bring was given up willingly enough. Besides this, quantities of breadfruit, plantain, bananas, and other fruit were brought aboard. Heavily stocked, the *Bounty* sailed again two weeks later for Tubuai. Morrison states that native stowaways were discovered: nine women, twelve men, and eight boys.

Assisted by their native companions, the mutineers had better luck this time in establishing a *rapport* with the Tubuaians. These islanders are closely related to the Tahitians and speak almost identical dialects. The chief of the island coöperated with his uninvited guests by giving them a plot of ground. Christian's first act was to build a fort 50 yards square, surrounded by walls and a ditch 20 feet broad. The guns of the *Bounty* were mounted as further protection. This elaborate fortification seemed more than ominous to the natives who naturally showed signs of resentment at the hostile gesture. Added to this, dissension broke out among the Englishmen. Those who had no active part in the mutiny looked askance at this digging which had all the signs of permanency. They wanted to go home. Finally, the matter was put to a vote, and the decision was reached to abandon the attempt to settle at Tubuai.

Three months after the last departure from Tahiti the *Bounty* was back again, landing at Matavai Bay, September 22. The crew of twenty-five was divided into two parties. One, consisting of sixteen men, elected to land at Tahiti. The other of nine men decided to seek another island where they might escape the increasingly long arm of British justice. Their names are as follows:

FLETCHER CHRISTIAN
EDWARD YOUNG
JOHN MILLS
MATTHEW QUINTAL
WILLIAM McCOY
ALEXANDER SMITH (later known as JOHN ADAMS)
JOHN WILLIAMS

Isaac Martin
William Brown

At dawn the next day, after spending his last few hours ashore with Stewart and Heywood at the home of a friendly chief, Christian bade his youthful companions a sad farewell. And as the *Bounty* slowly gained speed the two midshipmen on the beach watched her disappear forever.

Tahiti welcomed the sixteen men left behind by Christian. Contact with white men had not yet engendered a feeling of contempt or indifference. Wherever they went, the Englishmen were surrounded by an eager band. Chieftains welcomed the prestige of their friendship. And natives of a lower order accepted them with traditional Polynesian hospitality, not unmixed with a love of novelty. Morrison and Millward became the protégés of Poenoo, a landowner at Matavai Bay. Stewart and Heywood were received into the household of Tippaoo, with whose daughter Stewart fell in love. The others scattered to various districts and households.

Not long after the arrival of the mutineers, the Tahitians experienced an example of the brutal conduct of which the Englishmen were capable. Matthew Thompson, who had adopted an overbearing attitude toward the natives, commanded one of them, whom he encountered walking with his wife and child, to stop. Not comprehending the order, the native advanced on his way. Thompson, infuriated by the indifference to his command, raised his musket and deliberately shot to death the unoffending native. Forced to retire into the interior to escape the anger of the islanders, Thompson joined Charles Churchill who had assumed the title of chief on the death of his *tyo* or patron. In a short time, Thompson quarreled with Churchill and slew him also. For this crime he was murdered by the enraged subjects of Churchill.

Morrison, however, soon grew dissatisfied with the

prospects of a life of exile and, joined by eight others, undertook to build a boat by which they might work their way back to civilization. To avoid obstacles from the natives, they explained that the craft was intended for cruising around the island. The boat was finally launched on July 30, 1790. She was a stoutly made boat, 30 feet long, with a beam of 9 feet 6 inches, and was named *Resolution*. Her builders, however, were never to employ her for their escape. On March 23, 1791, H.M.S. *Pandora* anchored at Matavai Bay, prepared to capture and return the mutineers to England for trial.

Edwards, captain of the *Pandora,* soon had the mutineers aboard, even though he had to chase Morrison, Ellison, and Norman, who had tried a get-away in the *Resolution.* The instructions delivered to Edwards were "to keep the mutineers as closely confined as may preclude all possibility of their escaping, having, however, proper regard to the preservation of their lives, that they may be brought home to undergo the punishment due to their demerits." There is nothing, however, in these orders which justifies the actual measures taken by their instrument, Captain Edwards. He had constructed on the quarter deck of the *Pandora* a cage about 11 feet long, entered only from the top through an opening 18 inches square. Into this chamber, known as "Pandora's box," were pressed fourteen men, heavily shackled with irons that were not supposed "to fit like gloves," as Mr. Larkin, the lieutenant, put it when the men complained of the swellings on their legs caused by their fetters. The only provision for air and light, except for the small entrance, was two nine-inch scuttles in the bulkhead of the box. Under these inhuman conditions fourteen men were forced to live and to perform the necessities of nature. Only once a week was this infernal trap cleaned with a hose. No commentary is necessary on the character of a man capable of confining fellow creatures in such a cesspool.

What must have been the horror of the natives when

they saw their friends treated in such fashion by their own countrymen. Many of the Tahitians loyal to their *tyo*ship brought daily supplies for the comfort of the mutineers, but only a few were permitted to visit them. Hamilton, the surgeon of the *Pandora,* was deeply moved by the sight of the reunion of the men and their native wives. "The prisoners' wives visited the ship daily and brought their children, who were permitted to be carried to their unhappy fathers. To see the poor captives in irons, weeping over their tender offspring, was too moving a scene for any feeling heart. Their wives brought them ample supplies of every delicacy the country afforded while we lay there, and behaved with the greatest fidelity and affection to them."

The grief of Peggy, Stewart's wife, was so heart-rending that, unable to bear the daily ordeal, he begged the captain not to allow her to visit him. The missionaries who arrived eight years later reported that Peggy died of a broken heart a few months after Stewart's departure.

On May 8, the *Pandora* left Tahiti. After a fruitless search among the neighboring islands for the remaining nine mutineers, Edwards gave up the hunt and started on the homeward voyage. While traversing the passage between Australia and New Guinea, the *Pandora* was wrecked on the Great Barrier Reef. Trapped like rats in Pandora's box, the men might have all drowned had not their despairing cries attracted the attention of the boatswain's mate. He was only able to draw some of the bolts before the ship lurched to her doom. Skinner and Hillbrant were drowned, still fastened to their chains. Stewart and Sumner, freed at the last moment, were struck by the gangway and sank. The folly of Edwards was colossal, and to him must be attributed these four violent deaths.

The surviving men of the *Pandora* and the ten captives made their way with much suffering to Timor where Bligh had preceded them two years earlier. Finally, on September 12, 1792, almost five years after their departure, the ten mutineers were held at Newgate for court-martial.

The trial lasted five days. Each man in his turn told his story, was cross-examined, and was then retired to await the decision of the Court. Norman, Coleman, McIntosh, and Byrne were acquitted. The remaining six, Heywood, Morrison, Ellison, Burkitt, Millward, and Musprat, were condemned to death, but the first two, Heywood and Morrison were recommended to the King's mercy. They were pardoned by a King's warrant. Musprat was also liberated. No hope, however, sustained the other three. Aboard the *Brunswick,* on October 29, 1792, Ellison, Burkitt, and Millward were hanged, thus expiating the crime of the mutiny on the *Bounty.*

Like a fallen rider who remounts, Heywood reëntered the service and distinguished himself under Lord Hood. When he retired after an honorable career, he was near the head in the list of captains. Morrison likewise saw service again and lost his life as gunner on the *Blenheim.* The others vanish into anonymity.

3

REDEMPTION ON PITCAIRN

When Christian, accompanied by eight mutineers and a number of natives, sailed from Tahiti, he sailed out of the world. As he watched the island blur with the distance, it was the last glimpse of what must have subsequently seemed like civilization. And how poignant a glimpse that was! Tahiti, with its deep, rich purples and greens, wet with the dawn, pouring down its spires and pinnacles, and with scarves of mist rising in the fiordlike valleys as the morning sun emerged.

Tight-lipped concerning his plans, or silent possibly because he had none, Christian left no clue to follow. When the punitive Edwards arrived on the *Pandora,* no one in Tahiti could give him any information about the hiding place of the leader of the mutiny. And none of the islands Edwards visited in the vicinity revealed traces of the vanished crew. In England, all expectation of ever seeing the departed was abandoned by the government, and after the single attempt of the *Pandora,* no further effort was made to apprehend them. As far as the world was concerned they were forgotten.

Then, in a letter dated Nantucket, 1813, Captain Mayhew Folger of Boston reported to the British Admiralty the discovery of Christian's retreat. He related that in 1808, while on a sealing voyage in the *Topaze,* he ran close to an island that he took to be Pitcairn, an uninhabited morsel of land, first sighted in 1767 by En-

sign Pitcairn sailing with Carteret. Putting over two
boats, Folger started for shore to seek water and seals.
His surprise was great when he observed a small boat
being launched from what he supposed was a deserted
shore. Even greater was his astonishment when he was
hailed in excellent English as the boats drew together.
There were three youths in the boat, and they asked for
the captain of the ship to whom they presented a gift of
cocoanuts. At the same time they invited Folger to visit
a white man who lived on the island.

Folger, in logbook style, records that he went on shore
and found there an Englishman by the name of Alexander Smith, the only survivor of the nine Englishmen who
last sailed the *Bounty*. In this manner was the last of the
mutineers accounted for about eighteen years after their
disappearance.

The events of the years intervening between their departure from Tahiti and Folger's visit were related by
Alexander Smith to his visitor. When the Englishmen left
Tahiti they took with them native wives and six men as
servants. Smith did not indicate whether Pitcairn was the
definite objective of Christian or was met by chance. At
any rate, Pitcairn appeared to be satisfactory, and the
Englishmen and their native followers landed with all
their goods and chattels. To prevent any desertion Christian had the *Bounty* run on the rock-strewn shore of
Bounty Bay where the surf completed the dismember-
ment begun by the men. This event took place in 1790.
A short time later the colony lost two of her Englishmen.
One ran mad and hurled himself into the sea. The other
died of fever. About four years later, the native men,
brutally treated by the seven Englishmen, rose in rebel-
lion and attacked their masters. They murdered six of
the Englishmen, leaving only Alexander Smith desper-
ately wounded by a pistol ball in his neck. Then Smith
and the widows combined, according to this version, to
destroy utterly the native men. There now remained
only Smith, eight or nine native women, and an unspeci-

fied number of children. Smith in his story to Folger concluded simply by saying that he went to work tilling the ground so that it produced plenty for them all and that he lived comfortably as commander-in-chief of Pitcairn's Island.

This, the first story of the events surrounding the settlement of Pitcairn, does not jibe with either the later accounts narrated by Smith himself or with the island tradition reported by Shillibeer and Miss Young. Shillibeer, a young lieutenant on board the *Tagus*, visited Pitcairn in 1815, and he describes his visit with enthusiasm.

Natives came out to greet the new arrivals. When requested to come alongside, the Pitcairn youths replied, "We have no boat hook to hold on by."

"I will throw you a rope," answered the captain.

"If you do we have nothing to make fast to," came the reply.

In spite of these difficulties, the islanders came on board. After the first few minutes of greeting and curious inspection on both sides, young McCoy asked, "Do you know one, William Bligh, in England?" In turn he was asked if he knew one Christian.

"Oh, yes," responded McCoy, "very well. His son is in the boat there, coming up. His name is Friday Fletcher October Christian. His father is dead now—he was shot by a black fellow."

The story extracted from these sons of the mutineers by cross-examination is given by Shillibeer as follows:

QUESTION: Christian, you say, was shot?

ANSWER: Yes he was.

QUESTION: By whom?

ANSWER: A black fellow shot him.

QUESTION: What cause do you assign for the murder?

ANSWER: I know no reason, except a jealousy which I have heard existed between the people of Otaheite and the English. Christian was shot in the back while at work in his yam plantation.

QUESTION: What became of the man who killed him?

ANSWER: Oh! that black fellow was shot afterwards by an Englishman.

QUESTION: Was there any other disturbance between the Otaheitians and English, after the death of Christian?

ANSWER: Yes, the black fellows rose, shot two Englishmen, and wounded John Adams, who is now the only remaining man who came in the *Bounty*.

QUESTION: How did Adams escape being murdered?

ANSWER: He hid himself in the wood, and the same night, the women enraged at the murder of the English, to whom they were more partial than their countrymen, rose and put every Otaheitian to death in their sleep. This saved Adams, his wounds were soon healed, and although old, he now enjoys good health.

QUESTION: How many men and women did Christian bring with him in the *Bounty*?

ANSWER: Nine white men, six from Otaheite, and eleven women.

QUESTION: And how many are there now on the island?

ANSWER: In all we have forty-eight.

QUESTION: And what became of the *Bounty*?

ANSWER: After everything useful was taken out of her, she was run ashore, set fire to, and burnt.

QUESTION: Have you ever heard how many years it is since Christian was shot?

ANSWER: I understand it was about two years after his arrival at the island.

QUESTION: What became of Christian's wife?

ANSWER: She died soon after Christian's son was born, and I have heard that Christian took forcibly the wife of one of the black followers to supply her place, and which was the chief cause of his being shot.

Not only does this story of the first years of the colony at Pitcairn differ materially from the narrative told to Captain Folger, but they both depart from the version recorded by Captain Beechey on his visit in 1825. This last is by far the most convincing on account of its greater detail, some of which Beechey quotes from Edward Young's diary. This journal seems to have been examined only by Beechey, and it has since disappeared.* The story follows:

"The mutineers now bade adieu to all the world, save the few individuals associated with them in exile. But where that exile should be passed, was yet undecided; the Marquesas Islands were first mentioned, but Christian, on reading Captain Carteret's account of Pitcairn Island, thought it better adapted to the purpose, and accordingly shaped a course thither. They reached it not many days afterwards; and Christian, with one of the seamen, landed in a little nook, which we afterwards found very convenient for disembarkation. They soon traversed the island sufficiently to be satisfied that it was exactly suited to their wishes. It possessed water, wood, a good soil, and some fruits. The anchorage in the offing was very bad, and landing for boats extremely hazardous. The mountains were so difficult of access, and the passes so narrow, that they might be maintained by a few persons against an army; and there were several caves to which, in case of necessity, they could retreat, and where, as long as their provision lasted, they might bid defiance to their pursuers. With this intelligence they returned on board, and brought the ship to an anchor in a small bay on the northern side of the island, which I have in consequence named 'Bounty Bay,' where everything that could be of utility was landed, and where it was agreed to destroy the ship, either by running her on shore, or burning her. Christian, Adams, and the majority, were for the former expedient; but while they went to the forepart of the ship, to execute this business, Matthew Quintal set fire to the carpenter's store-room. The vessel burnt to the water's edge, and then drifted upon the rocks, where the remainder of the wreck was

* A recent letter in the London *Times* reports the existence of Edward Young's Journal in England, but inquiry has not succeeded in bringing it to light.

burnt for fear of discovery. This occurred on the 23rd
of January, 1790.

"Upon their first landing they perceived, by the remains of several habitations, *morais*, and three or four
rudely sculptured images, which stood upon the emi-
nence overlooking the bay where the ship was destroyed,
that the island had been previously inhabited. Some ap-
prehensions were, in consequence, entertained lest the
natives should secrete themselves, and in some un-
guarded moment make an attack upon them; but by de-
grees these fears subsided, and their avocations proceeded without interruption.

"A suitable spot of ground for a village was fixed
upon, with the exception of which the island was divided into equal portions, but to the exclusion of the poor
blacks, who being only friends of the seamen, were not
considered as entitled to the same privileges. Obliged to
lend their assistance to the others in order to procure a
subsistence, they thus, from being their friends, in the
course of time became their slaves. No discontent, however, was manifested, and they willingly assisted in the
cultivation of the soil.

"In clearing the space that was allotted to the village,
a row of trees was left between it and the sea, for the
purpose of concealing the houses from the observation
of any vessels that might be passing, and nothing was
allowed to be erected that might in any way attract attention. Until these houses were finished, the sails of the
Bounty were converted into tents, and when no longer
required for that purpose, became very acceptable as
clothing. Thus supplied with all the necessaries of life,
and some of its luxuries, they felt their condition comfortable even beyond their most sanguine expectation,
and everything went on peaceably and prosperously for
about two years, at the expiration of which Williams,
who had the misfortune to lose his wife about a month
after his arrival, by a fall from a precipice while collecting birds' eggs, became dissatisfied, and threatened to

leave the island in one of the boats of the *Bounty*, unless he had another wife; an unreasonable request, as it could not be complied with, except at the expense of the happiness of one of his companions: but Williams, actuated by selfish considerations alone, persisted in his threat, and the Europeans not willing to part with him, on account of his usefulness as an armourer, constrained one of the blacks to bestow his wife upon the applicant. The blacks, outrageous [sic] at this second act of flagrant injustice, made common cause with their companion, and matured a plan of revenge upon their aggressors, which, had it succeeded, would have proved fatal to all the Europeans.

"Fortunately, the secret was imparted to the women, who ingeniously communicated it to the white men in a song, of which the words were, 'Why does black man sharpen axe? to kill white man.' The instant Christian became aware of the plot, he seized his gun and went in search of the blacks, but with a view only of showing them that their scheme was discovered, and thus by timely interference endeavouring to prevent the execution of it. He met one of them (Ohoo) at a little distance from the village, taxed him with the conspiracy, and in order to intimidate him, discharged his gun, which he had humanely loaded with powder only. Ohoo, however, imagining otherwise, and that the bullet had missed its object, derided his unskilfulness, and fled into the woods, followed by his accomplice Talaloo, who had been deprived of his wife. The remaining blacks, finding their plot discovered, purchased pardon by promising to murder their accomplices, who had fled, which they afterwards performed by an act of the most odious treachery. Ohoo was betrayed and murdered by his own nephew; and Talaloo, after an ineffectual attempt made upon him by poison, fell by the hands of his friend and his wife, the very woman on whose account all the disturbance began, and whose injuries Talaloo felt he was revenging in common with his own.

"Tranquillity was by these means restored, and preserved for about two years; at the expiration of which, dissatisfaction was again manifested by the blacks, in consequence of oppression and ill treatment, principally by Quintal and M'Coy. Meeting with no compassion or redress from their masters, a second plan to destroy their oppressors was matured, and unfortunately, too successfully executed.

"It was agreed that two of the blacks, Timoa and Nehow, should desert from their masters, provide themselves with arms, and hide in the woods, but maintain a frequent communication with the other two, Tetaheite and Menalee; and that on a certain day they should attack and put to death all the Englishmen, when at work in their plantations. Tetaheite, to strengthen the party of the blacks on this day, borrowed a gun and ammunition of his master, under the pretence of shooting hogs, which had become wild and very numerous; but instead of using it in this way, he joined his accomplices, and with them fell upon Williams and shot him. Martin, who was at no great distance, heard the report of the musket, and exclaimed, 'Well done. We shall have a glorious feast to-day,' supposing that a hog had been shot. The party proceeded from Williams' towards Christian's plantation, where Menalee, the other black, was at work with Mills and M'Coy; and, in order that the suspicions of the whites might not be excited by the report they had heard, requested Mills to allow him (Menalee) to assist them in bringing home the hog they pretended to have killed. Mills agreed; and the four, being united, proceeded to Christian, who was working at his yam-plot, and shot him. Thus fell a man, who, from being the reputed ringleader of the mutiny, has obtained an unenviable celebrity, and whose crime, if anything can excuse mutiny, may perhaps be considered as in some degree palliated, by the tyranny which led to its commission.

"M'Coy, hearing his groans, observed to Mills, 'There was surely some person dying,' but Mills replied, 'It's only Mainmast (Christian's wife) calling her children to dinner.' The white men being yet too strong for the blacks to risk a conflict with them, it was necessary to concert a plan, in order to separate Mills and M'Coy. Two of them accordingly secreted themselves in M'Coy's house, and Tetaheite ran and told him that the two blacks who had deserted were stealing things out of his house. M'Coy instantly hastened to detect them, and on entering was fired at; but the ball passed him. M'Coy immediately communicated the alarm to Mills, and advised him to seek shelter in the woods; but Mills, being quite satisfied that one of the blacks whom he had made his friend would not suffer him to be killed, determined to remain. M'Coy, less confident, ran in search of Christian, but finding him dead, joined Quintal (who was already apprised of the work of destruction, and had sent his wife to give the alarm to the others), and fled with him to the woods.

"Mills had scarcely been left alone, when the two blacks fell upon him, and he became a victim to his misplaced confidence in the fidelity of his friend. Martin and Brown were next separately murdered by Menalee and Tenina; Menalee effecting with a maul what the musket had left unfinished. Tenina, it is said, wished to save the life of Brown, and fired at him with powder only, desiring him, at the same time, to fall as if killed; but, unfortunately rising too soon, the other black, Menalee, shot him.

"Adams was first apprised of his danger by Quintal's wife, who, in hurrying through his plantation, asked why he was working at such a time? Not understanding the question, but seeing her alarmed, he followed her, and was almost immediately met by the blacks, whose appearance exciting suspicion, he made his escape into the woods. After remaining there three or four hours, Adams, thinking all was quiet, stole to his yam-plot for a supply of provisions; his movements, however, did not escape the vigilance of the blacks, who attacked and shot him through the body, the ball entering at his right shoulder, and passing out through his throat. He fell upon his side, and was instantly assailed by one of them with the butt end of the gun; but he parried the blows at the expense of a broken finger. Tetaheite then placed his gun to his side, but it fortunately missed fire twice. Adams, recovering a little from the shock of his wound, sprang on his legs, and ran off with as much speed as he was able, and fortunately outstripped his pursuers, who seeing him likely to escape, offered him protection if he would stop. Adams, much exhausted by his wound, readily accepted their terms, and was conducted to Christian's house, where he was kindly treated. Here this day of bloodshed ended, leaving only four Englishmen alive out of nine. It was a day of emancipation to the blacks, who were now masters of the island, and of humiliation and retribution to the whites.

"Young, who was a great favourite with the women, and had, during this attack, been secreted by them, was now also taken to Christian's house. The other two, M'Coy and Quintal, who had always been the great oppressors of the blacks, escaped to the mountains, where they supported themselves upon the produce of the ground about them.

"The party in the village lived in tolerable tranquillity for about a week; at the expiration of which, the men of colour began to quarrel about the right of choosing the women whose husbands had been killed; which ended in Menalee's shooting Timoa as he sat by the side of Young's wife, accompanying her song with his flute. Timoa not dying immediately, Menalee reloaded, and deliberately despatched him by a second discharge. He afterwards attacked Tetaheite, who was condoling with Young's wife for the loss of her favourite black, and would have murdered him also, but for the interference of the women. Afraid to remain longer in the village, he escaped to the mountains and joined Quintal and M'Coy, who, though glad of his services, at first received him with suspicion. This great acquisition to their force enabled them to bid defiance to the opposite party; and to show their strength, and that they were provided with muskets, they appeared on a ridge of mountains, within sight of the village, and fired a volley which so alarmed the others that they sent Adams to say, if they would kill the black man, Menalee, and return to the village, they would all be friends again. The terms were so far complied with that Menalee was shot; but, apprehensive of the sincerity of the remaining blacks, they refused to return while they were alive.

"Adams says it was not long before the widows of the white men so deeply deplored their loss, that they determined to revenge their death, and concerted a plan to murder the only two remaining men of colour. Another account, communicated by the islanders, is that it was only part of a plot formed at the same time that Menalee was murdered, which could not be put in execution before. However, this may be, it was equally fatal to the poor blacks. The arrangement was, that Susan should murder one of them, Tetaheite, while he was sleeping by the side of his favourite; and that Young should at the same instant, upon a signal being given, shoot the other, Nehow. The unsuspecting Tetaheite retired as usual, and fell by the blow of an axe; the other was looking at Young loading his gun, which he supposed was for the purpose of shooting hogs, and requested him to put in a good charge, when he received the deadly contents.

"In this manner the existence of the last of the men of colour terminated, who, though treacherous and revengeful, had, it is feared, too much cause for complaint. The accomplishment of this fatal scheme was immediately communicated to the two absentees, and their return solicited. But so many instances of treachery had occurred, that they would not believe the report, though delivered by Adams himself, until the hands and heads of the deceased were produced, which being done, they returned to the village. This eventful day was the third October, 1893. There were now left upon the island, Adams, Young, M'Coy, and Quintal, ten women, and some children. Two months after this period, Young commenced a manuscript journal, which affords a good insight into the state of the island, and the occupations of the settlers. From it we learn, that they lived peaceably together, building their houses, fencing in and cultivating their grounds, fishing, and catching birds, and constructing pits for the purpose of entrapping hogs, which had become very numerous and wild, as well as injurious to the yam-crops. The only discontent appears to have been among the women, who lived promiscuously with the men, frequently changing their abode.

"Young says, March 12, 1794, 'Going over to borrow a rake, to rake the dust off my ground, I saw Jenny having a skull in her hand: I asked her whose it was? and was told it was Jack Williams's. I desired it might be buried: the women who were with Jenny gave me for answer, it should not. I said it should; and demanded it accordingly. I was asked the reason why I, in particular, should insist on such a thing, when the rest of the white men did not? I said, if they gave them leave to keep the skulls above ground, I did not. Accordingly when I saw M'Coy, Smith, and Mat. Quintal, I acquainted them with it, and said, I thought that if the girls did not agree to give up the heads of the five white men in a peaceable manner, they ought to be taken by force, and buried.' About this time the women appear to have been much dissatisfied; and Young's journal declares that, 'since the massacre, it has been the desire of the greater part of them to get some conveyance, to enable them to leave the island.' This feeling continued, and on the 14th of April, 1794, was so strongly urged, that the men began to build them a boat; but wanting planks and nails, Jenny, who now resides at Otaheite, in her zeal tore up the boards of her house, and endeavoured, though without success, to persuade some others to follow her example.

"On the 13th of August following, the vessel was finished, and on the 15th she was launched: but, as Young says, 'according to expectation she upset,' and it was most fortunate for them that she did so; for had they launched out upon the ocean, where could they have gone? or what could a few ignorant women have done by themselves, drifting upon the waves, but ultimately have fallen a sacrifice to their folly? However, the fate of the vessel was a great disappointment, and they continued much dissatisfied with their condition; probably not without some reason, as they were kept in great subordination and were frequently beaten by M'Coy and Quintal, who appear to have been of very quarrelsome dispositions; Quintal in particular, who proposed 'not to laugh, joke, or give anything to any of the girls.'

"On the 16th August they dug a grave, and buried the bones of the murdered people; and on October 3rd, 1794, they celebrated the murder of the black men at Quintal's house. On the 11th November, a conspiracy of the women to kill the white men in their sleep was discovered; upon which they were all seized, and a disclosure ensued; but no punishment appears to have been inflicted upon them, in consequence of their promising to conduct themselves properly, and never again to give any cause 'even to suspect their behavior.' However, though they were pardoned, Young observed, 'We did not forget their conduct; and it was agreed among us, that the first female who misbehaved should be put to death; and this punishment was to be repeated on each offence until we could discover the real intentions of the women.' Young appears to have suffered much from mental perturbation in consequence of these disturbances; and observes of himself on the two following days, that 'he was bothered and idle.'

"The suspicions of the men induced them, on the 15th, to conceal two muskets in the bush, for the use of any person who might be so fortunate as to escape, in the event of an attack being made. On the 30th November, the women again collected and attacked them; but no lives were lost, and they returned on being once more pardoned, but were again threatened with death the next time they misbehaved. Threats thus repeatedly made, and as often unexecuted, as might be expected, soon lost their effect, and the women formed a party whenever their displeasure was excited, and hid themselves in the unfrequented parts of the island, carefully providing themselves with fire-arms. In this manner the men were kept in continual suspense, dreading the result of each disturbance, as the numerical strength of the women was much greater than their own.

"On the 4th of May, 1795, two canoes were begun, and in two days completed. These were used for fishing, in which employment the people were frequently successful, supplying themselves with rockfish and large mackerel. On the 27th of December following, they were greatly alarmed by the appearance of a ship close in with the island. Fortunately for them there was a tremendous surf upon the rocks, the weather wore a very threatening aspect, and the ship stood to the S.E., and at noon was out of sight. Young appears to have thought this a providential escape, as the sea for a week after was 'smoother than they had ever recollected it since their arrival on the island.'

"So little occurred in the year 1796, that one page records the whole of the events; and throughout the following year there are but three incidents worthy of notice. The first, their endeavour to procure a quantity of meat for salting; the next, their attempt to make syrup from the tee-plant (*dracaena terminalis*) and sugar-cane; and the third, a serious accident that happened to M'Coy, who fell from a cocoa-nut tree and hurt his right thigh, sprained both his ankles and wounded his side. The occupations of the men continued similar to those already related, occasionally enlivened by visits to the opposite side of the island. They appear to have been more sociable; dining frequently at each other's houses, and contributing more to the comfort of the women, who, on their part, gave no ground for uneasiness. There was also a mutual accommodation amongst them in regard to provisions, of which a regular account was taken. If one person was successful in hunting, he lent the others as much meat as they required, to be repaid at leisure; and the same occurred with yams, taros, etc., so that they lived in a very domestic and tranquil state.

"It unfortunately happened that M'Coy had been employed in a distillery in Scotland; and being very much addicted to liquor, he tried an experiment with the tee-root, and on the 20th April, 1798, succeeded in producing a bottle of ardent spirit. This success induced his companion, Matthew Quintal, to 'alter his kettle into a still,' a contrivance which unfortunately succeeded too well, as frequent intoxication was the consequence, with M'Coy in particular, upon whom at length it produced fits of delirium, in one of which, he threw himself from a cliff and was killed. The melancholy fate of this man created so forcible an impression on the remaining few, that they resolved never again to touch spirits; and Adams, I have every reason to believe, to the day of his death kept his vow.

"The journal finishes nearly at the period of M'Coy's death, which is not related in it; but we learned from Adams, that about 1799 Quintal lost his wife by a fall from the cliff while in search of birds' eggs; that he grew discontented, and, though there were several disposable women on the island, and he had already experienced the fatal effects of a similar demand, nothing would satisfy him but the wife of one of his companions. Of course, neither of them felt inclined to accede to this unreasonable indulgence; and he sought an opportunity of putting them both to death. He was fortunately foiled in his first attempt, but swore he would repeat it. Adams and Young having no doubt he would follow up his resolution, and fearing he might be more successful in the next attempt, came to the conclusion, that their own lives were not safe while he was in existence, and that they were justified in putting him to death, which they did with an axe.

"Such was the melancholy fate of seven of the leading mutineers, who escaped from justice only to add murder to their former crimes; for though some of them may not have actually imbrued their hands in the blood of their fellow-creatures, yet all were accessory to the deed.

"As Christian and Young were descended from respectable parents, and had received educations suitable to their birth, it might be supposed that they felt their altered and degraded situation much more than the seamen who were comparatively well off; but if so, Adams says, they had the good sense to conceal it, as not a single murmur or regret escaped them; on the contrary, Christian was always cheerful, and his example was of the greatest service in exciting his companions to labour. He was naturally of a happy, ingenuous disposition, and won the good opinion and respect of all who served under him; which cannot be better exemplified than by his maintaining, under circumstances of great perplexity, the respect and regard of all who were associated with him up to the hour of his death; and even at the period of our visit, Adams, in speaking of him, never omitted to say, 'Mr. Christian.'

"Adams and Young were now the sole survivors out of the fifteen males that landed upon the island. They were both, and more particularly Young, of a serious turn of mind; and it would have been wonderful, after the many dreadful scenes at which they had assisted, if the solitude and tranquillity that ensued had not disposed them to repentance. During Christian's lifetime they had only once read the church service, but since his decease this had been regularly done on every Sunday. They now, however, resolved to have morning and evening family prayers, to add afternoon service to the duty of the Sabbath, and to train up their own children, and those of their late unfortunate companions, in piety and virtue.

"In the execution of this resolution Young's education enabled him to be of the greatest assistance; but he was not long suffered to survive his repentance. An asthmatic complaint, under which he had for some time laboured, terminated his existence about a year after the death of Quintal, and Adams was left the sole survivor of the misguided and unfortunate mutineers of the *Bounty*. The loss of his last companion was a great affliction to him, and was for some time most severely felt. It was a catastrophe, however, that more than ever disposed him to repentance, and determined him to execute the pious resolution he had made, in the hope of expiating his offences."

Thus at Folger's arrival in 1808 the colony consisted of one surviving mutineer, eight or nine Tahitian women, and twenty-five children. These last were the progeny of the Englishmen and their Tahitian wives, the native men having left no offspring. The eldest was Thursday (Friday in the island records) October Christian, then eighteen years old and already a tall, powerfully built man. While still infants, these twenty-five children lost their fathers, and they turned to Smith, or John Adams as he preferred to be called, for guidance and paternal support. On him devolved the responsibility of their training and education which he attempted to execute to his best ability. Fortunately, just before his death of asthma, sometime about 1800, Young sought to make use of his education by instructing the children. Morning and evening family prayers were made a regular practice and services were held on Sabbath. Another and no doubt apocryphal story relates that Adams had two vivid dreams in which were reënacted his past transgressions and the dire punishment awaiting him. In one, he saw a terrible being, a devil, threaten him with a spear, and in the other were painted the lurid details of hell. These so terrified Adams that he resolved to mend his ways and bring up the guiltless children in the true light. His success has been abundantly testified by the first visitors to Pitcairn. Beechey found them "a happy and well-regulated society."

Adams,* whose formal education had been extremely limited, was just able to write his own name, and he could, with some difficulty, spell out the words of the *Bounty's* Bible and prayer book. What little he knew he imparted to the children with the aid of the King James version, a text that could hardly have been better.

From 1790, the year of the landing on Pitcairn, until 1808, four ships were seen by the islanders—one every four and a half years. None of them stopped, and it was not until 1808, as has already been mentioned, that Folger discovered the settlement of some forty-five people on the island. The next visitor arrived in 1815. Captains Staines and Pipon, in the *Tagus,* were in the South Pacific under orders to track down Porter who had ravaged British shipping in the Pacific until the British Admiralty had been forced to take notice of his depredations. Staines and Pipon were only dimly aware of the colony on Pitcairn, Folger's report having been received skeptically in England, so that when the *Tagus* approached Pitcairn those aboard were surprised to see a small boat come out to welcome them. The officers were impressed by the stalwart, vigorous youths who visited their ship. Although the eager curiosity of the islanders betrayed an intelligent and lively interest which, however, never overstepped the bounds of good breeding, the new world that these ships from the ends of the earth represented could sometimes be terrifying. Young McCoy, seeing a small black terrier for the first time, became very alarmed and ran to one of the officers for protection. Somewhat ashamed at his display of timidity,

* John Adams (Alexander Smith in the Admiralty records) was, according to tradition, the son and brother of London lightermen. I have, however, received from Mrs. J. F. McGowan, of Pittsburgh, a letter in which she claims descent from Alexander Smith, who she says lived in County Armagh, Ireland, until he deserted his family. Mrs. McGowan doubts that he ever saw London.

he pointed to the animal, saying, "I know what that is, it is a dog. I never saw a dog before—will it bite?" And then, turning to another islander, he remarked, "It is a pretty thing too to look, is it not?" But the slight condescension of the officers turned to embarrassed shame when, before eating breakfast to which they had been invited, the islanders said their usual grace.

Here is the scene in Shillibeer's own words. "I must here confess I blushed when I saw nature in its most simple state, offer that tribute of respect to the Omnipotent Creator, which from an education I did not perform, nor from society had been taught its necessity. 'Ere they began to eat; on their knees, and with hands uplifted did they implore permission to partake in peace what was set before them, and when they had eaten heartily, resuming their former attitude, offered a fervent prayer of thanksgiving for the indulgence they had just experienced. Our omission of this ceremony did not escape their notice, for Christian asked me whether it was not customary with us also. Here nature was triumphant, for I should do myself an irreparable injustice, did I not with candour acknowledge, I was both embarrassed and wholly at loss for a sound reply, and evaded this poor fellow's question by drawing his attention to the cow, which was then looking down the hatchway, and as he had never seen any of the species before, it was a source of mirth and gratification to him."

Folger, the discoverer of the Pitcairn colony, being an American, created no misgivings among the islanders. Staines and Pipon, however, were the first Englishmen to confront Adams since the mutiny, and his sense of guilt at the sight of officers in His Majesty's Navy was keen. Hannah, the daughter of John Adams, met the visitors at the top of the cliff overlooking Bounty Bay. The visitors had an intuition that she had come to test out the situation so that ample warning might be given her father to escape if their attitude seemed hostile. Reassured of their kindly intentions she led the guests to her parent. The younger officers evinced as much if not more interest in Hannah than in her rather more notorious father. In the words of one of them, "She was arrayed in nature's simple garb, and wholly unadorned, but she was beauty's self, and needed not the aid of ornament. She betrayed some surprise—timidity was a prominent feature."

Although the English officers suspected that Hannah's fears reflected a similar state of mind in Adams, they discovered that he had a longing to see England before he died. He was offered a passage home with any of his family who chose to go. But this proposal was met with an emotional outbreak. Hannah, in tears, cried, "Oh, do not, sir, take from me my father!" To her sobs were added those of the aged Tahitian wife of Adams and other members of the community. The possibility of losing their patriarch filled them with dread and sorrow. Reassured that Adams would not be removed contrary to their wishes, calm was again restored, and our smitten officer noticed that Adams' "daughter too had gained her usual serenity, but she was lovely in her tears, for each seemed to add an additional charm."

The susceptible British described the young women as "having invariably beautiful teeth, fine eyes, and open expression of countenances, and looks of such simple innocence, and sweet sensibility, that renders their appearance at once interesting and engaging, and it is pleasing to add, their minds and manners were as pure and innocent, as this impression indicated. No lascivious looks, or any loose, forward manners, which so much distinguish the characters of the females of the other islands."

The little colony which aside from Adams and the surviving Tahitian women consisted of twenty-odd youngsters, none more than twenty-five years old, made a deep impression on the visitors. The patriarchal Adams was the father of this flock, adored by all, and their instructor in religion and learning. Everyone looked to him for guidance, and his word was the final appeal. Happily it was not necessary, since quarrels were rare. Those which in the natural course of human affairs did arise were trivial and were "nothing more than a word of mouth quarrel."

Ten years later, Captain Beechey in the *Blossom* found little change. Adams had grown older, fatter, and even more patriarchal, more of the children of the mutineers had married, and a thriving crop of grandchildren had appeared. Adams, his fears allayed that he might be punished for his part in the mutiny of thirty-five years ago, came out to the ship this time. His old fo'c'sle manners reasserted themselves automatically, and he respectfully reached to his bald head for a forelock long since vanished. The young men of the island aroused a friendly response from Beechey. He found them "tall, robust and healthy, with good-natured countenances." Their manners were simple and their patent anxiety to give no offense was effective in promoting good-will. "Please may I sit down?" "Please may I open the door?" and similarly polite and, no doubt, tedious requests disarmed the officers of the *Blossom*. As Staines and Pipon were bombarded by questions, so Beechey found himself exploited as an encyclopedia for the eager curiosity of the islanders.

In their desire to emulate the costume of their visitors and to show off their few prized articles of European clothing acquired from their previous visitors, the islanders were a "perfect caricature." Some wore long black coats on bare torsos, others a simple waistcoat without shirt or coat. And all lacked shoes and stockings.

The charm of those islanders aboard his ship, added to the romance surrounding their origin, intensified Beechey's desire to see more of the natives and the manner in which they lived. The hazardous landing was willingly relinquished to the hands of the Pitcairn islanders who landed their guests two by two. That fascinating young lady, Hannah Adams, who had already conquered at least one Englishman's heart, was waiting to greet the

newcomers who thereby felt themselves rewarded for the
dangers of the landing. Clad in the island cloth manufactured from the bark of the mulberry tree, she was a
graceful and charming figure. Hannah's demonstrative
and unpremeditated affection for her father pleased the
officers. Under her guidance, they proceeded to climb the
arduous cliff, clinging to tufts of grass as they laboriously
advanced. Having arrived at the neat village of five
houses, Beechey found himself engulfed in the warm and
simple hospitality of the island. He spent that day and
the next in exploring the island and enjoying the homely
life of the natives. Among the services he was able to
render his hosts in return for their generosity was one
specially requested by old John Adams. Having lived
thirty-five years in unsanctified union, it was Adams' desire that he now be formally married to his aged Tahitian
consort. As captain of the *Blossom*, Beechey had the
power to satisfy this request.

The islanders had been educated, according to the
traditions of their fathers, to look to England as their
mother country. The display of their loyalty to the
Crown touched a sentimental chord in the hearts of
the visiting Englishmen. This devotion to England and
the eagerness of the islanders to identify themselves with
the Empire, even though only with the ragged hem of
her skirt, led them to view the visiting men-of-war as a
tangible thread with "home." Already they had initiated
the custom, later to become traditional, of appealing to
the captain of a British man-of-war for final decision in
disagreements they could not decide themselves.

One of the first cases brought to Captain Beechey was
the affair of George Adams vs. Polly Young. Old John
Adams had trained the youth to regard their word once
given as sacred. This lofty standard had resulted in an
unforeseen and difficult situation. George Adams, having
become deeply smitten by Polly Young, a young lady
slightly older than he, proposed marriage to her. Polly,
for reasons known only to herself, had firmly and em-

phatically stated that she *never* would give her hand to
George. But George, either from lack of choice (girls being scarce) or from a divine persistency common to
lovers, plied Polly with all the blandishments in his ar-
mory. There was no problem until the efforts of George
began to make an impression on Polly, and she found herself regretting her rash statement. But so well had Adams
taught that Polly felt herself bound to her foolish vow,
and for want of a solution the lovesick couple languished
in the bonds of honor. Beechey remarks that "the
weighty case was referred" to him for consideration,
"and the fears of the parties were in some measure relieved by the result, which was, that it would be better to
marry than continue unhappy, in consequence of a hasty
determination made before the judgment was matured."
But so strong were these early habits that the couple,
though yearning for each other, could not be prevailed
upon to accept the inevitable at once.

The reader, curious about the solution of this impasse,
may rejoice to know that my records show that George
married Polly on All Fools' Day, 1827. He had three
sons: John, Jonathan, and Josiah; and after Polly's
death in 1843, he found consolation in Sarah McCoy.

When Beechey went on shore, he discovered that the
population had been increased by normal multiplication
and by the arrival of two Englishmen. The colony now
contained sixty-six persons of whom thirty-six were
males. The two Englishmen were John Buffett, who
hailed from Bristol, and John Evans, the son of a Long-
acre watchmaker. Both these men had been sailors
aboard the *Cyprus* of London which touched at Pitcairn
in 1823. The simplicity and harmony of the little colony
had strongly appealed to Buffett who had secured permission to remain behind. When the *Cyprus* had departed, Evans was discovered ashore, having jumped
ship.

Buffett, a man of some education, undertook to teach
the children, to maintain a register of island affairs, and

to conduct the religious exercises. Beechey found his sermon to be very good but tedious, since it was repeated
three times in succession in order to fix it firmly in the
minds of the islanders. This passion for exhaustive performance also led Adams to read not only the appropriate
prayer but also all those intended only as substitutes.

Even at this early date, 1825, the nightmare of overpopulation had troubled Adams. He anticipated serious
difficulties if the population continued to grow as rankly
as it had commenced. Consulting with Beechey he requested the British government to come to their assistance. On Beechey's representations, the Admiralty and
the Colonial Office prepared to take steps to remove the
population to a more commodious place. But the reluctance of the islanders, when it came to actual removal,
to leave their beloved though constricted Pitcairn caused
the plan to remain in abeyance.

Three years after Beechey's memorable sojourn on
Pitcairn, a momentous event in the colony's history occurred. In November, 1828, George Hunn Nobbs came
to reside among the islanders. Nobbs is a somewhat
mysterious person. Nothing very definite is known about
his origin. It has been averred without evidence that he
was the illegitimate son of a daughter of the Irish gentry and fathered by a marquis. The following brief account of his life and adventures is drawn from the pious
pages of the Reverend Thomas B. Murray.

Nobbs was born in Ireland in 1799, and at an age now
regarded as tender entered in the British Navy. In 1813
he sailed on the *Indefatigable* to New South Wales and
Van Diemen's Land. On the succeeding voyage he jour-
neyed to Valparaiso where he served in the Chilean navy
under Lord Cochrane, later Earl of Dundonald, and was
rewarded with a lieutenancy for his services. From Chile
Nobbs, whose itinerary reads like a modern aviator's,
proceeded to Naples. Wrecked *en route* from that city
to Messina, he endured a voyage in an open boat to
Messina. In 1823, he went back to England, but not for

long. The lust had gripped him again, and he was off for Sierra Leone as chief mate of the *Gambia*. Again Providence saved him for Pitcairn, for of the nineteen men who manned the ship, only the captain, Nobbs, and two Negroes survived. On the next voyage of the *Gambia* Nobbs was in command. This time fever nearly took him off. In the course of his globe-trotting Nobbs had heard of the already famous Pitcairn colony, and true to form he conceived a passion for visiting the island. We next find him aboard the *Circassian* in November, 1825, bound for Pitcairn via Calcutta. At this point the Reverend Mr. Murray points out that Nobbs had already been four times around the world and that he wished to lead a life of peace and usefulness. Detained at Calcutta until August, 1827, Nobbs finally obtained a passage on an American ship, *Ocean,* for Valparaiso. Again shipwreck threatened in the Straits of Sunda, but no doubt Nobbs was able by this time to regard it with nonchalance. At Callao, Nobbs fell in with an American named Noah Bunker, with whom he secured, for £150, an 18-ton bark. These two after a six-week voyage reached Pitcairn in November, 1828. The charmed Nobbs survived the arrival, but his companion succumbed.

Nobbs' education and aggressiveness were superior to those of anyone else's on the island, and he took it upon himself to act as registrar, schoolmaster, and pastor. For these services he expected to be supported by the natives. This poaching on the preserves of John Buffett caused some dissension, though the island soon settled back to its wonted if not impervious calm.

But not for long. On March 5, 1829, John Adams, the last survivor of the mutiny, died. A chapter ended, but so well had he labored and so amenable to his precepts were his "children" that something of his spirit carried over to the next generation. Adams was sixty-five when he died, but he seemed much older to his flock. Just before his death, he called in the islanders and urged them to select a head who would maintain harmony and order. His wise counsel was not adopted, however, and Nobbs extended and consolidated his influence. Although the character of Nobbs was not wholly ingratiating, his addition to the colony was not entirely regrettable. He was the best schoolmaster available, and under his tutelage the children acquired a quite adequate education. At worst, he encouraged some of the natives to adopt an attitude of odious cant and self-conscious religiosity, though this phenomenon is perhaps not to be laid entirely at Nobbs' door. No doubt, the uniform reaction, the universal praise that their simple and unpremeditated devotion had excited in their visitors encouraged some to a more calculated effort to achieve this sweet adulation. Witness the Pitcairn woman who met Waldegrave on his visit in 1830.

"I have brought you a clergyman," announced the captain.

"God bless you, God bless you!" came the response.

"To stay with us?"

"No," replied Captain Waldegrave.

"You bad man, why not?"

"I cannot spare him, he is the clergyman of my ship. I have brought you clothes, which King George sends you," explained Captain Waldegrave.

"We rather want food for our souls," came the reply.

Fortunately, this tendency was not universal, nor is it just to create the impression that the Pitcairn Islanders were given to sanctimony. There is decisive evidence that their piety was genuine. Waldegrave was able to confirm all previous impressions of the people. He wrote, "It was with great gratification that we observed the Christian simplicity of the natives. They appeared to have no guile. Their cottages were open to all, and all were welcome to their food."

In the five years since Beechey's visit, Waldegrave found that fifteen people had been added to the population. When he asked the islanders their total number, they replied eighty-one. But on the actual counting of names the answer persistently came to seventy-nine. Finally one of them quietly solved the difficulty by giving the Christian names of two others previously withheld. But the parents' names were not divulged. "It would be wrong to tell my neighbors' shame," was the explanation. This lapse from the celebrated chastity of the Pitcairn Islanders was a source of great shame to the natives who had already come to take pride in their virtue. In defense of the islanders, it should be placed on record that John Buffett was the father of at least one of these two illegitimates. This episode illustrates two things of interest; one, that the genealogical records were being kept with care and were therefore reliable for modern research, second, that the serpent had made its entrance into the South Sea Eden.

The specter of a water shortage and of famine never left the subconscious minds of the leaders of the colony, so that when in 1830 a severe drought and failure of crops occurred, the islanders decided that the time had come to migrate to a larger island. Pomare, King of Tahiti, offered to set aside a fertile tract of land for these stepchildren of Tahiti, and arrangements were made by the British admiralty to remove the population of Pitcairn to their new home. Captain Sandilands, H.M. sloop *Comet,* was dispatched together with a transport bark, the *Lucy Anne,* to Pitcairn, where they arrived on February 28, 1831. Assembling the heads of the families, Captain Sandilands explained his mission. One half of them gave their names immediately as ready to depart, but the others proved reluctant to quit their homes. The next morning, however, the opposition had disintegrated, and the entire colony prepared to abandon their world for another, rendered attractive by distance and legend. Eighty-seven persons, with their most cherished lares and penates, embarked on the *Lucy Anne* on the 7th of March. During the voyage of sixteen days,

Lucy Anne Quintal was born, making a total of eighty-eight returning to one of the homes of their ancestors.

The arrival at Papeete, Tahiti, found Pomare dead and his daughter on the verge of a civil war with rebellious chiefs. But the gentlemanly and chivalrous Tahitians temporarily laid aside their quarrels to greet the new-comers. Natives from all the districts came to seek among the little band the girls and the men who had left them forty-two years before. One old lady found a sister among the four surviving Tahitian women who had accompanied the mutineers so bravely long ago. Sandilands arranged subsistence for the islanders until their first crops might mature and then departed, leaving them established on a rich stretch of land.

But the Pitcairn Islanders were not to remain for long in their happy state. Tahiti requires more resistance to withstand her sweet and poisonous blandishments than these innocents could muster. The Pitcairn recorder notes "soon after arrival at Tahiti the Pitcairn people were taken sick." And the more responsible of the party viewed with distinct and mounting alarm the debauching of the youthful and even some of the older members of the group. On April 21, Thursday October Christian died. On the 24th, John Buffett and family, Robert Young, Joseph Christian, Edward Christian, Charles Christian 3rd, Matthew Quintal, and Fredine Young decided to leave Tahiti and sailed on a small schooner for Pitcairn. Adverse winds, however, forced them to land at Lord Hood Island where they remained until they were rescued by a French brig and carried to Pitcairn on June 27. Meanwhile the deaths continued at an alarming rate, finally driving the remainder of the colony to charter the American brig *Charles Dogget* of Salem, with the copper bolts of the *Bounty* as part payment. On September 2, the last of the surviving islanders had returned to their haven on Pitcairn. Aside from other losses, this adventure had exacted a toll of, perhaps, seventeen lives.

This misadventure need not have taken place had the

Pitcairn Islanders not feared to displease the British government by refusing to accept its offer of transportation. Or so the islanders declared to Captain Freemantle in 1833, when he found them "not improved by their visit to Otaheite (Tahiti), but on the contrary much altered for the worse, having, since their return, indulged in intemperance to a great degree, distilling a spirit from the tee root, which grows in great quantities on the island." The most intelligent of the men "agreed that they never had been happy or contented" since leaving Pitcairn, and they affirmed their intention never to leave it again. Despite their joy at returning home, "They had nothing to complain of respecting their treatment at Otaheite, but disliked the character of the people, and were alarmed at the sickness which prevailed among themselves."

"It is impossible," wrote Captain Freemantle in a long summary, "for any person to visit this island without being pleased with a people generally so amiable, though springing from so guilty a stock, and brought up in so extraordinary a manner. And although I have no hesitation in saying that they have lost much of that simplicity of character which has been observed in them by former visitors, they are still a well-disposed, well-behaved, kind, hospitable people, and, if well advised and instructed, would be led to anything; but I fear, if much left to themselves, and visited by many ships, which now is not an uncommon occurrence, that they will lose what simplicity they have left, and will partake of the character of their neighbors the Otaheitians. I found even now that it was a difficult matter to obtain the truth on any point which told at all to their prejudice; and it was only by cross-questioning them that I could arrive at it. The present generation of children is the finest I ever saw; and out of the whole number, seventy-nine, there are fifty-three under twenty years of age, who appear to have been well instructed, many of them capable of reading, and nearly on a par with children of the same age in England. It certainly is desirable that this system of instruction should be kept up, and that a clergyman should be sent to them, who would be most acceptable. The Englishmen who have been on the island have on the contrary done much harm, particularly Buffett, who, although a married man, has seduced one of the young girls, by whom he has two children."

This censure, mixed with praise, is somewhat unjust. For my part, I cannot find fault with a people who object to retailing to every comer the scandal concerning their companions.

4

DICTATORSHIP: CHAPTER AND VERSE

Despite its isolation a century ago, life on Pitcairn was far from dull. At the end of 1832, an elderly gentleman, named Joshua Hill, arrived from London with letters, subsequently discovered to be spurious, giving him authority to act as governor of the island. Recognizing in the Englishmen Nobbs, Buffett, and Evans possible adversaries to his ambitions, he commenced activities calculated to remove them from the island. On Captain Freemantle's arrival four or five months later, he informed him that Nobbs was habitually drunk. One of Hill's first moves was to form a temperance society to eradicate the growing practice of imbibing intoxicants. To punish Buffett who opposed him, he had the poor unfortunate publicly flogged and even threatened similar chastisement to some women who, he said, had gossiped about him. Finally Hill's despotism went to the extreme of banishing the three Englishmen from Pitcairn: Buffett and Evans to the Gambiers, Nobbs to Tahiti. The plight of these men is revealed by their own statements.

The humble Petition of George Hunn Nobbs, late
*Teacher at Pitcairn's Island**

"*Sheweth,*—That your petitioner went to Pitcairn Island in 1828, with the intention of assisting the late John
Adams in teaching and schoolkeeping; that, on your petitioner's arrival, he was kindly received by the natives,
and, at their request, and with the consent of John
Adams, your petitioner immediately commenced keeping school. On the death of John Adams your petitioner,
at the desire of the natives, undertook the charge of their
spiritual affairs, and your petitioner's conduct gave general satisfaction, as will appear by the accompanying
certificate. For the space of two years things went on in
an amicable manner, when H.M.S. *Comet* arrived, for
the purpose of removing the inhabitants to Tahiti. After
some deliberation, the natives determined to remove.
Your petitioner, thinking he could be of no further service to them (as they would be under the guidance of
the missionaries at Tahiti), wished to remain with his
wife and family on the island of Pitcairn. This the islanders objected to, and insisted on your petitioner accompanying them to Tahiti. Your petitioner complied
with their desires; and, previous to Capt. Sandilands (of
H.M.S. *Comet*) quitting Tahiti, he (Capt. S.) sent for
your petitioner, and told him he must not quit the Pitcairn people, but continue to be their teacher, under the
direction of the missionaries: adding, 'You have been of
service to them, and may be so still; you are married
amongst them, and in fact become as one of themselves;
therefore you ought not, and it is my request you will
not, leave them.' After the departure of H.M.S. *Comet*,
sickness appeared among the late inhabitants of the Pit-

---

* This, together with the following appeals by Buffett
and Evans, were apparently directed to the commanding
naval officer of the British station on the Western coast of
South America and were transmitted to the Admiralty.

cairn's, and ultimately twelve died. During their sickness
the attention paid them by your petitioner obtained the
approbation of the missionaries and other gentlemen residing in Tahiti. Your petitioner was also indefatigable
in obtaining subscriptions to assist them in returning to
their native land. Previous to their departure from Tahiti,
they went, of their own accord, to the missionaries, and
requested your petitioner should be appointed 'their sole
minister and teacher,' which the missionaries agreed to,'
and signed a paper to that effect, a copy of which ac-
companies this petition.

"A short time after our return to Pitcairn's Island, some
of the natives (Edward Quintal, William Young, and
Fletcher Christian), determined to re-commence distilling rum—a practice they had been accustomed to in
John Adams's time. Your petitioner remonstrated with
them on the impropriety of their conduct, but to no purpose; the answer they gave to your petitioner's advice
was, 'We are our own masters; we shall do as we like; no
one shall control us.' Many times your petitioner talked
with them, and begged them to desist from distilling
spirits; but your petitioner always received abuse in return, and twice narrowly escaped a beating from Edward Quintal. Afterwards a Mr. Hill arrived, who assumed great authority, said he was sent out by the
British Government to adjust the internal affairs of the
island, and the British ships of war on the coast were under his direction.

"He furthermore told the natives that he had resided
for a considerable time at Oahu, where he possessed
great influence, by reason that your Honour had served
under him on board one of the Honourable East India
Company's ships, which he (Mr. Hill) commanded.

"Believing these things to be true, your petitioner gave
Mr. Hill an apartment in your petitioner's house, and
used every means to make him comfortable; but, before
one month had expired, Mr. Hill had succeeded, by
villainous misrepresentations, atrocious falsehoods, and

magnificent promises of presents, to be obtained through his influence from the British Government and several British of Mr. Hill's acquaintance, in ejecting your petitioner from his house. Mr. Hill then told the natives he should act as their teacher, until a qualified teacher was sent out from England. Soon after, H.M.S. *Challenger* touched at Pitcairn's Island from Tahiti. Capt. Freemantle assembled the inhabitants, and informed them that Mr. Hill was not acting under the authority of the British Government; also, that he, Capt. Freemantle, came on shore with the intention of removing Mr. Hill from the island; but, on hearing that your petitioner had partaken of the spirits distilled by the natives, he, (Capt. F.) informed your petitioner that he could not re-instate him in the situation of which Mr. Hill had deprived him; at the same time Capt. F. told Mr. Hill he did not approve of his (Mr. H.'s) conduct, as he acted without authority. Capt. F. also told Mr. Hill he must not interfere with the laws, as the administration of them was vested in the natives.

"Capt. F. asked your petitioner what he intended to do. Your petitioner replied, it was his wish to leave the island. Capt. F. said he thought it was the best thing your petitioner could do, under existing circumstances, but that he certainly might remain if he chose. Before Capt. F. departed, he told the natives it was his belief that Mr. Hill wished to get the other Europeans off the island, that he, Mr. Hill, might make himself king over them. Capt. F. also sharply reprimanded Mr. Hill for calling the other British residents, 'lousy foreigners,' etc.; and bade him desist from doing so. Mr. Hill promised to obey, but never kept his promise. Shortly after Capt. F.'s departure, Mr. Hill began again to oppress your petitioner and the two other Englishmen. He ordered the natives to turn us out of their houses; and our nearest relatives dared not come and visit us.

"As soon as a ship appeared off the island, a canoe was dispatched on board, forbidding the officers and crew coming to our houses, and we were threatened with stripes if we offered to go on board. In May last, an act was passed (by force) to deprive our children of their mothers' inheritance, merely because their fathers were foreigners (Englishmen). In August Mr. Hill sent his colleagues to seize the muskets of those persons whom, he said, were opposed to the governor of the commonwealth. As soon as Mr. Hill obtained possession of the muskets, he loaded them with powder and ball, and deposited them in his bedroom, for the use of the magistracy of the island. Every Sunday a loaded musket is placed beneath his seat in church, to intimidate his hearers. Since that period your petitioner has been in continued alarm for the lives of himself and family. Your petitioner dared not go out of his house after dark, nor up to his plantation at any time, by himself, for fear of being maltreated by the colleagues of Mr. Hill. Several of the natives protested against such conduct; Mr. Hill threatened to give them a flogging, and, moreover, said, that if they did not obey him, he would cause a military governor to be sent out from England, with a party of soldiers, who would take their land from them and treat them as slaves. In the month of November last your petitioner was seized with the dysentery, and for three months was confined to his bed. Your petitioner could not obtain medicine, although there was a medicine-chest on the island, and of which your petitioner was a part proprietor. In fact, it was the declared intent of Joshua Hill and his colleagues to bring about the death of your petitioner, either by hanging, flogging, or starvation.

"Your petitioner at last, by sickness, deprivation of common necessaries, and anxiety of mind, occasioned by Joshua Hill's wicked counsel and conduct, was brought to the verge of the grave, when, providentially, a ship appeared in sight, which proved to be the *Tuscan* of London, Capt. Stavers; who, on seeing the miserable condition of your petitioner, kindly consented, at your petitioner's earnest request, to give him a passage to Tahiti. Owing to the professional and benevolent endeavours of Dr. Bennett, surgeon of the *Tuscan*, your petitioner is recovering, and hopes, ere long, to be re-instated in health. And now, Honoured Sir, will you permit your unfortunate petitioner to implore your Honour's protection? Driven from family and home by an unauthorized person, without friends or money, and almost without clothes, your petitioner is at a loss what course to pursue. Your petitioner cannot support the idea of being separated for ever from his wife and family; but, alas! he can scarcely hope to see them again unless your Honour condescends to espouse his cause. Convinced that his cause is just, and knowing that Capt. Stavers and Dr. Bennett can corroborate the most material statements in this petition, the fervent prayer of your petitioner, and the other two unfortunate Englishmen with him, to be restored to their families and possessions on Pitcairn's Island; and your petitioner, in duty bound, will ever pray, etc.

"Your petitioner has no desire to be replaced as teacher, but simply to employ himself in agricultural pursuits, for the support of his family."

To this should be added the following complaints of John Buffett and of John Evans.

"HONOURED SIR,—I hope you will excuse the liberty I take in writing to you, which I doubt not you will, when you are informed in what critical circumstances I am placed. In December, 1823, on our return to England, we touched at Pitcairn's Island, and by desire of the natives and consent of our captain, I went on shore to teach their children to read, etc., which I did to their satisfaction. Mr. Nobbs arriving soon after, became their teacher; since then I have lived as a private individual, on good terms with the natives. After going to Tahiti with them, and remaining there about three weeks, I

procured a passage for myself, my wife, and family and
arrived at Pitcairn's Island about three months before
the rest of the natives. After they all arrived, we all lived
together upon friendly terms, until the arrival of Mr.
Joshua Hill from Tahiti, in October, 1832, who stated
that he had been sent out by the British Government,
and whatever he was in want of he would procure from
England, New South Wales, or Valparaiso.

"By means of such promises, and by his making them
believe that whatever heretofore has been sent out, was
by his influence, he has gained the favour of a few natives, and appointed three elders and two privy council-
lors. He has framed laws and built a prison; and should
any of the natives refuse to obey him, let his proposals
be ever so unjust, he tells them he will send to England
for a governor and a regiment of soldiers. By such means
he has persuaded the natives to sign a petition to Government to deprive us Englishmen and our children of
their lands; and I am ordered, with my wife and five
children, to leave the island. His plea (J. H.'s) is, that
there is not land sufficient. At the same time, he has proposed to send to England for English ladies, for wives
for the youth of the island; and because I made known
his plan of sending my wife and family off the island, I
had a mock-trial, on which Mr. Hill was judge, jury, and
executioner.

"After Mr. Hill's beating me over the head, breaking
it in two places, likewise my finger, I was suspended by
my hands in the church, and flogged until I was not able
to walk home, and confined to my bed for two weeks,
and it was several weeks before I was able to work or
have the use of my hand; my wife, at the same time,
was ill and not able to work, and Mr. J. Hill would not
allow the natives to visit me or my wife, not even her
own sister, but literally tried to starve us. Charles Christian, the oldest man on the island, was brutally treated,
and turned out of his house, for trying to prevent my
being flogged; and because the women assembled crying

shame on his (Mr. J. H.'s) proceedings, he, Mr. J. Hill, on the Sunday following read the riot act, and told them, should they do so again, the authorities would be justified in shooting them. He then sent his colleagues, as he is pleased to call them, to take possession of our firearms, which they loaded with ball, and Mr. J. Hill has since kept them in his possession.

"Since this, Sir, not only the lives of us English residents, but some of the natives, have been in danger from the malicious temper of Mr. J. Hill. He has been the means of depriving one of my children of the land left her by her grandfather, and he proposes to deprive the others also, and as they grow up to send them to sea as cabin boys, etc. He wished Capt. Freemantle, of H.M.S. *Challenger,* who touched at Pitcairn's Island, in February, 1832, to remove me from the island; but he (Capt. F.) would not. Since that he has been trying all in his power to prejudice the natives against me. Capt. T. Stavers has been so kind as to give me a passage to Tahiti, when I shall endeavour to get a passage for my family, either to Lord Howe's Island or Rappa. In the meantime, I humbly hope, Sir, you will use your influence to get Mr. Hill removed from Pitcairn's Island; it is the desire of most of the inhabitants. The land that Mr. Hill wishes to deprive my children of, is their mother's portion, left by her father (Edward Young of the *Bounty*). If, Sir, you would condescend to write me a few lines, informing me how to act, to the care of Mr. Pritchard, Tahiti, you would greatly oblige your most humble servant,"

(Signed)   J. Buffett.

The humble Petition of John Evans, two (sic)
years resident on Pitcairn's Island

"*Sheweth,*—That your petitioner landed on Pitcairn's in the year 1823, and after a residence of twelve months was united in marriage with the second daughter of the late John Adams (by his consent). From that period your petitioner continued to live in peace and harmony with the natives, and maintained himself and family in a comfortable manner. Your petitioner accompanied the Pitcairn people to Tahiti, and while there, assisted them as much as lay in his power. At their return, the natives were perfectly agreeable that your petitioner should return with them, and resume possession of his wife's land, etc. Things went on in their usual train for twelve months after our return, when a Mr. Joshua Hill arrived at Pitcairn's, who informed your petitioner he was come by authority of the British Government to adjust the internal affairs of the island, and that he had sent orders to Valparaiso for H.M.S. *Dublin* to come and take him on board, and convey him to the Marquesas Islands in a diplomatic capacity.

"Your petitioner gave credit to Mr. Hill's assertions, and treated him with all possible respect, also cheerfully contributed to his support; but scarcely had Mr. Hill been on shore three weeks, when he attempted to persuade your petitioner's wife to leave him, saying he would take her under his protection, and supply her with everything she wanted; adding, 'I will cause the first captain of a man-of-war who arrives to remove these lousy foreigners from the island.' My wife refused to do as he wished, and from that time forth he became her declared enemy. Shortly after a ship of war arrived, the captain of which declared he knew nothing of Mr. Hill, neither had he (Mr. Hill) any authority from the British Government.

"Mr. Hill used every means in his power, by misrepresentation and gross falsehood, to induce Capt. Freemantle to remove me from the island. This Capt. F. refused, saying, he had a good opinion of me, and should not separate me from my family. Capt. Freemantle severely reprimanded Mr. Hill for his conduct towards the

English residents, and desired him to alter his conduct towards them; this Mr. Hill promised to do, but malice and falsehood are prominent traits in the character of Joshua Hill. No sooner was Capt. Freemantle gone, than Mr. Hill (vexed that he had not gained his point) became more outrageous than ever; he still asserted he was sent out by the British Government, that Capt. F. was no gentleman, and denounced vengeance on every native that did not join with him in oppressing the lousy foreigners. Whenever a ship appeared in sight, two confidential men were dispatched on board to forbid the captain and officers holding any communication with foreigners on shore; and we were prohibited, under pains and penalties, from going on board. In May last a prison was built, for the avowed purpose of confining the Englishmen and their friends, and a law passed (by force) depriving our children of their mothers' inheritance; and all the genuine natives, from seven years and upwards, were compelled to sign a paper, declaring they would never intermarry with the foreigners—a term applied to our children as well as ourselves. In July a law was enacted relative to high treason.

"Your petitioner requested a copy as a guide for his future conduct; Mr. Hill refused to give him one, flew into a violent rage, and shortly after, your petitioner was dragged to the church, underwent a mock-trial, no witnesses being allowed, and received one dozen lashes with a cat-o'-nine-tails, each tail being the size of a man's little finger. Your petitioner was so much hurt about the head, eyes, and ribs, as to be confined to his bed for ten days. From this time the state of things became desperate, and your petitioner was under continual alarm for the lives of himself and family. Mr. Hill and his colleagues were continually threatening the life of someone or other, and your petitioner firmly believes, had it not been for the opportune arrival of the ship *Tuscan*, Capt. R. T. Stavers, murder would have been shortly committed. Capt.

Stavers, seeing the untoward state of affairs, humanely consented to give your petitioner a passage to Tahiti. And now, Honoured Sir, will you permit your petitioner to hope you will commiserate my unhappy condition? Neither the natives nor Mr. Hill can bring any serious charge against me, as Capt. Stavers and Dr. Bennett can certify, and yet your petitioner is banished from family and home, merely to gratify the malevolence of Mr. Hill. Your petitioner humbly begs that your Honour will restore your petitioner again to his wife and family, that he may support them by his labour.

"And your petitioner as in duty bound, will ever pray."

But so completely had Hill deluded the simple-minded, unsophisticated islanders that either of their own volition or out of fear, some of them signed the following petition addressed to Hill. The style of this extraordinary document suggests, however, that its composition was the product of Hill himself.

Copy of a Letter, dated Pitcairn's Island, 3rd October 1833, from the Public Functionaries and others, to Captain Joshua Hill, Teacher, etc.

"Respected Sir.—We, the undersigned, being all public authorities, as well as other natives, who are earnestly desirous for the prosperity and welfare of our dearly beloved island, beg not only that you will be pleased to accept our most sincere gratitude for all which you have done for us, in various respects, both before your arrival here in October last, and since, especially in thus saving and snatching us so providentially, as it were, from the brink of infidelity itself, and as well as other crying and besetting sins (now too painful for us to contemplate), which otherwise must have been our entire and total ruin. But, moreover, we entreat that you will not think of leaving us yet awhile, or until we become, with the blessed Lord's help, settled somewhat in safety. For, indeed, we have too good reason to know, that so long as one of these profligate foreigners is among us on Pitcairn's, we never shall be able to go on aright, or resist their corrupting or destructive practices. Hence we implore you, dear friend, to consider our unfortunate case; and remember that, on your arrival here (aforesaid), we had two cursed stills up—without a school, without a church!—and, alas! alas!—'tell it not in Gath'—we were living without God, in the world!

"We pray you, therefore, leave us not thus to the enemy, or we fear again that we shall be for ever lost!

"We hereto subscribe ourselves, respected Sir, your most sincere friends, and very obedient servants."

(*Signed etc.*, by all.)

Hill's reply sounds curiously like the petition itself.

J. Hill's Answer to the foregoing, dated Pitcairn's Island, October 4th, 1833

"My very dear Friends,—The lively interest which, from the beginning, I have taken in your welfare is well known to our mutual friends in England. And thus, since my arrival here, on the 28th October, 1832, you know yourselves. I can only observe, at this moment, in answer to the request which you have deemed requisite thus to reiterate, that is repeat, in your joint letter to me of the 3rd instant, which you handed to me at our prayer-meeting yesterday, P.M., in reference to my continuing a while longer with you, etc., I would say that, notwithstanding the importance of time, I shall not, with the blessed Lord's will, think of leaving you until hearing from home; i.e. from the British Government, nor until my presence becomes no longer necessary in furtherance

of the established welfare of your commonwealth and beloved little island. Being always,
            "My friends, really and faithfull,
            "Your well-wisher,"
        (*Signed*)   JOSHUA HILL,
                                    Teacher, etc.

Having assumed the reins of government, such as they
were, Hill appointed from among the principal men on
the island four elders, three subelders, and four cadets.
He continued to dominate the island, while correspondence to, from, and about him passed back and forth
across the Pacific. I am tempted to extract additional
documents relating to the extraordinary Mr. Hill, but
I shall conclude these engrossing quotations with a
lengthy self-testimonial by Joshua Hill himself.

"I am aware that pedantry and egotism become no
one, and myself perhaps less than any. (Pro. xxvii. 2.)
But for certain reasons, the following credentials, as a
memorandum, I hope will be pardoned on the present
occasion—they are truths.

"I observe, *in limine,* that I have visited the four quarters of the globe, and it has ever been my desire to maintain, as far as lay in my power, the standing of an English gentleman. I have lived a considerable while in a
palace, and had my dinner parties with a princess on my
right, and a General's lady upon my left. I have had a
French cook, a box at the opera. I have drove my dress
carriage (thought the neatest then in Paris, where I
spent five or six years; as well I have known Calcutta),
and the handsomest lady (said), Madame R——, to grace
my carriage. I have drove a curricle with my two out-
riders, and two saddle-horses, besides a travelling-car-
riage. A valet, coachman, footman, groom, and, upon
extraordinary occasions, my *maître d'hôtel.* I have (at
her request) visited Madame Bonaparte, at the Tuileries,
St. Cloud, and Malmaison. I might thus mention many
others of note abroad.

"I have frequently dined with that remarkable woman, Madame Carburas, afterwards the Princess de C——. I have had the honour of being in company; i.e. at the same parties, with both his late Majesty George IV. then Prince Regent, and his present Majesty William IV. then H.R.H. Duke of Clarence, as well with their royal brothers. I have ridden in a royal Duke's carriage, with four horses and three footmen, more than once, and have dined at his table, and drunk the old hock of his late father, George III. I have visited and dined with some of our first families, and have been visited by a Duke, and others of the first noblemen. I have known and dined with (abroad and in England), Madames Catalini, Grassini, Georges, etc. And I have given the arm to Lady Hamilton (of Naples renown), whom the hero of the Nile has given his (one) to more than once. I have dined with a Viceroy Governor (who was a General and a Count), and with Admirals, both on board their ships and on shore. I have entertained Governors, Generals, Captains (R.N.), on board my ship, more than once. And I have commanded several ships, and went to sea at the beginning of the French Revolution.

"I have been acquainted with many military and naval officers. I have since 1807, my admittance, from the late President, Sir Joseph Banks, to the sittings of the Royal Society. I have occasionally breakfasted with Sir Joseph, and visited, and even presented a friend (the actual President of the bank of the N.N.S. of America) to his evening parties. My admittance to the Royal Society has always admitted me to similar institutions abroad. I received the dress sword, and nautical instruments, etc. of a noble lord (at his death), a Vice-Admiral of the Red. I sailed from England (Portsmouth, May 1st, 1794) to the East Indies and China, in the largest fleet, possibly, that ever was; it was under Lord Howe, down the British Channel, just one month before his great victory. I have visited the Falls of Niagara and Montmorency, the natural bridge in Virginia, the great Reciprocating Fountain in East Tennessee, the great Temple of Elephants at Bombay.

"I have dined with a prince, as well as with a princess; and with a count, a baron, an ambassador, a minister (ordinary and extraordinary), and have dined with a Chargé d'Affaire, and lived with consuls, etc. I have visited and conversed with 'Red Jacket,' the great Indian warrior. I have visited and been visited by a bishop. I have frequently partook of the delicious Hungarian wine (tokey), Prince Easterházy's; as also of Prince Swartzerburgh's old hock, said to have been 73 years old; and I was intimate with the brother-in-law of this last German nobleman. I have dined with a principal Hong merchant at Canton. I have sat next to the beautiful Madame Recamier and Madame Carbanus, at the great dinner parties. I have written to the Prime Minister of England; and have received the (late Earl of Liverpool's) answer with his thanks, etc.

"I was at Paris when the allies were made there. I have visited and breakfasted with the late Warren Hastings, Esq., at his seat in Gloucestershire. I have had permission with a party of friends to hunt over his grounds. Entertained etc. two or three days at the sporting lodge of an Earl, now a Marquis. I have made a crimson silk net for a certain fashionable Marchioness, which she actually wore at her next great party of five or six hundred persons. I have danced with the Countess Bertand; i.e., Mademoiselle Fanny Dillon, before she married the Marshall. I was at Napoleon's coronation. I have been invited to the Lord Mayor's, and to the dinner of an Alderman of London; to those also of the first merchants and bankers, as the late Mr. Thelusson (afterwards Lord Rendlesham), the formerly rich Messrs. A. and B. Goldsmiths, etc. And at Paris I have had a credit of 400,000 francs, at one time, on the house of Perregan, Lafitte, etc., and other bankers at Paris for considerable sums. Delepent and Co. for 40,000 francs, and Recamier's, at one time, for upwards of 100,000 francs. Lafitte's house at another time for 50,000 francs; again for 12,000 francs. I have had at a time, nearly 5000 sterling at the Bank of England.

"I wrote and published in the London *Morning Post* (7th March, 1811), on naval power. I have seen the Vestrises, father, son, and grandson, at once (the only time), dance on the stage at the opera at Paris. I have given a passage to many on board my ship, but never in my life received a farthing as passage-money from any person. I am decidedly against the use of ardent spirit (malt liquor may do for those who like it), tobacco, etc. And as for wine, that only at dinner; it even then ought to be good, if not the very best, as the Gourmet would have it, when speaking of Clas-Vangeat, and Romance, etc. I have had a fine band of music on board my ship, and my four kinds of wine on my table. (I am not sleeping on a 'bed of roses' now, but in a humble hut or cabin.) After all, what does the foregoing amount to?— vanity of vanities. I will merely add, that I have had a year in the Church of Christ, and that I am a life member of the Bible Society. That I am looking with the blessed Lord's help to something of far more intrinsic worth and consideration—'the price of our high calling' —the life to come. I am now in my sixty-second year of age, and of course it is high time that I should look upon this world as nearly to close on me. I might perhaps say much more, but must stop. I am now an humble teacher upon Pitcairn's Isle for the time being.

"June, 1834."

(*Signed*)   J. HILL.

The entire tragi-comedy ended ignominiously for Joshua Hill when Captain Lord Edward Russell visited Pitcairn on H.M.S. *Actaeon* in 1837. Hill had let it be known that "he was a very near relative of the Duke of Bedford, and that the Duchess seldom rode out in her carriage without him." Nemesis at last appeared in the guise of Lord Edward, who was the son of the Duke of

Bedford. Unable to remove Hill without instructions from London, Lord Edward immediately reported to his superiors. In the following year, H.M.S. *Imogene* arrived and quietly removed Hill to Valparaiso.

Released from the domination of the magnetic and grandiloquent Hill, the principal men of the island now signed a petition to restore the exiled Englishmen in their adopted homes. And in due course Nobbs, Buffett, and Evans were returned to their families and to their former occupations.

5

HEGIRA

The year of Mr. Hill's downfall, 1838, also marked a definite regularization of the island's official position and the formal establishment of an internal organization. These events were engineered by Captain Elliott, H.M. sloop *Fly*, who landed at Pitcairn in November, 1838, but their need had long been recognized by the islanders. The episode of Joshua Hill had made apparent the wisdom of an ordered government. And the increasing contact with the outside world, represented by whaling ships, made some formal authority imperative.

It is necessary to pause here to describe the relationship of the Pitcairn colony to the whaling industry. The discoverer of the settlement, in 1808, was the first in a wave that was to mount to extraordinary proportions. The American whalers, having exhausted the Atlantic of its cetaceans in the eighteenth century, had already found a new and rich field in the Pacific by the beginning of the nineteenth. In increasing numbers, hundreds of little harbors up and down the New England coast were sending out whaling expeditions, financed by "stocking" capital. Of these centers Nantucket and New Bedford were the most flourishing. By 1849, the peak year, some 4000 whalers from New England ports were at sea, mainly in the Pacific. Out often four years at a stretch, the captains greatly needed convenient ports of call where they might secure water and fresh provisions and where they might shelter their wives during parturition. Pitcairn, lying near one of the South Pacific whaling grounds, proved to be so handy that the number of ships calling there annually increased enormously. The island's register gives a list from which the following figures are derived:

NUMBER OF SHIPS		NUMBER OF SHIPS		NUMBER OF SHIPS	
1823	1	1833	6	1843	29
1824	3	1834	4	1844	18
1825	4	1835	2	1845	22
1826	3	1836	7	1846	49
1827	3	1837	4	1847	19
1828	2	1838	10	1848	9
1829	7	1839	13	1849	18
1830	4	1840	10	1850	47
1831	6	1841	20	1851	24
1832	5	1842	30	1852	14

These figures represent all ships that called at the island, but the great majority were American and practically all of these were whalers. The honesty and friendliness of the islanders were so renowned that most of the captains welcomed the opportunity to visit Pitcairn. Lady Belcher quotes one sailor "that if any insult were to be offered to any of them (the Pitcairn Islanders), and especially to the female part of the community, a man would not be long alive after he came on board." Laudable as this sentiment was and typical as it might have been, unfortunately whaling crews did not always measure up to such standards. Melville's description of at least one job lot complement leads one to suspect that some rather tough customers sailed on those "stinking trypots." On one occasion on Pitcairn part of "the ruffian crew of a whale ship were on shore for a fortnight, during which time, they offered every insult to the inhabitants, and threatened to violate any woman whose pro

tectors they could overcome by force." To eliminate
recurrence of such raids, Captain Elliott formally declared the island to be under the protection of the British
crown; and both to protect them from successors to Mr.
Hill, and to preserve them from taunts that they had no
government or country, he endowed the islanders with
a simple form of self-government. To administer the affairs of the island, Edward Quintal was elected the first
magistrate.

For the most part the annals of the island, preserved
in the *Pitcairn Island Register,* record with monotonous
regularity the births of the new Janes and Mary Anns,
Edwards and Arthurs, varied by arrivals of ships and attacks of illness. But in 1845, the chronicler had three subjects worthy of his pen. The first concerned the *Bounty's*
guns. "January 19th. During the past week we have been
employed fishing up two of the *Bounty's* guns (long
nines, I believe). For fifty-five years they had been deposited at the bottom of the sea on a bed of coral guiltless of blood—(during the time so many thousands of
mankind in Europe became 'Food for Cannon'); but on
Saturday last one of these guns resumed its original vo-
cation; at least the innocuous portion of it, to wit, belch-
ing forth fire and smoke, and causing the island to rever-
berate with its bellowing: the other gun is condemned
to silence having been spiked by someone of the *Bounty's*
crew."

The second event called forth an essay on the "salubrity" of Pitcairn. The islanders for some years past had
been suffering, as many island populations suffer after
the visits of ships, from recurrent epidemics of influenza.
In 1845, another hit the colony, and its course was faithfully recorded in the Register. "March 27th. The fever is
on the decline, cheerful faces are again seen, and I hope
grateful hearts are praising God whose mercies endureth
for ever.

"I will now say a few words respecting the salubrity of
the island: it is generally supposed to be a healthy spot;

indeed, appearances seem to justify such a conclusion; but the reverse is found by experience, to be the fact. Asthmas, Rheumatism, Consumption, Scrofula and last but not least Influenza under various modifications is prevalent. Five times within the last four years have the fever been rife among us, and though it has not been so severe latterly as it was on its first appearance, this, I think, may be accounted for by the teacher becoming more acquainted with the nature of the disease (thanks to Dr. Gunn [*hiatus*]) and also with the appropriate remedies—when the influenza first appeared among us it did not spread so rapidly as it has done on its subsequent reappearance, but the cough was more violent then, than it has been since. This I attribute to the teacher's not giving them emetics as soon as the disease attacked them; since then he has invariably given them vomits on the first appearance of the disease; which seems to prevent any considerable degree of cough. But there is one particular in which the recent fever differs from the previous ones; viz. in the total absence of a cold fit at the very commencement. I have seen some of the patients when first attacked tremble as violently, and apparently from the same causes, as ever I saw anyone under the influence of ague.

"Now, in this last sickness it was not thus; only one person complained of cold and he was but slightly affected. The first person attacked was a man of full habit of body, plethoric and subject to fits, he had attended Divine service in the morning, it being the Sabbath, after evening service I found him under the influence of a raging fever; his eyes seemed ready to start from their sockets and the heat of his skin caused a disagreeable sensation to those who touched him;—he complained of violent pains in his head, back and thighs and said he felt as if 'live things were creeping between his flesh and skin.' Fearing it might bring on one of the fits to which he was subject the teacher bled him, and gave him a sudorific which had a good effect; the next day a dose of

calomel and jalap was administered, and two days after
that he was well; though very weak.

"I do not think the fever was infectious; and though in
the space of six days not less than sixty out of one hundred and twenty-two were attacked yet I attribute it
solely to the peculiar state of the atmosphere: whenever
we have been visited by this epidemick the circumstances, as respects the weather have been invariably the
same. A long drought succeeded by two or three weeks
of wet; and the wind settling into the north west; in fact
a north west wind is always the precussor [sic] of rheumatism, catarrh, and slight febrile affection. Bleeding is
not to be recommended; vomits are the sovereign
remedy, for certainly no community of persons secrete
greater quantities of bile than the inhabitants of this island. March 31st. There is now but one person sick and
she is recovering,—a few have a slight cough but that is
wearing away.

"And now it behoves us to offer up our grateful thanksgiving to Almighty God, Father, Son and Holy Spirit,
to Whom be glory now and for ever. Amen."

The third occurrence to exercise Mr. Nobbs' pen was
a phenomenon startling to the islanders. During the
night of April 16, "a perfect typhon" raged over the island, "the whole concave of the heavens" being in a "continued blaze and roar of the thunder." "Very frequently
through the night loud crashes were heard, which we
supposed were the trees in the higher parts of the island
yielding to the fury of the storm;—the noise did proceed
from the falling, and smashing of trees, but from a cause,
of which we were, at that time happily ignorant.

"At daylight a man, much alarmed, came to my house
saying, 'A part of the island had given way and was
going into the sea;—' From the door of my house I obtained an imperfect view of the spot from which a portion of the earth had been detached and felt certain it
was an avalanche occasioned by the wind acting upon
the trees, and the torrents of rain which fell detaching

the earth from the parts above it. So great was the consternation and amazement of many of the natives that although they had seen the spot from which the earth had slidden almost every day of their lives, yet they could not so far collect their ideas as to remember the original appearance of the place, whose property it had been; nor the locality of the parts near it;—As to the cause of the disruption various opinions prevailed some said it was occasioned by a waterspout, others that a thunderbolt had fallen there and a third party were anxiously enquiring if it were not probable the sea had perforated a hole from the under side of the island and so washed it away.—That they had considerable occasion for alarm cannot be disputed, and what may easily be referred to natural causes (and those not very recondite either) would by persons so inexperienced as our community, appear mysterious and awful.

"I will endeavour, in a few words, to describe what presented itself to our view at daylight. On going out of doors we saw that a considerable portion of the earth had been detached from the side of the [?] but to what extent we could not then ascertain;—the place in question was situated at the head of a ravine which debouched into the sea; the rain mixing with the falling earth (which was of clayey nature) brought it to the consistancy of thick mud but sufficiently liguified to glide very slowly down the inclined plane of the valley;—nothing with which it came in contact could resist its force,—the large trees at the head of the ravine, and immense pieces of rock, were borne slowly but unresistingly along and about three hundred cocoa nut trees were torn up by the roots and swept into the sea.

"So tenacious was the heterogeneous stream that some of the cocoa nut trees from forty to fifty feet in height, after being displaced from their original situation remained in an upright position some minutes, and when they fell it was many yards from the spot in which they had come to maturity.—A considerable portion of this aquatic lava (for indeed its appearance had a distinct resemblance to the molten streams of an active volcano) had reached the sea before daylight: and when some of our people ventured to the edge of the precipice, they found to their dismay the boat houses, and boats left there, had disappeared. Two families whose houses were adjacent to the ravine removed their household goods, fearing the foundation of their dwellings might become undermined, and whelm them in the ruin;—but in a few hours the stream ceased to flow, and confidence was in a measure restored. We had now time to turn our attention to other parts of the island; at Bounty Bay a great quantity of earth had been washed away, a yam ground containing a thousand yams totally disappeared, several fishing boats destroyed, the *Bounty's* guns washed to the edge of the surf and large pieces of rock so encumbered the harbour that if a ship should come it is doubtful whether a passage could be found for her boat to pass through.

"In the interim all the plantain patches are levelled, about four thousand plantation trees are destroyed, one half in full bearing; the other half designed for the year 1846 so that this very valuable article of food we shall be without for a long time to come. The fact is, from this date until August we shall be pinched for food; but 'God tempers the wind to the shorn lamb.' I humbly trust the late monitions of providence viz. Drought sickness and storm which severally have been inflicted upon us this year may be sanctified to us, and be the means of bringing us, one and all, into a closer communion with our God; may we remember the rod and who hath appointed it; may we flee to the cross of Christ for safety and for succour in every time of need; always bearing in mind our heavenly Father doth not willingly afflict the children of men."

On January 23, 1850, the islanders celebrated the six-tieth anniversary of the founding of the Pitcairn community. Everyone enjoyed the event so fully that it was decided to repeat it annually.

"This day was observed as the anniversary of the settlement of the colony, sixty years since. One survivor of that strange event and its sanguinarry results; witnessed the celebration. At daylight one of the *Bounty's* guns was discharged and wakened the sleeping echoes and the more drowsy of the inhabitants. At ten o'clock divine service was performed. Text [*hiatus*]. After the sermon the various letters received from the British Government and principal Friends were read from the pulpit and commented upon. At twelve a number of musketteers assembled under the 'Flag Staff' and fired a volley in honor of the day. After dinner the community male and female assembled in front of the church, where the British flag was flying and gave three cheers for Queen Victoria, three for the Government at Home, three for the Majestrates here, three for absent friends, three for the Ladies and three for the community in general; amid the firing of the muskets and the ringing of the Bell.—At sunset the gun of the *Bounty* was fired again and the day closed in harmony and peace—Much, very much have we to be grateful for, both to God and man.—It is voted that an annual celebration be observed."

In July of the same year Susannah, a Tahitian woman, died—the last link with the *Bounty* and her crew.

Since 1819 the Society for Promoting Christian Knowledge had taken a deep interest in the welfare of the Pitcairn Islanders. Presents of religious books, clothing, and other articles were frequently sent from England to this remote spot from the Society and its friends. Through the officers of the Society and others in England interested in the island, the wishes of the islanders, and of Nobbs himself, to have a pastor duly accredited by the Church of England, were finally granted. Admiral Moresby arrived in 1852 and, substituting his own chaplain, Mr. Holman, gave Nobbs passage to Valparaiso *en route* to England where, after some months of instruc-

tion, he was first ordained a deacon by the Bishop of
Sierra Leone, then a priest by the Bishop of London. Be-
fore quitting England, Nobbs was appointed a mission-
ary with a small salary by the Society for Promoting
Christian Knowledge. Nine months after his departure
Nobbs once more landed on Pitcairn, May 16, 1853.

Through their benefactor, Admiral Moresby, whose
name has been preserved in the memory of the community as a given name among their own members, the
Pitcairn Islanders presented a gift to Queen Victoria. The
letter of presentation bears its own stamp of authenticity.
A part of it follows:

"We humbly trust we may be allowed to consider ourselves your Majesty's subjects; and Pitcairn's Island a
British Colony as long as it is inhabited by us in the
fullest sense of the word. Several years since the Capt.
of your Majesty's ship *Fly* took formal possession of our
little Island; and placed us under your Majesty's protection; and if your Majesty's government would grant us a
document declaring us part of your Majesty's dominion;
we should be freed from all fears (perhaps groundless)
on that head; and such a gracious mark of Royal favour
would be cherished by us to an exertion in the discharge of the various duties incumberent on British
subjects. . . .

"At the suggestion of our worthy benefactor Rear Admiral Moresby we have ventured to present your gracious Majesty with a small chest of drawes of our own
manifacture from the Island wood; the native name of
the dark wood is *miro;* the bottoms of the drawers is
made of the breadfruit tree; our means are very limited;
and our mechanical skill also; and we will esteem it a
great favour if your Majesty would condersend to except
of it; as a token of our loyalty and respect to our gracious
Queen."

The memory of Tahiti and the activities of Mr. Hill
had been effective for a time in banishing all thought of
leaving Pitcairn. As late as 1849 Captain Wood had of-

fered to move the islanders, an offer which was refused after some deliberation. In the same year Captain Fanshawe wrote: "I could not trace in any of them the slightest desire to remove elsewhere. On the contrary, they expressed the greatest repugnance to do so, whilst a sweet potato remained to them." But even while the islanders were expressing themselves so strongly, a change in attitude was appearing. If the island was regarded as cramped for the 1831 population of eighty persons, now that it contained twice that number the need for a larger island began to seem inevitable. Each year the leaders of the community noted another crop of babies to be supported. The hive was full, and the bees must swarm.

A year after the visit of Captains Fanshawe and Wood, the community's views tended to removal. We read in Mr. Brodie's account of a brief visit in 1850 that Pitcairn was inadequate for its population, and that practically nothing was left for barter after the limited acreage supplied the needs of the islanders.

The decision to be made no longer was whether or not to move, but where to go. A large tract of land in Huahine, one of the Society Islands, had been inherited by the Pitcairners through one of the wives of the mutineers, but this did not suggest a solution. The islanders still retained a vivid memory of the disastrous experiment at Tahiti, another of the Society Islands. Once bitten twice shy. The choice of the community favored an uninhabited island where they could develop as a homogeneous community, unimpeded and unmolested. Juan Fernandez appealed to them, but Selkirk's hermitage belonged to Chile and was not available.

A famine and scarcity of water now forced the colony to act, and a petition was directed to the British Government to remove them as a body. Norfolk Island, abandoned in 1855 by Great Britain as a penal colony, was the island suggested, because there they expected to find a climate similar to their own and because there they could continue to be isolated and untrammeled. The

British government, ever complaisant to the requests of its subjects on Pitcairn, decided to grant the request and informed the governor of Norfolk to hold the island for the Pitcairners, not allowing squatters to settle on it.

Norfolk Island is situated roughly in latitude 29° S and longitude 167° 50′ E, about one thousand miles northeast of Sydney, Australia, and over four thousand miles west of Pitcairn. It is a volcanic island about twenty miles in circumference, five to six miles at its greatest breadth, and contains upward of eight thousand acres. The highest point, Mt. Pitt, has an altitude of one thousand feet. The soil is very rich, bearing a wide variety of tropical and subtropical fruit and vegetables, and the surrounding waters abound in edible fish. The island also contained a large number of buildings: compounds for the prisoners, a government house, two churches, and various small cottages, the quarters of the officers and the barracks for the soldiers. Most of these structures were solidly built of gray stone, their dour institutionalism emphasized by an austere type of Georgian architecture. Livestock, consisting of cattle, sheep, and horses, were also left for the benefit of the new tenants of the island.

The transfer from Pitcairn took place in 1856. Captain Mathers, the *Morayshire*, arrived at Pitcairn in April and, after the natural reluctance of the islanders was overcome, sailed with the entire population of 187 persons. The *Morayshire* reached Norfolk thirty-six days later. The first view of Norfolk was a severe disappointment to some of the islanders. They missed the rugged beauty of Pitcairn and their cozy little houses embowered in a rich foliage; they wanted the snug security that their own island gave them. The parklike tranquillity of Norfolk seemed immense. It lacked the dramatic beauty of their wild and romantic Pitcairn. One could, to be sure, slip off a precipice into the sea at Pitcairn, but one couldn't get lost in pathless forests or swampy gullies. On Norfolk, one could wander for days without seeing another friendly human. It was uncomfortable.

The three-storied stark stone buildings, the oxen, and the horses filled the islanders with astonishment. But a mere two weeks later Nobbs* noted a change. He wrote, "Some are employed tending sheep, some driving cattle, and two or three at the wind-mill grinding maize; and it is really wonderful with what facility our people comprehend the details of these complicated employments." Sir William Denison, governor of New South Wales, urged the inhabitants to build habits of self-reliance in their new home. There was sufficient, he maintained, for their needs without the gifts of charity that had become increasingly necessary to support life on Pitcairn.

Doctor Selwyn, Bishop of Melanesia, had secured permission to establish his Melanesian mission at one corner of the island, and the colony found a new teacher in Mrs. Selwyn, his wife. Arrangements were made in England to send out Thomas Rossiter as teacher, James Darve as miller, wheelwright, and smith, and H. J. Blinman as mason and plasterer. Of these new settlers, only Rossiter remained. Thus the new life of the Pitcairn colony was established auspiciously on Norfolk. The land was divided into fifty-acre allotments, one for each family. A thriving trade was commenced with the whalers, dripstones were manufactured from a suitable rock discovered on the island, and offshore whaling became a possibility where beaches were accessible.

* Nobbs continued as the spiritual guide of the colony on Norfolk until his death. He raised twelve children who in turn have helped swell the population of Norfolk Island.

6

HOME SWEET HOME

Even though some were tending sheep, some driving cattle, and two or three working the windmill, still others were finding it difficult to forget Pitcairn and "home." There are always such. Nowadays we have a glib word for these people. And we call their nostalgia a fixation. Towards the end of 1858, after a two-year trial of Norfolk, two families decided that they preferred to return to their former home—to the Pitcairn they loved. These were Moses Young with his wife and five young children, and Mayhew Young and his wife together with seven children. Of these last, six were the offspring of Mrs. Mayhew Young by a former marriage to Matthew McCoy. The sixteen pilgrims took passage on the *Mary Ann* and reached Pitcairn in January, 1859.

Aunt Mary Ann, who was one of the children returning to Pitcairn, told me that the little band arrived at the island just in time, for, according to her tale, soon after their landing a French man-of-war appeared with the intention of claiming the abandoned island for France. Having saved Pitcairn for the Empire, they climbed the cliff eagerly anxious to see their beloved homes. But a ruin faced them. Most of the houses had been destroyed, the gardens had run wild, and desolation chilled their hearts. Later the returning islanders discovered that during their absence on Norfolk a crew of sailors had landed from neighboring Oeno, where they had been shipwrecked. That desert island offered no asylum, and the shipwrecked crew had made their way to Pitcairn only to find it abandoned. After living on the island for a short time, and tiring of the pastime of carving their names on the school benches, the shipwrecked sailors decided to construct a craft by which they might sail to Tahiti. The planks and nails of the houses were handy to their purpose, and, without much compunction, they wrecked what was necessary.

With fortitude and increasing joy, the little band of islanders fell to the task of rebuilding their dwellings and planting their crops. The plantations, fallow for more than two years, now yielded crops more abundant than ever before in the memory of that generation. The elder girls, profiting by Mrs. Selwyn's instruction, undertook to preserve among the younger ones the few elements of learning they possessed.

Five years after the arrival of the first lot, a second arrived. News of the successful resettlement of Pitcairn had reached Norfolk and stirred up dormant longings in others to return to the island of their birth. This time four families deserted Norfolk. These were Thursday October Christian, 2nd, wife, nine children, and mother-in-law (the aged Mrs. Young, née Elizabeth Mills, the only child of John Mills of the *Bounty*); Robert Buffett and wife; Simon Young, his mother Hannah (the daughter of John Adams), his wife, and their eight children; and finally a newly married couple, Samuel Warren and his wife Agnes Christian. The last man, Samuel Warren, was a sailor who had recently joined the colony at Norfolk. Hailing from Providence, R. I., he had found life among the islanders more seductive than that aboard a whaler. Throwing in his lot with the Norfolk Islanders, he married a daughter of Thursday October Christian, and when the latter decided to return to Pitcairn, daughter and son-in-law determined to accompany him. Samuel Warren left a large brood of prolific children who have in turn added to the island population. It was a grandson of old Samuel, Burley Warren, who was my devoted host on Pitcairn, and it was Burley's quarter of American ancestry that gave him first claim to a fellow American.

No dissuasion had any effect on the second lot, although much pressure was brought to bear on these diehards to remain on Norfolk. Amid sad partings which the participants knew were for ever, the little band of thirty-one set sail on the *St. Kilda*. They left Norfolk on December 18, 1863, and on February 2, 1864, joined their predecessors at Pitcairn. Thus in all forty-seven, about one quarter of the total colony, found their way back to the place from which they had started.

Unknown to the islanders ashore, the *St. Kilda* arrived at night with her load of homesick passengers. In the joy of reaching their destination and in their eagerness to announce their coming, a terrific din of shouts and musket fire was let loose to attract the attention of the friends and relatives ashore. But it had the unforeseen effect of creating stark terror in the hearts of the children and devastating dread in the parents. The next morning brought a doubled rejoicing—the removal of fear and the discovery of friends.

Among the newcomers was Simon Young, a man of superior parts and with a high sense of social responsibility. With a keen realization of the needs of the rising generation, he established a school, revivified the religious services, and in general took a leading part in guiding the growth of the tree cut back to its stump. Not the least of his influence was felt by his young daughter, Rosalind Amelia. This girl was the most apt of her father's pupils and ultimately became the most literate of all the children of Pitcairn.

The succeeding years were full of peace and calm, broken only by the visits of passing ships. As the years passed and with them the prosperity of the whaling industry, fewer ships brought the world to Pitcairn's shore. The time had almost come when Pitcairn once more was nearly as isolated as it had been at the beginning of the century.

In 1868, the Norfolk Islanders for the last time attempted to entice the Pitcairn Islanders to rejoin them. Their letters offered every inducement even to paying for the charter of a transport; but although some of the experimental youth were ready to try another trek, the conservative judgment of their elders prevailed, and the offer was refused.

The year 1875 was marked by two shipwrecks. The first was that of the *Cornwallis*, which crashed on the rocks of Pitcairn Island itself. The second took place on the nearby coral island, Oeno, where the *Khandeish* ran aground. One of the crew settled for a time on Pitcairn and married one of the women. This shipwreck of the *Khandeish* proved profitable to the natives, for the stories of their kind reception that the crew told on their return to San Francisco inspired its citizens to send to Pitcairn quantities of gifts, among them an organ which created great enthusiasm on the island.

So rapidly had the colony been increasing that at the time of Admiral de Horsey's call at Pitcairn in 1878, the population, consisting of ninety persons, had almost doubled itself since 1864.

In 1880 the islanders underwent a psychological experience that left a deep impression and that was regarded at the time as a "visitation." We are indebted to Rosalind Amelia Young for the account. Only eleven or twelve of the younger members of the colony were affected. The victim first became subject to hallucinations of a terrifying but unspecified nature. In some cases they heard voices calling. Then apparently exhausted by these emotional crises, the subjects were unable to recall the memory of past events, the power of speech was temporarily lost, and their faces froze into an empty rigidity as though the mind had flown from its abode. Usually the victim was not violent. A peculiarity often accompanying this state was the seeming transformation of large objects into miniature ones or the reverse, so that children grew miraculously to gigantic size and full-grown men shrunk to dwarfs.

The "visitation" was not confined to the natives alone. A shipwrecked youth, who was confined to the island until he might find passage on a ship, was also a victim. He began by seeing his mother's coffin pass above his head and out the window. Soon after he became oblivious to the world about him and lost the power of speech. When speech and consciousness returned, he started to seek an unjustly persecuted friend who had been thrown into prison. Later he was found by a search party at the opposite side of the island sleeping under a rock and rolled in a scout's blanket. At that stage, he was Davy Crockett on the trail of Indians.

The last case was the longest. One of the girls fell under this strange spell in 1884 and was not restored to normality until 1886.

No explanation of this series of mental disturbances has ever been offered. Once at a meeting of physicians, I cited these cases, and a friend of mine, Dr. Ramsay Spillman, suggested that a noxious weed might conceivably have induced the phenomena described. He cited the effect of the Jimson weed on the settlers of Jamestown who, unfamiliar with its qualities, became temporarily deranged on eating it. It is not impossible, however, that most of the seizures on Pitcairn might have been the result of suggestion. Such an explanation is probable when we remember the youth of the victims.

Three more outsiders joined the colony at this time when the *Acadia* was wrecked on Ducie Island, a coral atoll about three hundred miles away. When the *Edward O'Brien* arrived a short time after the shipwreck and removed the sailors, three elected to remain on Pitcairn. Two of these married Pitcairn girls, one remaining on the island, the other after three years returning with his wife and two children to Wales. The third man left by the *Acadia* aroused a hornet's nest by winning the affections of a girl already betrothed to an island man. The family of the fickle young lady was infuriated by this state of affairs and succeeded in antagonizing the chief magistrate against the newcomer, who was subsequently dismissed from the island at the first opportunity. Captain Clark of H.M.S. *Sappho* was the *deus ex machina,* and as a sequel to this affair he officially forbade, at the request of the islanders, all marriages with strangers. The law was afterwards amended to permit marriage with anyone whose admission might be deemed beneficial to the community.

In 1886, a major event in the religious life of the Pitcairn Islanders took place. John I. Tay, a missionary of the Seventh Day Adventists, came among them. This visit had been well prepared, for ten years earlier, Elders James White and J. N. Loughborough had sent to Pitcairn a box of literature concerning the tenets of the Seventh Day Adventists. These writings were regarded first with horror, then tolerated, and at last embraced. The islanders, always interested in churchly affairs and devoted to the reading of religious tracts, could hardly resist the temptation to examine the documents of this new sect. Nothing, however, was done to change their academic interest into one of active faith until the arrival of Tay in October, 1886. During a brief stay of six weeks he was able to persuade a large part of the colony to adopt the new articles of belief. A minority, however, at first refused to abandon the church of their fathers, thereby threatening a schism in the community. So closely knit, however, was the community that the reluctant minority wisely decided to adopt the new faith in order to preserve a unanimity in religious observances.

The islanders, ever sensitive to the opinion of their friends in England and America and fearful of criticism, were concerned about the reception the news of their conversion would receive. They were not long in waiting, for after the visit of H.M.S. *Cormorant* in 1887, they discovered that many "viewed with regret" and the rest lamented their religious "debauch."

Partaking easily of the prevailing opinion in the mother country, the Pitcairn Islanders had assumed with the most loyal of Englishmen a reverential attitude toward Queen Victoria. Prayers for her welfare were never forgotten, and inquiries as to her health and happiness were punctiliously made of all visiting British ships. None of her subjects bestowed a greater devotion on Queen Victoria than did these, the least important of them. It was, therefore, a labor of love for the islanders to add their mite to the bounty showered on the Queen on the occasion of her jubilee in 1887. A box of island curios together with a letter of presentation was prepared and dispatched to Her Majesty by the Pitcairn Islanders.

Queen Victoria, who took a keen interest in the colony, replied to their gift by sending a present of commemoration coins, ranging from six-penny to four-shilling pieces. These were distributed among the women and girls who cherished the token of their Queen's remembrance.

In 1890 the inhabitants celebrated the centenary of the settlement on Pitcairn. Although the affairs of the island were of no importance to the world, and the life of the community was but slightly affected by the historical events of the century; yet within the microcosm of the colony much had happened, and far beyond most isolated communities, this one had enjoyed the attention of the world. They had undertaken in a body two remarkable migrations. To their shores had come a long list of ships, many of them containing men distinguished in their day, and within their island they had suffered oppression and had experienced release.

To celebrate the one hundredth birthday of their community the islanders characteristically chose a hymn as the most appropriate form of verse in which to sing their thanks to God. The following was composed by a native and sung by the participants in the celebration:

Our Father, God, we come to raise
Our songs to thee in grateful praise;
We come to sing. Thy guiding hand,
By which supported still we stand.

To this fair land our fathers sought
To flee their doom their sins had brought,
In vain—nor peace nor rest was found,
For strife possessed th' unhallowed ground.

Darkness around their path was spread;
Their crimes deserved a vengeance dread;
When, lo! a beam of hope was given
To guide their erring feet to heaven.

The holy word, a beacon light,
Had pierced the shade of sin's dark night.
And poured a flood of radiance where
Had reigned the gloom of dull despair.

We own the depths of sin and shame,
Of guilt and crime from which we came;
Thy hand upheld us from despair,
Else we had sunk in darkness there.

We, their descendants, here today
Meet in thy house to praise and pray,
And ask thy blessing to attend
And guide us to life's journey's end.

Oh, that our lives henceforth may be
More consecrated, Lord, to thee!
Thy boundless favours to us shown
With gratitude we humbly own.

Thou know'st the depths from whence we sprung;
Inspire each heart, unloose each tongue,
That all our powers may join to bless
The Lord, our Strength and Righteousness.

The Pitcairn Islanders, eager for fresh tides rolling in from the world, were thrown into considerable excitement their centennial year by the news that the Seventh Day Adventist missionary ship, *Pitcairn,* was bound for the island where it would make its first "parochial" call. The visit meant more to them than visits of other ships, welcome as these were. It was a flattering recognition by the mother church and an unusual opportunity for religious and social diversion. The *Pitcairn* arrived on November 25, 1890, bearing Elders Gates and Read, their wives, and Mr. and Mrs. John I. Tay. The entire community was baptized, and a rich fare of theology was easily digested by the communicants. After a short visit the *Pitcairn* departed, taking three island men aboard.

In July, 1892, the ship was back again, and this time Elder Gates remained on the island. This gentleman injected into the quiet waters of Pitcairn life a current of activity which was strong enough to bear the burden of a class, a literary society attended by over forty members, and the first newspaper. This periodical had a somewhat collegiate name, the *Monthly Pitcairnian,* and consisted of laboriously hand-written pages. Its reportorial staff was overburdened by six news gatherers whose lack of activity explained their abundance. Rosalind Amelia Young, who no doubt was energetic and prolific in her contributions, described the paper as having its first page devoted to an original poem, followed by an editorial page over which Elder Gates presided. Moral and Religious Topics, the Home Circle, News Items, Pleasantries, and All Sorts constituted the remaining departments. It would be interesting to see a copy of Pitcairn's solitary journalistic effort, but I have never come across one. Perhaps they suffered the usual fate of all old newspapers.

The zeal of Mrs. Gates spent itself in schemes of dubious utility. She started a kindergarten according to the latest pedagogical methods; and perhaps from exuberance attempted to teach stenography to some of the young people who, wiser than their instructress, lost interest in the impractical endeavor.

Having disposed of their religious welfare, the islanders turned now to their political housekeeping. For some time they had wanted a change in the form of local government, and when H.M.S. *Champion,* Captain Rookes, arrived on October 3, 1892, the principal men of the group took the opportunity to consult with this official representative of Great Britain. The result of the conference produced this resolution and a modification in the number of government officials.

Resolution

"Whereas, we have witnessed in the past, that thro' lack of strength and firmness, on the part of the government officers, some evil has resulted, and, Whereas, we believe that a larger number of officers would tend to make a stronger government, and that plans for the public welfare would be executed with better success, therefore,

"Resolved, that we heartily endorse the plan of having a government consisting of a parliament of seven, with power to legislate, to plan for the public good, to execute all decisions of the court, and to see that all public demands are attended to without unnecessary delay."

Then follow a list of duties pertaining to various offices and a list of laws. These will be described in detail later. The resolution with its attendant features was approved on January 1, 1893, by the voters.

This code and the administrative offices were modified later in 1904 and, with the exception of minor changes since then, have endured to the present time.

In February, 1893, the missionary ship *Pitcairn* again touched at the island. Mr. Gates took passage on this trip, but his place was taken by a newcomer, Hattie André. This young lady, fresh from college, had come to teach school on the island. She started classes for adults as well as for the children and very soon won the affection of the islanders.

When the *Pitcairn* departed, she carried a manuscript history of the island written by Rosalind Amelia Young. A daughter of the gentle and devoted Simon Young, she had inherited from her father a love of learning and a sweetness of character that still make her name blessed among the Pitcairn Islanders. Miss Young had literary ambitions and, besides the account of Pitcairn published by the Seventh Day Adventist Press, was also the author of numerous verses. She is the best example of a type common in the colony: a deeply religious nature schooled to a gentle and deprecating tolerance for the weaknesses of the less rigorously faithful members of the community. For the best part of her life, Rosalind Young continued her father's task: the teaching and guiding of the children. But in 1907, Miss Young married David Nield, a minister of the Seventh Day Adventist Church. The couple had met three years before at Tahiti, where Miss Young had gone to attend a church conference. This meeting led to a correspondence in which, says the Reverend Mr. Nield, "All points of Doctrine, Health Reform, Food, Ages, Business, and Mission work were carefully considered." Rosalind Young, emerging without blemish from this inspection, arrangements were made for her to join her prospective husband in Auckland, N. Z., where they were joined in holy wedlock. She threw herself into her husband's work and, until her death in 1924 while visiting Pitcairn, maintained a deep interest in churchly affairs.

At the beginning of the present century, Pitcairn was again an almost forgotten island. The whaling days with their stream of free-lancing ships had passed, the World War inhibited the visits of British men-of-war, and the opening of the Panama Canal diminished the use of the route around the Horn. Fewer and fewer ships paid their friendly calls. Rapid voyages and refrigerating systems eliminated the lure of the fresh vegetables that Pitcairn

had to offer. This increasing isolation made the fewer
visits paid the island greater events.

When Mr. and Mrs. Routledge called at Pitcairn on
their yacht, *Mana,* in 1915, they were welcomed with
enthusiasm. Two island youths, Edward and Arthur
Young, shipped aboard the yacht and accompanied the
Routledges to London. This sort of temporary seafaring
was no novelty among adventurous Pitcairn boys. Bred
to the sea and fearless of her moods, they make excellent
sailors. Many of the older Pitcairn men now alive have
traveled widely among the islands of the Pacific. The
Youngs' sortie was, therefore, no cause for wonder, but
seeing the United States and England was a bit of good
fortune that made the two lucky ones the envy of their
fellows.

Within the last few years, Pitcairn once more has
been brought into more regular communication with the
world. The New Zealand Shipping Company steamers
on their way to and from Panama stop for about a half
hour as a diversion for their passengers. The natives come
out to sell their curios, and the passengers have an opportunity to inspect the "strange creatures" and to ask
impertinent and ill-advised questions.

III. CULTURAL

7

EARLY VICTORIAN EDEN

The attention that Pitcairn has received during the last century and more arises mostly from the romance and the drama of its history and a little from the appeal that all isolated and lonely communities exert, especially when they are situated on a lovely Pacific islet. For some the chords of the imagination vibrate more readily to the story of the mutiny; others respond more keenly to the tale of crime and the toll of murder that accompanied the first days on Pitcairn. An older and more godly generation succumbed to the spectacle of redemption rising like a sweet flower from a dung heap. But varied as the human interest of Pitcairn is and wide as the range of emotions in its history, it has still another claim that has been strangely neglected. The very sequence of events which produced a unique and absorbing story in its own right also created, as a by-product, a social and biological experiment of profound importance. My desire to study the mixture of races on Pitcairn led to my earlier attempt to reach the island in 1923 and to my successful try about twelve years later. Therefore, I shall now turn to Pitcairn in its scientific aspect. In the present chapter, however, I intend to consider only the "social experiment."

Perhaps I should begin by explaining exactly what I mean by the somewhat pretentious phrase *social experiment*. Pitcairn was not the scene of a Utopia or an

Erewhon. No social or political theories stimulated its founding. But it was an unconscious and spontaneous experiment none the less. The problems it illuminates are those of culture contact. This is a phenomenon as ancient and as widespread as the existence of culture itself, and some of its more dramatic phases are represented by the contacts of European civilization with those of the native peoples with whom it collided during the European expansion of the last four centuries. Classic Attica itself was the fruit of a grafting of a sophisticated Cretan civilization on a rude Greek culture. So, too, the civilization of France has grown from the fertilization of Gallic culture by the seed of Rome.

America, North and South, illustrates dramatically nearly all phases of culture contact. The Europeans arriving on these shores came to grips with a preëxisting, firmly established population living according to a cultural pattern inimical or antithetical to that the invaders brought. The Europeans automatically proceeded to establish various types of contact depending on the character of their culture, the nature of the country, and reaction of the Indians. They came as exploiters, colonizers, conquerors, traders, and missionaries. As a result of these varied forms of impingement, some Indian tribes folded up and vanished, if not like a mist into thin air, then into the less favored areas. A few tribes resisted and were able to preserve their integrity. A great many resisted but were conquered and absorbed. Still others, and by far the most important, were normally conquered but never really digested by their conquerors. These last, however, unlike those who had vanished, or had been absorbed, integrated their native culture with that of their conquerors and are now undergoing a renascence of the utmost significance. The Mexican is such a rebirth of Indian culture. In the dynamics of culture the importance of the phenomenon is self-evident.

Similarly in Polynesia culture contact with Europeans, beginning in the eighteenth century, has had a tremendous effect on native life. Here the contact was largely trading and missionary in origin, and—I need not add— amorous. Military conquest has played a very minor part. And yet, except for Samoa and Tonga, where native life has been protected, Polynesian culture has been almost completely destroyed. The expert can still find a few fragments surviving into modern times, but to a Captain Cook the present culture would bear about as much resemblance to what he saw in the eighteenth century as would life in his native Yorkshire to that in Chicago. He would find the once sacred *maraes* now tumbled piles of rocks overgrown with brush and trees; he would recognize in the modern outrigger canoe a sad degeneration from the skill that built the ancient war canoes; he would see no connection between the modern Tahitian woman in her European clothing and the *tapa*-clad houri of his day.

At the risk of overwhelming little Pitcairn with these mighty examples, I have expatiated somewhat on this theme to illustrate a fact of great importance in all cultures. On Pitcairn, we see an experiment in culture contact—the impact of European, or English, civilization and Polynesian. It occurs, to be sure, on a small scale, but it is a reduction in degree only. Here we have a number of advantages for the study of the phenomenon. The situation has been simplified to its basic elements. Most of the imponderables which affect other foci of culture contact and the complex reactions that obscure the design are absent on Pitcairn.

The Englishmen and Tahitian women who set up housekeeping on Pitcairn were completely shut off from the rest of the world for eighteen years and practically so for the thirty-five years from the date of landing in 1790 to Beechey's arrival in 1825. The initial ingredients, therefore, in the Pitcairn pudding were allowed to set without an added pinch of salt from England or an extra spoonful of sauce from Tahiti. Moreover, the stigmata and the disabilities, invariably attached to such "experiments" as these, did not exist. No social pressure, no external economic forces, no cultural reinforcements were brought to bear.

In addition to the importance of isolation in this social experiment, there is the added advantage of contact not only between two divergent cultures but between cultures relatively well known. Between Polynesian and English customs there is a gulf as wide as the geographical distance which separates them. Such contrast makes the resulting pattern easier to decipher.

We must not neglect to point out still another element in this unique set-up. That is the attitude of the culture-bearers themselves. Today we have become familiar through novels and cinemas with Polynesia; or if not familiar, at least cognizant. The romantic literature of escape has inflamed the heated imaginations of countless readers, many of whom would be ready to abandon everything for a cocoanut tree, a blue lagoon, and a brown maiden, voluptuous if not fair. The inherited culture of such romantics would have but little chance against the Polynesian. The English sailor, however, of the eighteenth century, much as he might enjoy the comfort of Polynesian life, was not conditioned by his reading, if he ever read, to regard the adoption of Polynesian life as the highest good. Therefore psychologically the mutineers on Pitcairn were ready to put up a good strong plea for England and the way they did things back home. I regard this state of mind as an element of incalculable importance. Few realize the revolution in the attitude of the white man towards native people. Familiarity has brought not contempt but a greater tolerance and even an insight that has led to a more profound appreciation of the achievements of people once held hardly better than slaves.

Pitcairn itself should not be omitted in this description of the birth of Pitcairn life. The very nature of the island, the fruit and vegetables it produced, its climate, all contributed to the character of the new colony. Had the

Bounty wandered farther south to a more inhospitable island or to one whose aspect was less like Tahiti, the inherited lore of the women would surely have been less useful and therefore less effective in shaping the manners of the colony.

Pitcairn was settled by a group of twenty-seven or twenty-eight persons, consisting of nine British mutinous seamen, six Polynesian men from Tahiti, and twelve, or by some counts thirteen, Tahitian women. Consider what that meant. Here was a group of Englishmen, hardly knowing the simplest elements of the Tahitian language and totally ignorant of the unguessed subtleties of that speech. Nor was this the extent of their ignorance of Polynesia, for they knew next to nothing of Polynesian life, its conventional manners and customs, and its rich traditional lore for supporting existence—a knowledge which was second nature to their native companions. Living in a more complex civilization where the activities of life were more specialized and divided into compartments, they lacked the knowledge to reproduce it entirely, even had they wished to do so. But if the mutineers had cherished such an ambition, they would have been immediately discouraged. The little group was confronted by a world without tools, equipment, or any of the necessities with which we manufacture other necessities. Even the fruits and vegetables of the land and the fish in the surrounding sea were not the varieties to which they were accustomed at home.

On the other hand, the Tahitians, both men and women, found Pitcairn similar enough to their own beloved Tahiti to feel at home. Living habitually closer to nature and employing simpler means of obtaining their livelihood, they were less at a loss as to how to take up the same pursuits here.

With such a set-up certain eventualities are predictable. It takes no profound insight to see that the mechanics of living would be Tahitian in origin. *Tapa*-making, underground cooking, and basketry were merely Polynesian transferals. But even though the first settlers derived much from Tahiti, the English stamped their character on the community life. And to this were added certain original developments, in response to local conditions.

Before describing the life of the Pitcairn Islanders of today, let us go back a century or more, before contact with Europe and America had begun to change the habits of the islanders, to a period when their existence and customs represented the products of their inherited culture plus the ingenuity of their wit. We are indebted to Captain Beechey for the most nearly complete account of the island in those days and to others, too numerous to mention, for additional details.

Since the first things to capture the attention of the stranger are usually the material manifestations, I shall begin by describing those aspects of the Pitcairn of one hundred years ago. The village was unlike the present one. The first settlers and their children built their houses around a rectangular plot of level ground, like a village green. The houses bore no resemblance to anything ever seen before in Polynesia, having been built by the Englishmen who naturally turned to familiar models. A Polynesian house is a light structure, consisting of a framework lashed together and covered with thatch or mats. Those on Pitcairn were solid, substantial cottages with sturdy plank walls. But there the resemblance to English cottages ceased. Lacking nails, glass, cut stone, mortar, cement, and similar building materials, the ingenious mutineers overcame these obstacles by evolving a house like a tree rooted to the ground. The few that have survived the hand of the wrecker are still sound.

The following account gives a brief description of the principal features of these houses. Since cellars and foundation walls were impossible, large rocks were set at each corner with a few more at intervals between to serve as supports. On these the builders laid heavy, roughly dressed logs, into which they mortised square uprights. Besides one upright at each corner, others were set at regular intervals along the sides. The tops of these uprights also were tenoned into cross pieces. The sides of the uprights were grooved so that a wall could be added without nails, and boards cut to the proper length were slid into these facing grooves. Shutters made in the same way, tongue and groove, were built into slots and could be pushed aside in good weather or closed in bad. The roofs were covered by thatch made in the Tahitian fashion. This consisted of folding a series of overlapping pandanus leaves around a palm stem or a similar stick. These leaves were then secured by a long wooden sliver which joined all the leaves like a simple running stitch. Lengths such as these were then laid on the roof in neat overlapping rows and made a very picturesque as well as practical covering.

The interior usually consisted of one long room divided by one or two partitions. Bunks like those on ships were built along the inner wall, while on the opposite wall was the long row of shuttered openings. A few houses had an upper story used for sleeping and reached by a ladder through a central trap door. The houses naturally were unpainted and soon weathered to a pleasing soft gray-brown, which blended into the rich, green foliage surrounding them.

The climate made fireplaces unnecessary, and the houses had no chimneys. For cooking, an outhouse, less substantially built, was attached to the main house, and the wide cracks in the walls permitted the smoke to escape. Besides the bakehouse, other outhouses included a poultry shed and a pigsty.

The furniture of these locally modified European houses was naturally of a very simple order. Cabinet work is a special craft. The best results require practiced hands and a series of tools that the islanders lacked. What furniture was made, therefore, was crude but sturdy. But note that the models were English. It is easy to understand why. Polynesians sit and sleep on the ground; they even squat on the ground when they eat.

Except for beautifully woven mats their house interiors are bare and simple. But the mutineers were accustomed to postures which require chairs, tables, and beds, and they proceeded to manufacture these articles of furniture as best they could. The beds or bunks, built against the inner wall of the main room, were usually raised about eighteen inches from the floor. Furnished with mattresses, consisting of palm leaves and about three layers of *tapa*-cloth, they were not uncomfortable. To these the children of the household retired, the parents shielding their own quarters by a partition.

The main room, always on the ground floor even in a two-storied house, had a large table and stools as its principal furnishings. Strangely enough, mats so indispensable in a Polynesian household were not used on Pitcairn. But sea chests were common articles of household furnishings. They were requisite for the storage of *tapa* and the scanty clothes of European origin.

In the evening, which comes soon after six o'clock on Pitcairn, these snug interiors were illuminated by the faltering light of the *doodoee* or candle nut. The use of these nuts for lighting once widespread in Polynesia today still lingers on remote islands such as Rapa. The oily kernels were strung on the midstem of the palm leaf, and as one nut burnt low the next would be ignited, thus producing a candlelike illumination satisfactory except for the cracking and spitting that Beechey found disconcerting.

Having housed themselves in ingenious dwellings the construction of which was variously derived from English, Tahitian, and native resource, the islanders revealed less eclecticism and ingenuity in the matter of their garb. In one respect choice played no part. Woven cloth was not available beyond the limited supply with which they arrived. Some source of apparel was absolutely essential, for even though the climate of Pitcairn is benign through the greater part of the year, there are periods of chill and damp. Moreover, the nights are cool and fresh, and bed-

clothes are a necessity. Fortunately there existed on Pitcairn the breadfruit and the paper mulberry tree whose
bark is suitable for making *tapa*, a kind of paper cloth.
In the manufacture of this fabric, the women, trained as
good Polynesian housewives, were expert.

The technique of *tapa*-making consists first of strip-
ping the bark from the paper mulberry or, in some
cases, from the breadfruit tree. The essential inner bark
is removed and soaked in water until it becomes soggy
and the fibers loosened. Then, kneeling before a stout
log, the women beat the pulpy mass to the appropriate
thickness with a *tapa*-beater. This implement, about a
foot and a half long, is square in cross section except for
the round, smooth handle. The four faces of the working
end of the beater are grooved with longitudinal ribbings
of different thicknesses on the various faces, the coarser
ones being used for the early stages and the finer ones
for the final beating. The work was laborious and slow,
and much of the women's time was occupied in making
rolls of *tapa* not only for clothing but for sheets as well.
Some of the *tapa* was dyed a rich red brown with pigment obtained by steeping the *doodoee* nut in water. Although the *tapa*-cloth was stiff when fresh from the
beater, it acquired softness after the repeated washings
that its toughness and durability permitted.

Lack of needles and thread may explain why the men
were forced to abandon the use of trousers. Or, possibly,
paper pants seemed a ridiculous solution, for on their
first discovery they were disclosed in heathen costumes.
The men wore, Polynesian fashion, a *maro*, which was
simply a length of *tapa* passed around the waist, with
one end drawn between the legs and then tucked in at
the waist. This garment, though abbreviated, was very
comfortable, modest, and convenient. In fact, even when
European clothing had been introduced and was accessible to all the men, they frequently preferred to wear
the *maro* when there were no visitors on the island.

The costume of the women, although more voluminous than the male attire, had a classic simplicity. A skirt or "petticoat," reaching from waist to ankle, was made by wrapping a length of *tapa* around the hips. It was then snugly secured by rolling down the top like the stocking of the erstwhile flapper.

Both men and women wore a subsidiary garment like the Tahitian *ahu buu*, which was simply a mantle thrown around the shoulder. The women dressed their hair like their Tahitian mothers, either braided or flowing unbound save for a wreath of flowers. Says Beechey, "It must be remembered, that these people, as with other Islanders of the South Seas, the custom has generally been to go naked, the *maro* with the men excepted, and with the women, the petticoat, or kilt, with a loose covering over the bust, which, indeed, in Pitcairn's Island, they are always careful to conceal; consequently, an exposure to that extent carried with it no feeling whatever of indelicacy; or, I may safely add, that the Pitcairners would have been the last persons to incur the charge."

Both sexes wore hats, for protection against the sun, cocoanut leaves and pandanus furnishing the fiber as in Tahitian hats. Friday October Christian, Folger's first visitor, had his headgear decorated with a black cock's feathers. And Captain Pipon, captivated by Pitcairn graces, exclaimed that the bonnets of the women would please a fashionable London dressmaker by their simplicity and good taste.

The women naturally took charge of another department of the island economy and practised an art acquired from Tahiti. This was the preparation and cooking of food. The principal method of cooking employed the underground oven—a device not unlike the clambake known and valued in New England. A pit was filled with stones and heated red-hot by a wood fire. After the embers had been removed, the meat or fish, wrapped in *ti*-leaves and surrounded by vegetables, was placed on the stones, and then covered by a matted layer of leaves and sticks. To retain the heat more effectively a final blanket of earth was placed over the whole. After an hour or two the removal of the covering layers revealed a superbly baked meal with all its delicate flavors retained.

Meals were generally prepared only twice a day, once late in the morning and again in the early evening after the day's labor. Such is the custom in Polynesia, and thus did the Pitcairn housewives plan their culinary labors. The main source of food was vegetable: yams, taros, sweet potatoes (*kumara*), pumpkins, peas, *yappai*, and sugar cane. In addition, there were abundant fruits such as bananas, oranges, plantain, breadfruit, cocoanuts, and watermelons. Once or twice a week fish was served and even more rarely meat, the principal source being the pigs which were kept in a sty adjacent to the house. Eggs, from chickens and from the sea birds that frequented the island at certain seasons, were another adjunct to the Pitcairn table.

Only one recipe for a blended dish has come down to us. It may be that on Pitcairn food was preferred in its simplest and purest elements. But it is more likely that the canons of the primitive Polynesian cuisine, which eschews mixed concoctions, also governed the Pitcairn kitchens. At any rate, I have discovered only one mixed dish. This is known on Pitcairn as *pillihai,* and is still in high favor on the island. It is made from boiled yams which are grated and mixed with cocoanut meat. The resulting paste is baked in a cake. A variant of this employs mashed bananas and cocoanut. These *pillihai* cakes are often sweetened with a molasseslike syrup extracted from the *ti*-root.

"Raw fish," a delectable dish that is widely appreciated not only in Polynesia but throughout Oceania even to Japan, seemingly was neglected in Pitcairn. According to the Tahitian ritual, the firm flesh of special species of fish is cut into small pieces, soaked for an hour or two in sea water flavored with lime juice, and then eaten with the fingers after each piece is dipped in a sauce of cocoanut milk. The more impatient Polynesians have been known to attack their fish while still wriggling on the hook. As the Russian yearns for *borscht*, the Marseillaise for the rich *bouillabaisse*, the Strasbourger for his *pâté* oozing goose fat, so the Polynesian craves raw fish. I have seen a look of positive beatitude on the face of a Samoan who, after months of deprivation, was able at last to satisfy his longing for this delicacy. It is therefore a matter of wonder that this form of fish consumption is absent on Pitcairn where raw-fish eaters controlled the kitchen. Had it once become established in the island diet, nothing could have shaken its hold, and it would have survived to this day among the islanders as one of the major requisites to the enjoyment of life.

Poë, another universally Polynesian article of food, is made by various methods in different parts of this island world. There is the breadfruit *popoë* of the Marquesas, the most obnoxious of all to the uncultivated taste. It is the habit, among these islanders, to reduce the breadfruit to a paste leavened with the yeasty remains of a more aged batch. Then after acquiring the proper ripeness in a subterranean pit it is served in a huge wooden bowl blackened by age and the polish of "poëy" hands. Just as the taste for it is a matter of cultivation, the trick of eating it requires skill. The participants, seated in a circle about the bowl, dip two fingers into the sticky viscous paste, the color of an ancient dish cloth, and with a practiced twist extract a mouthful which is adroitly speeded to the mouth, eagerly opened to receive it. The novice, however, requires a bath and a strigil after the banquet.

On other islands taro instead of breadfruit forms the base of *poë*. And in Tahiti *poë* has undergone numerous refinements to tickle the European palate. On Pitcairn, however, the only trace of it lingers, fittingly enough, in the name of the food on which infants are weaned. This, called *popoë* on Pitcairn, was a paste made from ripe plantains and boiled taro.

The principal beverage of the Pitcairn Islanders was and, for that matter, still is, water. Stronger drink had proved disastrous among the mutineers. William McCoy, lacking a more orthodox material for the exercise of his Scotch instincts, found a worthy substitute in the *ti*-plant, and his retentive mind reproduced from a youthful experience an efficient distillery that left an indelible impression on Pitcairn tradition. *Ti*-whiskey, if it may be so termed, was abhorred, and, until the contact with Tahiti had corrupted the islanders, never revived. Tea, however, brewed from the homonymic *ti*-plant was permitted. Milk was never used, although nanny goats were plentiful. Perhaps its flavor degenerates as a result of Polynesian grazing, or it may be that something in the Polynesian constitution finds it repellent; in any event, the natives esteem neither cows nor goats for their lactic glands.

Beechey thus describes a rather special meal prepared for him and the other officers visiting the island.

"The smoking pig, by a skillful dissection, was soon portioned out to every guest, but no one ventured to put its excellent qualities to the test until a lengthened Amen, pronounced by all the party had succeeded an emphatic grace delivered by the village parson. 'Turn to' was the signal for attack, and as it is convenient that all the party should finish their meal about the same time, in order that the one grace might serve for all, each made the most of his time. In Pitcairn's Island, it is not deemed proper to touch even a bit of bread without a grace before and after it, and a person is accused of inconsistency if he leaves off and begins again. So strict is their observance of this form, that we do not know of any instance in which it has been forgotten. On one occasion I had engaged Adams in conversation, and he incautiously took the first mouthful without having said the grace; but before he had swallowed it, he recollected himself, and feeling as if he had committed a crime, immediately put away what he had in his mouth, and commenced a prayer.

"Welcome cheer, hospitality, and good humour, were the characteristics of the feast, and never was their beneficial influence more practically exemplified than on this occasion, by the demolition of nearly all that was placed before us. With the exception of some wine we had brought with us, water was the only beverage. This was placed in a large jug at one end of the board, and when necessary, was passed round the table—a ceremony at which, in Pitcairn's Island in particular, it is desirable to be the first partaker, as the gravy of the dish is invariably mingled with the contents of the pitcher: the natives who prefer using their fingers to forks, being quite indifferent whether they hold the vessel by the hands or the spout."

One characteristic of a Pitcairn meal which caused considerable disappointment among the officers of the *Blossom* was the separation of the sexes. The women, as in Tahiti, never ate with the men, but took their meal afterwards. The officers had to be content to chat with the women who served them, standing behind their chairs brushing the flies away with whisks. To anyone accustomed to traditional Tahitian manners such a scene would be distinctly familiar.

The most important activity on Pitcairn as in other communities is getting a living. But the inhabitants of this island are more fortunate than the majority of mankind, for with moderate toil they reap rich harvests from the land and by what many men regard as a sport they garner food from the sea. The plantations on Pitcairn are situated on the rolling plateau that constitutes the roof of the island. In the early days of the colony, before there were enough men to till the fields, the women also shared the burdens of agricultural labor.

It is unfortunate that no description has come down to us of the details of Pitcairn agriculture. It would have been of interest to know more than we do of the agricultural techniques that sailors could evolve for raising food plants unfamiliar to them. One might reasonably assume that English seamen despite their calling would perhaps have had a little knowledge of the husbandry of English foodstuffs, but they could have known nothing of the cultivation of the Polynesian plants which constituted the crop on Pitcairn. On the other hand, the natives would certainly have been well acquainted with the methods of raising such plants as the taro and the *kumara*.

It is, however, clear that the agriculture of the islanders was primitive and that the foods were crude. Hoe culture appears to have been prevalent. Such refinements as subsoil ploughing were unknown. Fertilizer, however, in the form of seaweed had become a necessity after a couple of decades of intensive cultivation. Many fields yielded two crops a year, but since the soil was not carefully replenished or allowed to lie fallow it tended to become exhausted in later years.

The principal crops raised included yams, taro, and *kumara* (sweet potato). Planted in September, the yams usually matured by April or May. The taro, grown from young shoots, required somewhat special treatment. Aside from these plants, the island also produced the following foods which served as a welcome variety: breadfruit, cocoanuts, plantains, bananas, pumpkin, watermelons, peas, *yappai*, sugar cane, ginger, and turmeric. After relations with the world were established in the early part of the nineteenth century, a great variety of food plants were imported to the island to furnish a richer supply of vegetables. One other plant infamous in the annals of the island, the *ti*-plant, was extensively cultivated for its root and leaves. The root yields a sweetish liquor, like molasses, and the leaves were used both as fodder for goats and hogs and as food wrappers.

Fishing, like agriculture, was chiefly carried on by the men, although the women sometimes joined them. Usually once or twice a week, a day would be devoted to angling. To the nonfisherman the technique and lore of catching fish may seem the same the world over. But such is by no means the case. The Polynesian fisherman had evolved numerous specializations and a body of piscine knowledge that differ sharply from European methods and lore. In Polynesia, the extraordinary development of these traditions culminated in the famous "nights of the moon," a kind of almanac that guided the Polynesian angler. By following the "nights of the moon" he knew when and where to seek for certain fish.

On the other hand sailors, such as the mutineers, must have entertained rather definite notions about the best method of capturing fish. And such Tahitian developments as fish-spearing and stone fish-traps must have appeared strange to them. Unfortunately, few details are known of the fishing methods practised on Pitcairn before European contact.

It is known, however, that the first settlers made fish-hooks, presumably of European type, from the *Bounty's* iron. Fishing lines also were made on the island and even continued to be preferred by the islanders to later European importations, since their own product had less tendency to twist in deep water. The Pitcairn Islanders adopted the Tahitian method of spearing fish, both because of its appeal as a sport and because of its effectiveness in the hand of an expert. To this day they are fond of catching fish in this manner. The spear tipped with five prongs was a type borrowed directly from the Tahitians. Polynesians also lent the torch which attracted the fish and made them fall easy prey to a sure and deft hand. I can find no mention on Pitcairn of nets or stone fish-traps, both common in Polynesia. The rocky coast and precipitous shore may well account for the absence of the latter.

The common varieties of fish caught at Pitcairn were cod, gray mullet, red snapper, and a kind of mackerel. The agile women often captured squid and crawfish among the rocks on the shore.

The nautical skill of the Pitcairn Islanders is eminently appropriate to a people descended from British seamen and Polynesian women. They inherit from both sides traditions of maritime prowess. When the settlement was discovered in 1808, the islanders already possessed a native craft in the form of a dug-out canoe light enough for two men to handle. The *Quarterly Review,* quoting Folger, referred to a "double canoe," but aside from this single mention I have found no other indication that the Polynesian outrigger principle was in use. Unfortunately, Folger's own statement does not elaborate on the type of canoe he saw, and we do not know whether or not the outrigger was adopted by the Pitcairn Islanders. It is certain, however, that the type of craft first employed was a dug-out with or without an outrigger. Perhaps this was made as are those of the present time in two longitudinal sections joined along the keel and caulked with a resinous substance extracted from the banyan tree.

The skill with which these frail craft were handled astonished all visitors. Landing at Pitcairn when there is a bit of weather requires expert judgment and experience. Says Captain Freemantle, "The landing is particularly hazardous; it being rarely that a ship's boat ought to land. The natives are very clever with their canoes and will land in almost any weather."

In addition to these pursuits, the island men were accustomed to hunt the goats and hogs which after a few years had multiplied until they overran the island and created havoc in the plantations. To control the breeding of these animals the islanders resorted to keeping the males penned but permitting the females to run loose. Somewhat later, when barter with whale ships assumed considerable proportions, these wild goats and hogs became a valuable source of fresh meat for sailors weary of salt beef.

But life on Pitcairn was not exclusively devoted to agriculture, hunting, fishing, *tapa*-making, and household duties. Even though the islanders exhibited a reluctance in the company of strangers to engage in levity or light amusement, they were capable of frivolous pur-

suits. When Beechey pressed them to put on an enter-
tainment, they complied but not without much giggling
and shyness. The dance, Beechey concluded, was rarely
enjoyed, but to entertain him the islanders organized one.
A large room was prepared, and the performers "glowing beneath a blazing string of *doodoee* nuts" were arranged along one side of the chamber. Along the other
side were ranged the musicians under the direction of
Arthur Quintal who was seated on the ground before a
large gourd. With his toes he worked a piece of musical
wood (*porou*) and he beat the gourd with two sticks in
his hands. With her hands Dolly beat a rapid tattoo on
another gourd which had a longitudinal slit at one end.
A third musician provided the bass on the copper fish-
kettle of the *Bounty*. The time was excellent and the co-
ördination of the musicians perfect. To this rhythm, three
adult women danced with shy reluctance, "as they consider such performances an inroad upon their usual innocent pastimes," adds Beechey. The dance, a deco-
rously abridged version of a Tahitian one, was merely a
kind of shuffling of the feet and a simple figure executed
by passing each other, the whole being accompanied by
snapping fingers.

During the performance Beechey remarked that some
of the spectators were overcome by amusement, and
that shyness paralyzed others from rising to join the
dancers. Nor did this terpsichorean effort continue long,
"from an idea," Beechey observes, "it was too great a
levity."

Nor did the Englishmen's attempts to entertain the islanders have any apparent success. One of the officers
brought out his violin and offered to play some tunes in
order to stimulate the dancing, but the island women declined to respond. Nevertheless, the violinist presented a
specimen of his art, but the performance, though well
executed, did not produce the anticipated effect. "They
had not yet arrived at a state of refinement to appreciate
harmony, but were highly delighted with the rapid mo-

tion of the fingers, and always liked to be within sight of the instrument when it was played. They were afterwards heard to say, that they preferred their own simple musical contrivance to the violin." The unfavorable picture of the musical tastes of the Pitcairn Islanders drawn by Beechey was further confirmed when they showed no aptitude or desire to learn another tune than the single one to which they sang all psalms and hymns.

However, I think that Beechey did the islanders an injustice in his judgment of their capacity for music and of their attitude toward the lighter diversions. No doubt, before distinguished visitors they had a natural desire, fostered by their religious training, to pretend to a greater sanctity than they usually maintained. But shyness in the presence of strangers proved more effective as a damper on gaiety. From Miss Young's descriptions of a celebration held years later, it is clear that modified forms of the Tahitian dance survived, indicating a continuous tradition. She speaks of the ancient Tahitian *ihara* and *uri* which were known in her day.

As for the musical reactions of the islanders, it is difficult to measure innate musical sense. We must remember that unaccustomed music often receives an ungracious welcome even in cultivated musical centers. Later visitors reversed Beechey's judgments. They found the islanders singing intricate part songs. Carleton, in 1850, declared himself amazed at their aptitude for choral singing. Indeed, the praise of the young and susceptible Fortescue Moresby is fulsome. "They sang two hymns in magnificent style; and really I have never heard any church singing in any part of the world that could equal it, except at Cathedrals."

Swimming was a favorite sport among both sexes. The feat of swimming around the island, a circuit of about seven miles, was common. One of their water sports, surf riding, was of Polynesian origin. "To have a slide" meant taking a surf board about three feet long, shaped like a canoe with a small keel, which the swimmer held before him as he dove into the sea. Swimming out from the shore, they would wait for a heavy sea. Then lying prone on the board, they were carried on the crest of the wave at a terrific speed hard on to the rocky shore. But just before disaster seemed inevitable, the rider would nimbly leap to his feet.

The younger part of the population was fond of kite flying, which was practised both in Tahiti and England, and they also found diversion in an undescribed game played with a ball.

But it was not only on these forms of activity that the mark of Tahiti or England was stamped. We find that even the domestic relations of the sexes also bore traces of the origins of the colony. In Tahiti, at the period of its discovery, although the women occupied positions of authority and enjoyed considerable freedom, they retired to an inferior status at meals. In Polynesia, women suffered ceremonial disabilities as well. They could not enter the sacred *marae* and in the Marquesas were forbidden to touch a canoe, so that Melville records with surprise that the female visitors had perforce to swim out to the ship carrying their vestments in one hand.

The only vestige evident on Pitcairn of the conventional status of Polynesian women cropped out in the aforementioned refusal of Pitcairn women to eat with the men, even at the invitation of their British visitors. The ceremonial concomitants were, of course, lost on Pitcairn where *maraes* were not held in reverence or canoes sacred. The rationalization of this custom on Pitcairn was drawn from Biblical sources. Man, said the islanders, was made first and ought, therefore, on all occasions to be served first. But this tradition did not reflect a genuinely inferior position of the women in the social structure of the island. In fact, the women, like their Tahitian ancestresses, took a leading part in social activities and did not allow themselves to be oppressed. They shared the labor with the men, even working in the fields before marriage. John Adams was said to oppose early mar-

1   Pitcairn Island.

Drawing of the *Bounty*.

3a   Housing the Long-Boat at Bounty Bay.

3b   Fishing Dugouts and Long-Boats.

Adamstown, Pitcairn Island.

4

5b   The Village School.

5a   The Island's Oldest House.

6a   Four Generations of Pitcairn Islanders.

6b   School Interior.

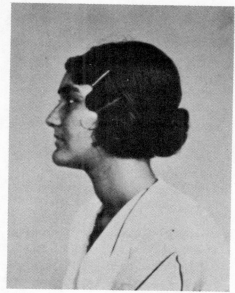

7a

Representing Pitcairn's Younger
Generation.

Burley Warren—the Author's Host
on Pitcairn.

7b

8a

Parkins Christian, Great-Great-
Grandson of Fletcher Christian.

Mary Ann McCoy—the Oldest
Woman on Pitcairn.

8b

riages for this reason, since the colony was deprived of a necessary worker when a girl married. "When once they become mothers," said Adams, "they are less capable of hard labour, being obliged to attend to their children." And Captain Pipon observed, "One may conclude they would be prolific." Later when a more formal governmental machinery was organized, the equality of women was recognized by granting them full rights along with the men in voting for administrative officers of the island. This, let it be remembered, was at a time when European women still labored under medieval disabilities.

The effects of accident are obvious in the social organization of the Pitcairn community. The orgy of violence which accompanied the founding of the colony resulted in reducing the population to a handful of Tahitian women, their twenty-five children by the mutineers, and a solitary man, John Adams. The children, rendered fatherless while they were still infants or young children, had come to look on Adams as their father, their teacher, and their guide. In fact, the colony was like a large family with a patriarch ruling its destiny. We know the startling series of events which created this situation. It was unique and it had unique consequences. The community on Pitcairn was an indigenous growth, pruned by massacre and trained by circumstance to grow around John Adams.

Unlike the material aspects of the community which had been shaped while the mutineers were still living, the social and governmental life changed its character as the children grew older, developing a pattern like nothing in Tahiti or England. It grew into a framework which accident had created and as its tender tissue hardened it preserved the design of its mold like a Chinese cricket gourd. The absence of a code of laws or a crystallized tradition did not make any the less effective the conditioning of Pitcairn life. All the children were raised together, the distinctions between "my" mother and "your" mother were vague as they often are in Polynesia, and the parenthood of the one surviving man, John Adams, was extended to serve all the mites of humanity who were growing up in a strange world that was the most normal they could imagine.

Under such circumstances, it never occurred to the islanders to consider a machinery of self-government necessary while Adams was still living. Having been trained in infancy to accept his dicta unquestioningly, they continued to do so even after reaching adult years. And to the day of his death, John Adams ruled the colony. He might have justly said, if he ever glorified his community by calling it a state, "*L'état, c'est moi.*" As a patriarch, he was just and kind, eager to do what was best for the common good, and as a leader, he was strict with himself in maintaining a standard for the conduct of his charges.

A true picture of Pitcairn social and family relationships would, of course, have to include the occasional difficulties, the rare disputes, and the infrequent bitternesses. The islanders were human. But the surprising thing is not the fact that such disagreements arose, but that they arose so seldom. The community, by universal testimony of its visitors, was remarkably harmonious and coöperative. The report of a Pitcairn idyll had elements of truth. "Adams assured his visitors that they were all strictly honest in all their dealings, lending or exchanging their various articles of livestock or produce with each other, in the most friendly manner; and if any little dispute occurred, he never found any difficulty to rectify the mistake or misunderstanding that might have caused it, to the satisfaction of both parties." Brodie contributed this description: "Quarrels and swearing were unknown amongst the islanders, who are as one large family bred up together; they are, in point of fact, all more or less related to each other, and look upon each other more as brothers and sisters than anything else. The children appear to be more nursed by their relations than by their mothers, which makes it often difficult to distinguish the married from the unmarried."

In times of stress or affliction, the entire population was always ready to render assistance, and this readiness reflected the warm ties of affection that bound the colony together. It was customary to wander into a neighbor's house as freely as into one's own. But unlike more sophisticated folk they deemed it a wrong to carry slander or gossip from house to house. Their homogeneity was so pronounced that it was a source of irritation to some visitors who were unsuccessful in extracting secret intimacies concerning the islanders.

Such a social pattern, common origin, and intimate family relationship inevitably led to a complementary attitude towards personal property. A Pitcairn Islander felt free to borrow a tool or a book from his neighbor without formal permission. But real property was not so loosely held. On arriving at Pitcairn, the mutineers had divided all the island, except the village and the common, into nine equal shares: one for each Englishman. The Tahitian men received no land, since their position was little better than that of servants. These allotments, held privately, were inherited equally by all the children of the family. The system eventually led to glaring discrepancies and hardships. After several generations the members of prolific families found themselves in possession of scraps of a divided and redivided estate, whereas the children of smaller families had considerable holdings. Indeed, the situation became acute enough to form a barrier to the marriage of some of the young people who could neither support a family on their inheritance nor sell their labor.

Not only was the land held privately, but the very rocks on the shore were also in the possession of various families. These rocks were of value for fishing and for the collection of sea salt which was an important element in the island economy.

In addition to personal and private property, certain

properties were held in common. The village and the green were owned jointly by all the community. But of greater interest in illustrating the foresight of the islanders was the general reserve supply of food and other articles maintained by the community. Food and other requirements were issued on account to any individual in need of them, to be repaid later. Or for an article in the common store which he lacked an islander might exchange something from an abundance in his own supply. Salt for fresh provisions, and vegetables and fruit for poultry, were typical exchanges.

We turn now to another aspect of Pitcairn life which developed in response to local conditions, *i.e.*, education. To use this dignified word for the informal instruction that the children received, carries perhaps too great a connotation of fixed curricula and prescribed training. It is true that, after the arrival of Buffett and Nobbs, a school was established and a regular system of education inaugurated, but at this period—the first thirty-five years of the colony—the education of the children had not yet reached such comparative perfection.

The responsibility of imparting instruction in reading and writing fell upon Young and Adams. Young had had a good education, but unfortunately he died in 1800, soon after undertaking the task. This left Adams with the duty of instilling the rudiments into tender minds. He could hardly have been more ill-fitted for the position of schoolmaster. Adams learned to write only near the end of his life, and indeed always read with difficulty. But persistence won out, and the children were able eventually to decipher the Bible. Some few principles of arithmetic completed the course.

After the arrival of Buffett and Nobbs in the second decade of the nineteenth century, the school system acquired greater formality as well as enhanced efficiency. To accommodate the steadily increasing number of scholars a schoolhouse was erected under Nobbs' direction. Attendance was by this time compulsory for all chil-

dren between the ages of six and sixteen. It is worthy
of note that compulsory and universal education, such as
it was, existed on this isolated scrap of land long before
it was ever enforced in most of the civilized lands of the
day. In fact, the islanders enacted a law to this end. The
enactment also required that the children be able to repeat the alphabet before entering school. Mr. Nobbs held
school from 7 a.m. to noon (the hours were changed at
various times) on all days except Saturdays and Sundays. The tax to support the school system was one
shilling per child per month. Since the sale of provisions
to an occasional passing ship provided the only source
of revenue, money was scarce. The canny island legisla-
tors therefore provided a list of equivalents which might
be accepted if shillings were not available.

One barrel of yams	8 shillings
One barrel of sweet potatoes	5 shillings
One barrel of Irish potatoes	12 shillings
3 good bunches of plantains	4 shillings
One day's labor	2 shillings

To insure the salary of the schoolmaster, it was also
provided that a parent could not escape the tax by removing his child from school. The tax was imposed for
each child within the age limits whether or not he or
she attended classes. Mr. Nobbs must have been in considerable demand as a godfather, since he was in the
habit of instructing his godchildren without charge.

The curriculum about 1850, although later than the
period under consideration, is not without interest. Each
day began and ended with "prayer and praise." Mon-
days and Tuesdays included a recital of weekly tasks, a
reading of Holy Scriptures, writing, arithmetic, and class
spelling. Wednesdays were devoted to history and geography. Thursdays were a repetition of the fundamentals
of the first two days. But Friday was the busiest day of
the week. On this day the scholars were asked to tran-
scribe words together with their meanings from Walker's

dictionary; hymns and other devotional and moral poetry were read for their edification; Watts' and the Church Catechism were repeated; and finally "arithmetical tables" and "emulative spelling" completed the full day.

Under such tuition the islanders acquired a facility in the fundamentals. Visitors, on whose reports we must depend, were lavish in their praise of the progress achieved by the Pitcairners. To illustrate the literacy of some of them I have culled bits from a letter too long to quote in full. It was from a Pitcairn Island woman to Admiral Moresby soon after the removal to Norfolk. She writes: "I cannot express my joy on receiving the kind letter you sent me by the *Iris,* and I heartily thank you for the scolding you gave me, and I only wish it was from your own dear lips. . . . And now I must tell you about our new home. . . . When we first came on shore everything looked strange to us, but it did not last long. Some of our people like Pitcairn best, but I think Norfolk Island is much better. We have such beautiful houses and gardens, which give lots of employment to keep them clean, and we have milked the cows and made butter. We have our men employed in the field, and I assure you they have enough to do. Norfolk Island is a much healthier climate than Pitcairn, although it is colder. We do not go so thinly clad as formerly, and I believe we are improving in everything; in fact, we are having everything after the English fashion. It is a great advantage for us to be so near the colonies; for we can easily get what we want. . . .

"The report you heard about our young men going to Sydney for wives is false, for there are many already engaged, and they are still preferring their countrywomen. . . . Dear, good, little Forty (Fortescue Moresby) has again come to see us. . . . Old times, and old associations and recollections, came vividly to my mind, and I did, in a measure, live over again a few of those happy hours spent at dear little Pitcairn. If you could only fancy to yourself a road some three and a half miles in length, with only two solitary persons upon it at first, and then one, and another, and another, and so on until half the population was hanging around, kissing and shaking hands, and expressing their joy in a thousand different ways, you may form some idea of Forty and his retinue, from his landing at the back of the island to the settlement. The delight at meeting was mutual. We were delighted, and so was Forty; but he had the worst of it—he saw and can learn for himself how all his Pitcairn friends are; but we, poor things, had to press him with a thousand and one questions concerning our very dear friends of the *Portland*. He was, I am sure, bewildered with the shower of anxious questions heaped upon him, and by the time he went to bed his patience must have been severely taxed. . . ."

In one respect I would hazard the guess that most prophets would have been wrong had they attempted to forecast the future of the Pitcairn colony from the circumstances surrounding its founding and from the characters of the founders themselves. Nor was there anything in the cultural background of the settlers or in the nature of the Pitcairn environment to foreshadow the spiritual characteristics of the mutineers' descendants. Most people would have predicted a dire end for the nascent population. Indeed, the feeling that the Pitcairn Eden was not a logical outcome of the planting of cutthroat mutineers was partially responsible for the great interest the civilized world showed in the news of its discovery.

After Staines and Pipon in 1814 greeted the Pitcairn youths on their coming out to the ship, they proceeded to quiz the young men, impatient to learn what they could of the island.

QUESTION: "Have you been taught any religion?"

ANSWER: "Yes, a very good religion."

QUESTION: "In what do you believe?"

ANSWER: "I believe in God the Father Almighty," and so on through the whole of the belief.

QUESTION: "Who first taught you this belief?"

ANSWER: "John Adams says it was first by F. Christian's order, and that he likewise caused a prayer to be said every day at noon."

QUESTION: "And what is the prayer?"

ANSWER: "It is: I will arise and go to my Father, and say unto Him, Father, I have sinned against Heaven, and before Thee, and am no more worthy of being called thy son."

QUESTION: "Do you continue to say this every day?"

ANSWER: "Yes, we never neglect it."

From this it is evident that Fletcher Christian had planted the first seed of religious observance on the island. How much of John Adams' subsequent zeal sprang from Christian's example, it is impossible to say. It is traditional that Young, too, before his death in 1800, had begun to impart religious instruction to the children. This Adams continued. Another tradition, previously mentioned, has it that Adams had several visions in which the fury of hell was depicted so vividly that he came to realize the necessity of saving the young Pitcairn Islanders from such a fate.

But whatever impulse may have moved him, the fact remains that Adams was the principal religious mentor of the community. To his congregation he was able to read chapters from Holy Writ, and for guidance in ritual he referred to a prayer book salvaged from the *Bounty's* library. So eager did Adams become to follow the letter as well as the spirit, that coming upon a reference to Ash Wednesday and Good Friday and recalling from a remembrance of things past that these were fast days, he decreed that Wednesday and Friday of every week be observed by abstinence from food. After John Buffett's arrival, the unnecessary regimen for these days was pointed out. Influenced perhaps as much by the strain under which his docile disciples had been laboring as by the error of his calculations, Adams was persuaded to give up Wednesday as a weekly fast day. He could not, however, bring himself to relinquish Fridays also. Habit had become too strong, and until his death the Friday of each week was scrupulously set aside as a day of fasting.

One of the observances most carefully maintained among the islanders was the saying of grace before and after every meal. Staines' and Pipon's youthful visitors from the island piously and distinctly pronounced, "For what we are going to receive the Lord make us truly thankful," before partaking of the food offered them. This simple and sincere grace made a deep impression on the Englishmen. Beechey, in a passage already quoted, observed the faithful adherence to the same custom.

John Adams was nominally an adherent to the Church of England, but since his acquaintance with ecclesiastical ritual was very limited we must conclude that the version of that Church's articles of faith and ritualistic practices that he attempted to foster among his charges was a very inadequate reproduction. The following is the dignified prayer preserved in his own quavering script, which he used for the Lord's Day Morning.

> *Suffer me not O Lord to waste*
> *this day in Sin or folly*
> *But Let me Worship thee with*
> *much Delight teach me to know*
> *more of thee and to Serve thee*
> *Better than ever I have Done Before,*
> *that I may Be fitter to Dwell*
> *in heaven, where thy Worship and*
> *Service are everlasting   Amen.*

After the arrival of Buffett in 1823, the conduct of the religious welfare of the islanders was entrusted to him. Nobbs' arrival in 1828 brought another and more permanent change. Nobbs by virtue of his superior education and greater ambition replaced Buffett and introduced services more nearly like those of the Church of England. The reader may remember that eventually

Nobbs was taken to England where he was ordained a priest after some months of instruction. But this takes us to a later period when the original adjustments of Pitcairn life were undergoing modifications.

Beechey's account is the only nearly complete one for this early period, and we must rely on him for our information concerning the details of the religious observances during these first three decades of the colony's history. It is impossible to know how much was the result of Buffett's influence, for he had already been settled on the island about two years at the time of Beechey's visit.

Each family both in the morning on rising and in the evening at sunset assembled for hymn-singing and family prayers. Again, before retiring, the family was accustomed to collect in the main room of the house for the same purpose. In addition to these collective pious observances, each individual offered up a private prayer before going to sleep. On the Sabbath the entire day was given over to devotion: prayers, reading, and meditation. No work of any kind was permitted. Beechey attended the church on Sunday and discovered that Adams read the prayers and Buffett the lessons. Hymns preceded the service. He observed that the congregation showed close attention, even the children evincing "a seriousness unknown in the younger part of our communities at home."

The loyalty of the islanders to their sovereign was scrupulously displayed by prayers for his welfare offered during the litany. "Adams," comments Beechey, "fearful of leaving out any essential part, read in addition all those prayers which were intended only as substitutes for others." The sermon which followed was delivered by Buffett who repeated it three times in order that none of it be "forgotten or escape attention." Finally the service was completed by the singing of hymns first by the adults and then by the children.

All told, the community assembled five times on Sundays, for religious purposes. Such a plethora of devotional exercises argues either a very sincere belief, fos-

tered and cultivated by Adams, or a substitute for the
absence of a more varied social life. It may have occurred to the reader from the anecdotes previously
quoted that a strong taint of sanctimony flavored all
this hyper-religiosity. And as far as one can judge from
miscellaneous accounts, such an impression seems justified by the actions and words of a few of the later islanders. It would have been a natural result, it seems to
me, of the hyperbole showered upon them by their
visitors for their simple and sincere faith. Pride in wor-
ship and eagerness to inspire a repetition of praise are
an insidious pair of human traits. But at this period, the
islanders were still fresh in their contact with the world,
and their devotions must be regarded as sincere and free
from cant.

All christenings and marriages on the island were performed by Adams. Only one ring existed, and this Adams
used for each couple whom he joined in holy wedlock.
With a religious training and tradition borrowed directly
from England, it would naturally follow that such a
socio-religious institution as marriage would also be derived from the same source and that the paganism of a
Tahitian marriage would not be tolerated. The license
traditional among Polynesian youths before marriage was
abhorrent to the islanders.

The foregoing outline is illustrative of a culture adjustment which spontaneously flowered from the grafting of one culture on another. It has been my purpose to
emphasize in this chapter only the first view we are
vouchsafed of the island and its life, leaving to the following chapter a description of the present-day Pitcairn
Islanders. And it has been my aim to indicate what the
Pitcairn Islanders, through the media of their mothers
and fathers, adopted from their culture-heritage, why
these particular customs, manners, or objects were selected, and, finally, how they responded to situations
which were novel and which required original solutions.
Certain clusters of culture traits were borrowed from

either Tahiti or England because of the dichotomy of sex. All the women were Tahitian, and most of the men, notably all of the dominant ones, were English. We should expect that such a division of cultural background, when associated with sex, would inevitably mean that the occupations of the women would be borrowings from Tahiti and that the activities of the males would be influenced by English usage. Such a simple explanation, however, does not always hold water. It is true that cooking, *tapa*-making, and like activities were merely Tahitian transferals. But the exigencies of life on Pitcairn, its lack of the necessities with which to reproduce English implements, and its exotic character enforced a different pattern upon the masculine contributions than we might have anticipated. The better to appreciate the significance of Tahiti and England in developing the characteristic life of the first generation of Pitcairn Islanders, I have prepared the following table. For each culture trait on which I have sufficient evidence to make a judgment I have indicated its principal source.

	TAHITIAN	ENGLISH	ORIGINAL
The Household Arts:			
Underground oven	x		
Food preparation	x		
Tapa-making	x		
Use of calabash	x		
Dress style	x		
Hats	x		
Houses:			
Building materials		x	
Structure		x	x
Roof thatch	x		
Arrangement			x
Household equipment:			
Furniture		x	
"Linens"	x		
Lighting	x		

	TAHITIAN	ENGLISH	ORIGINAL
Fishing:			
Gear		x	
Methods	x	x	
Boats	x		x
Agriculture:			
Tools		x	
Methods	x	x	
Family life			x
Social life:			
Social organization			x
Separation of sexes at meals	x		
Position of women			x
Dance	x		
Music	x	x	
Surf-riding	x		
Kite-flying	x	x	
Private ownership of land		x	
Common fund			x
Education		x	
Religion		x	x

Summarizing the situation by this method, it becomes apparent that the Tahitian contributions outweighed the English. For reasons already mentioned this is not unexpected: Pitcairn is more like Tahiti in its resources; the Tahitian women coming from a simpler plane of life were more efficient in adapting their culture to its new home; the Englishmen conditioned by specialization and hindered by the absence of the necessary materials were less able to draw upon their own background for contributions to their new existence.

But the most unexpected findings of this survey concern the relatively large number of original adaptations to the exigencies of Pitcairn life which this handful of people developed on a pinhead of land. Merely to list some of them is impressive: the original architecture, the modified Tahitian canoe, the patriarchal social organization, the development of a community chest from which an individual could draw and by which inequalities in production could be equalized, the position of women, which in spite of certain Tahitian conventions, permitted them greater freedom than was customary in the age and allowed them equal franchise and inheritance rights, and, finally, a simple but personal faith that evolved from a crystallized, conventional religious system.

In their small way and without placing on their frail structure the weight of a top-heavy analogy, these developments of culture integration and fertility on Pitcairn are consistent with the conclusions of students of culture who have found that culture contacts are prolific in producing new combinations and original contributions. As race-crossing in nature reshuffles the genes and opens new possibilities for gametic pairings that result in a richer variety in the offspring, so the impact of cultures may, and often does, produce evidences of originality even under unfavorable circumstances.

8

THEY EAT THE APPLE

Over a century has elapsed since the days I have been describing in the last chapter—one hundred years of immense consequence to the Pitcairn colony. In the beginning came the whalers. A dribble at first, only a ship every other year. Then the numbers increased until 1846, when forty-nine ships in a single year called at Pitcairn —an average of almost one a week. In these ships came the articles of the civilized world: pots, pans, tools, cloth, knives, forks, plates, books, and pictures. And with their coming, the few simple, homemade manufactures of the islanders departed.

Less tangible but more profound in their consequences, however, were the subtler influences of English and American ideas and attitudes. These have tended to convert a simple, carefree people into a very self-conscious one. I don't mean to imply a generally unpleasant quality. Strangely enough, for a community unaccustomed to the attention of the world, the Pitcairn Islanders behaved extremely well under the spotlight of public notice. And among the present-day islanders, there are a large number of well-poised, self-contained individuals whose demeanor is full of dignity. But the naive charm of unspoiled children has vanished. And one does encounter islanders who are unpleasantly eager to impress the visitor with their sophistication or who are too anxious to reflect the standards of the outside world—

with a conspicuous lack of success. Fortunately they are few, even though the impression they make lingers in the memory.

But European and American contacts were not the only forces remolding Pitcairn life. The population increased by leaps and bounds. Birth control was unheard of during the early days on Pitcairn, and huge families were produced generation after generation. Population pressure grew to the point where release was sought, first in the abortive and disastrous movement to Tahiti and then in the mass hegira to Norfolk Island. But this concentration of inhabitants had other consequences; the old patriarchal order became inadequate, and the value of private property was enhanced.

Still another significant influence on the community was exerted by the newcomers to the colony—the three Englishmen in the 1820's: Evans, Buffett, and Nobbs; and later the three Americans: Warren, Coffin, and Clark. These men brought in new ideas and foreign methods.

Even though whaling contact declined after the middle of the last century until Pitcairn returned to an isolation almost as profound as in the beginning, nevertheless the changes wrought were fixed, and today life on Pitcairn is different from what it was a century ago.

But all things are relative. While Pitcairn was undergoing its modification, the world of America and Europe was experiencing even more radical innovations and alterations. Therefore, today Pitcairn remains as relatively simple to the modern world as its prototype of a century ago did to the early nineteenth century voyagers.

The first thing visitors to Pitcairn notice about the inhabitants is that they wear European clothes. Why the traveler should be mildly disappointed by such a costume is not difficult to explain. The sentimental voyager likes to see native people in no clothes at all or in picturesque garb. But the experienced traveler in Polynesia knows that practically all the natives now take pride in their imported clothing and that *tapa* is a thing forgotten.

Fortunately for the Pitcairn Islanders, they can secure cast-off clothes from passing ships. But to the despair of the women most of these are male garments. Nevertheless, the women have another source of supply. Friends of the colony in England and America occasionally dispatch bundles of clothing which are distributed to the various families. One woman on the island made a comment that will strike every woman as pathetic. She told me that she had never had a new dress or enjoyed the feminine ecstasy of selecting a dress for herself. But conditions are not quite as desperate as this sounds. Money earned from the sale of curios sometimes permits a housewife to order material by mail. The children, of course, are clothed in hand-me-downs retailored to suit their diminutive proportions. Jewelry was rarely displayed during our visit. Homemade necklaces of seeds are common, but they are usually reserved as gifts to visitors. Occasionally a frangipani flower is stuck behind the ear, but wreaths are never worn although I saw some made.

Sewing by hand and by machine is a general accomplishment since the nondescript clothing received on the island usually requires revamping. The few antiquated sewing machines I saw often served a number of families. The art of dressmaking was introduced by foreign women. In whaling days, wives of the skippers sometimes took long voyages and Pitcairn was often a favored spot at which to deposit, until the return trip, a wife who either had become fatigued by the privations endured on a whaler or had become *enceinte* and required the ministrations of her own sex. Such occasional visitors, usually New England women, introduced not only sewing but other household and culinary arts. These culture-bearing functions have in more recent times been the by-products of the visits of missionaries and their wives. Two articles of local dress are, however, still manufactured on Pitcairn. These are the hats nicely woven from bleached pandanus leaves and the slippers made of canvas and rope soles, like the canvas shoes of Southern France.

Having read the old descriptions of Pitcairn life, I was immediately struck, on landing, by another change. The snug, fitted houses of the first settlers were no longer in evidence. They had with a few exceptions been destroyed around 1857 or 1858 by a shipwrecked crew who had dismantled them during the absence of the entire community on Norfolk Island. With the timbers taken from these sturdy houses, the desperate sailors constructed a boat in which they reached Tahiti. Other houses, replacing these, were then built on more conventional models and I was successful in discovering vestiges of only a few of the previous habitations. But the remodeled structures, built to suit the altered needs and standards of their present occupants, still retained enough of the features described by Beechey to make their discovery a distinct delight.

Nowadays Pitcairn dwellings are frame houses on whose walls rough boards are laid in overlapping courses like huge clapboards. The roofs are covered by corrugated iron and the interior is covered with fitted planks like match boards. The windows are furnished with glass. One story high, these dwellings by accretions often acquire a careless shabby charm. The unpainted exterior weathers to a rich brown and gray that harmonize well with the deep red brown of the soil and the mature greens of the foliage.

The interiors lack any regular plan, each house having its own arrangement. Usually there is a living room, a dining room, and a varying number of bedrooms. A few living rooms are decorated with wall paper, now tattered, but most of them are modestly and neatly painted either white or blue. The floors are covered with wide hand-sawn boards.

The kitchens are always in an attached shed where the ovens and fireplaces are kept, the remaining outbuild-

ings consisting of a privy and storage or work sheds.
Plumbing, of course, does not exist. Water is carried by
hand from a spring or more often from a stone-lined
vat. Most houses have such storage tanks where the rain
water is conducted by a flue from the corrugated iron
roof.

The lumber used in construction is cut and dressed on
the island. A rough elevated platform serves as a mill.
The sawyer lays the logs on this structure, standing on
the openwork scaffold, and with the aid of an assistant,
saws out planks which are later trimmed to the purposes for which they are designed.

Hammers, saws, chisels, planes, nails, and other house-
building equipment are imported. The ancient *Bounty's*
anvil which has rung to blows of generations of Pitcairn
mechanics is used now mainly for repair work and as an
historic monument. Its adamantine back no longer serves
for beating out homemade tools.

The furniture of the Pitcairn home is a mixture of late
nineteenth-century importations and of native manufacture. Chairs, tables, old harmoniums, and bureaus from
England and America have flooded the island, making
the living rooms and bedrooms look as though they had
been furnished from an unpretentious suburban attic.
The only note of distinction is the heavy sea chests,
products of native craft. Burley Warren, adept in handling wood, has in his house beds which he made himself. Unadorned and sturdy, they added a peasant
quality to an interior otherwise notable only for its
gimcrackery.

Needless to add, the other household paraphernalia,
linens, dishes, cutlery, are all cheaper varieties of well-
known articles. As means of illumination the *doodoee* nut
has now been superseded by lamps and kerosene. And
the drums and musical wood have been replaced by the
victrola, several of which blare raucous music from ancient, scratched records.

I was struck by a curious lack of any innate decorative

impulse. An occasional print, a picture from an illustrated magazine, or an illuminated text sometimes adorns a wall. But neither on the exteriors nor in the interiors of their dwellings do the islanders apply any native art. This absence of aesthetic development has a curious parallel in the relative inferiority of both the English among European peoples and the Tahitians among the Polynesians in graphic or plastic expression.

In the kitchen, perhaps more than in any other department of Pitcairn life, one still may see the lingering influence of Tahiti. It is true that flour, once unknown, has brought in the use of bread and the oven. Each kitchen possesses a large squarish chamber built of stone and set up on a support. A coat of cement makes it air-tight, and with an iron door added it becomes a satisfactory oven. The old underground oven, though not used as widely as it once was, has not yet completely lost favor. An open fireplace and an iron pot-rest, however, remain the principal apparatus for cooking food.

When first partaking of a Pitcairn meal, the foreign visitor tends to confine his choice to those dishes most like the ones to which he is accustomed at home. His selection would be based indubitably on aesthetic considerations. *Pillihai,* the most characteristic of Pitcairn dishes, is not a confection designed to make the mouth water. It looks heavy and soggy, and it is. But its flavor is not unpleasant after several trials. The island recipe requires either bananas and *kumara* (sweet potato) or taro. The *kumara* or taro is grated on a peculiar grid which consists of a flat stone deeply scored by crossing lines, thus leaving stony elevations that reduce the vegetable to small fragments. Cocoanut milk, from the grated meat, is added to the bananas and *kumara,* and the resulting doughy mass is baked in a shallow pan and served cold. *Pillihai,* I suppose, once took the place of bread, and it remains a favorite even though bread is now available. Another native preparation, arrowroot pudding, contains cubes of pineapple.

The Pitcairn table is heavily laden with food, mostly of vegetable origin. The more recent additions to the vegetable resources of the island include potatoes, cabbage, squash, manioc (cassava), carrots, beets, corn, onions, and radishes.

Being observant Seventh Day Adventists, the more devout eat only vegetables, although some weaker vessels occasionally succumb to temptation and consume fowl, fish, and goat-meat. Pork, however, once the principal flesh food, is now regarded as an unworthy food. All the pigs, it is said, were killed so that the temptation to eat their succulent flesh might be removed. One wonders if a huge pork banquet was prepared from this slaughter— the last porcine orgy.

Fruits such as oranges, lemons, limes, pineapples, bananas, watermelon, grapes, wild strawberries, rose apples, breadfruit, passion fruit, melons, custard apples, pawpaws, mangoes, and guavas include recent importations and are numerous and very good. Bananas are sometimes hastened in their ripening by being buried for forty-eight hours between layers of pandanus nuts covered by earth.

Even to this day the islanders abhor intoxicants. None were to be seen, and no one privately dropped a word that a wee drop might be good for the health. As a matter of fact, the islanders are as abstemious in respect to drink as to food. The standard bearers of the community disapprove of coffee and tea, confining themselves instead to pure water or "tea" steeped from bran husks. Since milk is not particularly relished the goats are not milked. Cows do not exist on the island at all, although well-meaning friends have several times shipped cattle to Pitcairn. Eggs are a staple food.

The meals I ate on Pitcairn were varied and except for the native dishes mentioned above were prepared in a manner similar to our own. Soups, boiled and baked vegetables, and, for my benefit, roasted goat-meat, fowl, and baked fish were on the menu. Pie—an odd New England touch—was a favorite dessert.

As in most communities the principal activities of the men are directly concerned with getting a living, the chief Pitcairn occupations being agriculture and fishing. The upland plateau is devoted to the former activity, although small gardens are also found on the lower reaches of the island near the settlement. In consequence of divisions of inheritance, the plantations have been cut up into a large number of individual plots which from a distance present a pleasant pastoral design of a kind familiar in many agricultural areas. Since no horses or other suitable beasts of burden exist on Pitcairn, plowing and harrowing are unknown. Spading and hoeing are the agricultural methods employed, and fertilizing with sea weed used to be practised and may still be in use.

Fishing, on the other hand, has become less important as a means of livelihood. The methods already described are still used, although hooks and lines are no longer made locally. One of the commodities most in demand from the store of the *Zaca* was fishing tackle. With a couple of men to each little dugout, the native fishermen cruise the coast in pursuit of the red snapper, rock cod, tuna, 'cuda (barracuda), and kingfish. Many of the local names for fish are still Tahitian in origin: *faafaia, upapa,* and *manue.* The last named is always caught by spearing. *Pickpick* and *whistlin'* and *dotter* are Pitcairn names for varieties of fish I could not identify. Shellfish, however, are not gathered by the islanders, since that form of sea life is not approved by the dietary regulations of their church.

In this connection mention should be made of the islanders' boats. Besides the light dugouts, they have some heavy whale boats of which I counted at least four. Both types are made by the natives and are worthy of high praise. Sometimes they carry sails. The dugout is mainly used for fishing since it can be easily managed by one or two men. It is usually eighteen to twenty feet long and thirty to thirty-four inches wide. It has a narrow keel and a flat bottom. The wood employed in its fabrication is obtained from the *doodoee*-nut and the *toonena* tree.

The dory, on the other hand, is modeled after the whale boats which were used by the whalers of the last century. The frame is constructed of native *purau* wood, and imported pine is employed for the planking. The oars for the big boats are imported, but those for the dugouts are made locally. In these sturdy craft the men make voyages of ninety miles to Henderson Island for the *miro*, a kind of wood favored for cabinet work. I have already commented on the ease and skill with which these heavy boats are maneuvered. Perhaps unfortunately, we had no opportunity to see the skill of the Pitcairn men put to a really severe test, since the weather was unusually fine during our visit. Nevertheless, what the natives regarded as a mill pond seemed to me to be fraught with numerous hazards, and I was grateful for their experience and their prowess. For protection against the weather the boats are housed in sheds on the beach. They form a clump of picturesque, thatch-roofed structures that are the first to greet the eye on "entering" Bounty Bay.

Besides these occupations, one finds the men engaged in a variety of chores. The goats tethered to the house post or penned in an enclosure must be fed and the *ti*-plant leaves gathered as fodder. The chickens have to be cared for and their eggs gathered. Ducks and turkeys are raised. Wood for the kitchen fire must be replenished and expeditions made to the wooded hill-slopes for timber. Coming down the steep hill-paths, I would frequently see an islander with his specially constructed, underslung wheelbarrow heaped high with knotty lengths of firewood. Then there are the repairs to the house that require attention and odd jobs that are too numerous to list.

The making of sugar or, rather, molasses is an intermittent activity. The press with its four huge spokes is housed under a huge open shed where the sugar cane is pressed and a thick molasses extracted. Lumber-cutting is carried on in quantity only when a house is under construction.

About once a year each family organizes an expedition to Tauma on the opposite side of the island where it boils salt day and night for two weeks. Great stacks of wood are piled high to keep the fires constantly banked. Sea water is let into wide shallow pans beaten out of corrugated iron and as the water evaporates in steam a deposit of salt is left behind encrusted on the pan.

Finally, the spare moments of the day are devoted to the turning, carving, inlaying, and polishing of wooden objects: cups, boxes, walking sticks, and other curios that are made to be sold on passing ships. The early accounts of the islanders mention this craft. On an occasion briefly noted in a previous chapter, an elegantly inlaid box with drawers was sent as a birthday gift to Queen Victoria. Small hand lathes are used for turning the cups. At intervals I would catch a glimpse of Burley busy at his work bench, cutting thin strips of orange wood for inlay and polishing the red *miro*. This last is a species of wood of very tough texture, once common on the island, but now almost exhausted.

After finishing their household duties, the women, too, have their moments of leisure, during which they occupy themselves plaiting hats and baskets. Pitcairn women plait baskets as countrywomen used to knit socks—automatically. With hardly a glance at their work and without interrupting their conversation, they deftly twist and turn the long fringe of pandanus fibers until the finished basket seems miraculously to flower from its own strands. In spite of their skill in basketry, mat-weaving is not carried on today. I was struck by the designs on the baskets which I learned were rather recent adoptions and not native inventions.

The constructive talents of the islanders are most ambitiously embodied in their public buildings which take three principal forms, aside from the tithe house, the boat-houses, and the sheds that house the smithy and cane press. The most imposing is, fittingly, for so religious a people, the church. It stands firmly rooted despite its sagging lines, which are due both to settling and to a slight departure from the true in the original construction. It is a two-story building with a rectangular ground plan. I had no opportunity to measure its dimensions, but some conception of its size may be formed by the fact that each side is long enough to accommodate eight windows on each story. A modest porch adorns the façade and leads into a small hall with a staircase on each side. Both floors are fitted out as meeting rooms for religious services, but the first floor is the principal one and is somewhat more pretentiously decorated. A series of round wooden pillars extends down the center aisle, on either side of which are arranged the pews— simple, unpainted, wooden benches. The pulpit stands on a rostrum on one end of which is the reed organ that supplies music during services. Hanging on the wall back of the pulpit is a huge map indicating the centers of Seventh Day Adventism throughout the world. On the side wall there is a print of a Melanesian black bearing the name: "James of New Hebrides," and below the portrait is the legend: "174 natives are now employed by us." Presumably in missionary endeavors. The light blue pigment with which the walls and the pillars are painted, adds a touch of color to the room. The upper hall, equal in size, is similar to the lower one.

Outside the church door a bell hangs from a wooden crossbar supported by two uprights. Its resonant and peremptory voice calls the inhabitants not only to church, but summons them for various other group activities such as road-work, public assembly, and manning the boats, or for any emergency that requires the people's effort or voice. Each duty has its allotted number of strokes so that the purpose for which the bell is tolled is immediately known to the entire settlement.

About a hundred feet away from the church stands the courthouse which, with the church, forms the opposite sides of a square that occupies a terrace overlooking the road about six feet below. Along the road side of the square is a long bench where one may sit while waiting for church or assembly. Here the islanders are accustomed to linger for a little gossip after services. The fourth and inner side of the square is formed by a denuded terrace on which perches the house of the recently deceased Philip Coffin, an American settler from Nantucket. This square is the community center of Pitcairn.

The courthouse is but one story high and smaller than the church, yet sufficiently commodious to seat all the adults. A veranda runs along almost its entire length. The interior is roughly finished, with one end partitioned off by wooden bars behind which the postmaster functions. During our visit the recovered rudder of the *Bounty* was visible here through the bars. As in the church, rows of backless benches provide the seating accommodations.

Just outside the door is the community bulletin board. Here was posted the list of voters eligible to cast a ballot for the candidates whose names were recorded alongside.

The third of the public buildings is the schoolhouse. Like the other two community structures, it is of relatively recent date. Standing apart from the church and courthouse, it is without exterior distinction. The interior is a large open room about fifty feet long, equipped with benches for the students and table-desks for the masters. The walls are hung with religious texts.

The social organization of Pitcairn, as far as I could judge in a brief visit, has undergone considerable changes, though it preserves a distinct flavor reminiscent of earlier descriptions. The patriarchal system of John Adams' day was, after all, the product of peculiar circumstances which could not well survive as conditions became more normal. As the children grew to maturity, mated, and produced offspring of their own, the natural tendency to split up into separate family units was not only desirable but necessary. Consequently, after Adams' death a system of family units was fully formed, ready to be released from the restraints of the patriarchate.

It must not be assumed from this that the young couples chafed under Adams' rule. On the contrary, the combined power of custom and of Adams' kindness and concern for the common weal was sufficient earnest in the minds of the islanders of his right to assume authority. As a matter of fact, the harmony of the Pitcairn Islanders was one of their greatest charms. More practically, it was one of the prerequisites to a tolerable life on so constricted an island. At present the inhabitants form family groups just as among us with, however, somewhat greater intimacy between the various families. This closer cohesion is natural. Not only do the islanders live in a geographically tight settlement where privacy is not easily maintained, but they all own a common origin, have a common tradition, and by constant inbreeding share the same ancestors.

Family life is consequently very informal. Young Edward, seeing a light in John's and Mary's house as he passes, just drops in and without a word sits down, may or may not join the conversation and may as unceremoniously depart. Similarly, Henry may decide on the spur of the moment to invite himself to a meal in progress at David's house. A place is made for him at once, without surprise and without question.

Under these circumstances, secrets, family or personal, are not easily concealed. The transgressor is known, and he (sometimes she) must suffer the judgment of the community. Some laxity or, by a kinder name, tolerance tempers this group control. A noticeable change has affected the sex morality of the community. The days when the virtue and chastity of Pitcairn women were recognized as inviolable by the hard-boiled crews of whaling ships have disappeared. Illegitimacy in the early part of the nineteenth century was unknown except in a couple of instances. All this has changed in the last fifty years. Practically 25 per cent of births at present are illegitimate and a considerable number of the permanent unions are not legitimatized, even though they may have produced large broods of children. The evidence of greater sexual freedom is shown by comparing the age of the women at marriage with their age at the birth of their first child (see Chapter 10). It is to some extent a distortion to consider some of these births illegitimate even when the parents have not been legally married. Extra-legal unions, as permanent as the legal variety, have been contracted, and are regarded as just as binding in the eyes of the community. Such marriages might well be considered as an expression of a community change in procedure and not as evidence of an alteration in attitude towards sex. But besides these respectably "illegal" matings there are many examples of a roving taste in sex relationships. The older members of the community are well aware of the change occurring among the younger people, and they lament the breakdown of the older *mores* in terms that seem very familiar. Not even Pitcairn has escaped the problem of the "younger generation."

Family life on Pitcairn is generally very harmonious. I know of only one exception. Divorce in a legal sense does not occur among the islanders, although in one or two instances a working agreement was reached by which the partners in marriage were able to lead their own lives.

Despite the greater publicity of family life than that to which we are ordinarily accustomed, it would be erroneous to conclude that no privacy exists at all. In practice it is usual to find each family carrying on its functions as a unit without undue inspection from the neighbors. Besides the biological and social cohesion of the family, there is, of course, the economic and the religious. The land is inherited through the family, and the labors of the family are devoted to its own maintenance.

As for the religious functions, each family conducts prayers together. In this rite, it is usual for the wider circle of the family to join forces, that is to say, grandpa and grandma, with all their married children and grandchildren, may congregate for hymn-singing, reading the Bible, and the joint offering of prayer.

I was interested to find that a disconcerting remnant of Tahitian custom—the separation of the sexes during meals—had vanished. Captain Beechey would no longer be annoyed by the absence of the ladies from the table, were he to visit Pitcairn now. And his younger officers would be able to continue their enjoyment of island beauty even during the meals. There is no recognition of any social or political distinction between the sexes. Nor is the position of women economically disadvantageous. They inherit property on equal terms with the men.

Land, as has always been the case on Pitcairn, is privately owned and may be disposed of as the owner sees fit. This also applies to houses and personal property, although in practice real estate transactions are very rare. Public property includes the church, the courthouse, the schoolhouse, the roads, the spring, and—take note—the boats. I consider this last an interesting extension of the limits of public property. If one speculates why this should be so, the size of the whale boats and the necessity of large crews to handle them immediately suggest the corollary of group ownership whenever the social pattern favors such a solution. The small dugouts, manageable by one or two men, are, on the contrary, the property of individual families.

Education has made vast strides on Pitcairn since the days when John Adams laboriously framed with hesitating lips the Biblical words by which he instructed the young in the mysteries of reading. A commodious building now houses the forty-four school children of Pitcairn. They have four teachers and are provided with textbooks which have been sent out to the island. The master of the school is Roy Clark. His father, Lincoln Clark, while a cabin boy was wrecked in 1881 on Henderson, an uninhabited island near Pitcairn. When he was rescued by a passing ship, he left his shipmate, Philip Coffin, an American like himself, behind on Pitcairn. Lincoln Clark returned to the United States, married, and begat a son. In 1906, after the death of his wife, Clark determined to return to Pitcairn which persisted in his memory as an island paradise. After some difficulty, Clark and his sixteen-year-old son, Roy, landed on Pitcairn. The father married an island woman and sired another family. Roy very easily adjusted himself to Pitcairn life and now with increasing years has taken on the responsibilities of a leader of the community. As elder, he conducts religious services, and because of his superior education in American schools he has been appointed schoolmaster. For his services in the school, Roy Clark receives £3 quarterly. The three other teachers are Pitcairn Islanders, educated in the island school. One has a quarterly stipend of £2 while the other two, of whom one is a woman, receive £1 10s. The general running expenses of the school are provided by church funds.*

According to Clark, my informant with regard to the school system, the curriculum reaches the level of the fourth grade in New Zealand. Reading, writing, and arithmetic are the principal studies, and history, geography, and kindred subjects are taught to the older pupils.

All children between six and sixteen years of age are required to attend school. On the whole, in the opinion of the master, the children are neither very eager nor apt pupils. But this opinion is based on a limited teaching experience. Evidence on the other side cites one of the island boys, Richard Christian. Eager to pursue his education, he left Pitcairn for New Zealand where he en-

---

* Since my visit to Pitcairn some changes in the educational system have taken place, and new teachers have replaced those I knew.

tered college, and, according to a report received by his parents, was doing satisfactory work.

As part of the education of the islanders the influence of their reading matter is enormous. Newspapers somewhat out of date but none the less acceptable are secured from passing ships. Books, frequently of a religious character, are received from abroad. And numerous magazines of the popular American variety and of the illustrated English type are often seen in the houses of the island. All these help to form a picture of world activities which has a more than ordinary appeal for the Pitcairn Islanders. They are interested in world events and eagerly questioned us on the possibility of another world war.

Their favorite reading has naturally kindled a desire in many of the young men to see the world. A surprising number have been off the island, voyaging mostly to New Zealand and Australia, though Polynesia also has come within their orbit. Some of the more ambitious and enterprising have established themselves permanently abroad. It was difficult to obtain accurate estimates of the number who have migrated, but twenty-odd would probably include all living emigrants.*

After school hours Pitcairn children have a variety of games and amusements. They fly kites much like ours but with banana-bark tails. Tops are easily manufactured by sticking the stiff midrib of the cocoanut leaf through a *doodoee* nut. It is spun like a spindle by a quick twist across the palms of the opposed hands. Swimming is a favorite sport of the children, but rarely of the adults. And surfing by lying prone on a small board is likewise a diversion of the young, as well as the more formal game of cricket. On New Year's Day there is an annual boat race—an occasion for considerable rivalry and merriment.

I frequently have been asked what the Pitcairn Islanders do in case of illness. They do exactly what any

* The number living off the island today is very much greater.

very isolated doctorless community does. They have a variety of home remedies, native herbs, infusions of ginger and of the *ti*-plant, and a small supply of standard pharmaceuticals. A few of the more skilful islanders are summoned when their services are required. If the complaint is a minor one and easily diagnosed, there is ordinarily no difficulty, but for serious illnesses nature takes its course, and the patient dies or recovers. They see the working of Providence when the surgeon of a passing ship can be secured for an ailing islander. Cases demanding surgery are, if possible, reserved for the ministrations of a ship's physician. Acute attacks of illness such as appendicitis find the islanders completely helpless. Fortunately these are rare.

The presence of Dr. George Lyman as physician on the *Zaca* was a great boon to the islanders who lost no time in making use of his presence. He was besieged by the elderly sufferers from chronic conditions common to old age and by the possessors of warts, encysted splinters, benign tumors, and such like, eager for minor surgical operations. On the whole, he found the islanders very healthy and free from any endemic diseases. The ailments for which he was consulted are of a kind that might occur in any random lot of Europeans of equivalent ages. His diagnoses included high blood pressure, cancer, osteomyelitis, fibroma, asthma, arthritis, varicose veins, arteriosclerosis, and tuberculosis.

Recently the islanders have been able to repair their dental defects. A New Zealand dentist, Cooze by name, has settled temporarily on the island. His membership in their church brought him into contact with them, and he determined to visit the island in search of health. Equipped with a rather primitive dental instrumentarium, Mr. Cooze has found a rich field for its use. He has furnished most of the islanders with sets of false teeth which not only have improved their appearance but also have increased their masticatory efficiency.

The tradition of piety for which Pitcairn was famed

has continued in full flower, even though to some the flower may seem slightly overblown. The naive and unadorned faith of the fathers has been replaced by a more self-conscious observance of religious rites. I do not wish to suggest that the islanders are insincere, for that would be utterly untrue. After witnessing their moving devotions no one can doubt the conviction that fills their hearts. But it seemed to me that religion had become formalized and, in some of its observances, mechanical.

The theological tenets held universally by the islanders are those of Seventh Day Adventism. The reader will recall that Pitcairn received a visit from John I. Tay in 1886, after the inhabitants had absorbed a box of Seventh Day Adventist literature which had been sent before his arrival. The community was baptized in a body, and Seventh Day Adventism replaced the faith of their fathers exactly a century after the landing of the mutineers on Pitcairn.

Among the articles of faith of Seventh Day Adventism to which the islanders, as devout believers, adhere is the belief in the imminent second coming of Christ. For that reason reports appear in the press at more or less regular intervals that the Pitcairn Islanders have ceased to cultivate their plantations from the conviction that Christ is due on a date close at hand. The islanders expressed to me a mild resentment at these misinformed rumors. But being the victims of more than one distorted news story, they have learned to adopt a resigned attitude towards the newspaper clippings they receive concerning themselves. I have already mentioned another precept they all obey faithfully: abstinence from pork.

The Sabbath on Pitcairn is celebrated, according to the custom of the church, on Saturday by three long services. Sabbath school at 7:30 in the morning, services again at 11 a.m., and young people's service at 3:30 in the afternoon. On the Sabbath I spent at Pitcairn there was in addition a quarterly business meeting held at 7:30 in the evening. Besides these Sabbath services, church meetings are also conducted during the week. Family prayers complete the list of formal religious observances.

Tithes constitute a final and interesting feature in the religious life of the islanders. Most of them are punctilious in their contributions which ordinarily take the form of garden produce. Money obtained from the sale of curios is also frequently added to the regular tithe. The fruits and vegetables received are stored in a small wooden building known as the tithe house. Except for a small proportion sold to passing ships, these perishable articles of food merely rot away.

Managing the affairs of their church as well as the temporal concerns of the island has given the islanders excellent training in the technique of democracy. Just as the town meeting in New England was one of the closest approaches to true democracy, so the community meetings for church affairs and for governmental matters on Pitcairn are genuine expressions of the popular mind. Accustomed to rise and state their views, both the men and the women are clear and forceful speakers, undisturbed by public attention. Self-government dates back a century. Up to the time of Adams' death in 1829, there was no formal machinery of any kind for self-government. It is said that Adams, foreseeing a troubled future without his established and accepted control, urged the adoption of some sort of mechanism for self-government. Nothing, however, was done until the tragi-comic dictatorship of Joshua Hill awoke the islanders to the necessity of a formal government to protect their rights. After the removal of Hill, Captain Elliott, H.M. sloop *Fly*, established a form of government that permitted the islanders to conduct their affairs with decorum and legality.

It was provided that a chief magistrate be elected annually on the first day of the year. Only a native of Pitcairn Island was eligible for office. The candidate receiving the greatest number of votes, cast by every islander and every resident of five years' standing, over the age of eighteen, was to be duly appointed to the office. The duties of the office were to exercise the chief authority on the island and to settle all differences which might arise between various members of the community. In these functions the chief magistrate was advised and assisted by the council, consisting of two members, one elected by the islanders, the other appointed by the chief magistrate. The officials were answerable in the fulfilment of their vows to the commanding officers of visiting British men-of-war.

The following oath was a solemn part of the induction into office. "I solemnly swear, that I will execute the duties of magistrate and chief ruler of Pitcairn's Island, to which I am this day called on the election of the inhabitants, by dispensing justice and settling any differences that may arise, zealously, fearlessly, and impartially; and that I will keep a register of my proceedings, and hold myself accountable for the due exercise of my office to Her Majesty the Queen of Great Britain, or her Representative. So help me God."

Continuing the history of the present government on Pitcairn, we are indebted to Brodie for the contents of the code of laws which existed in 1850. He cites ten regulations besides a number of other rulings by which the island theoretically was governed. Aside from defining the conduct and the prerogatives of office, they exposed what were matters of public concern and what in the opinion of the natives required formal regulation. It is interesting to note that the increasing number of American ships calling at Pitcairn had brought about the substitution of dollars for shillings in the currency of the island and in the value of fines. The first law stated precisely the duties of the chief magistrate. He was to convene the public on occasions of complaint and after hearing both sides to commit the affair to a jury. He was to levy all fines and direct all public work. Only with the sanction of the people might he assume power or responsibility beyond that which was assigned to his office.

The second law concerned dogs. The owners had to pay a fine of a dollar and a half if their pet was found chasing goats; a dollar to be given the owner of the goat and a half dollar to the informant. The latter reward might have been a temptation to abuse, but we have no record of the existence of professional informants. Full damages, however, were exacted from the owner of the dog if the goat were killed.

Cats were regarded highly on Pitcairn. The third law protected them by imposing corporal punishment on children up to ten years, if they were guilty of killing a cat. If the offender were older, from ten to fifteen, he had to pay a fine of twenty-five dollars. This time the informer was to be rewarded by half the proceeds. The offense became a very expensive luxury for anyone over fifteen, since the fine was then raised to fifty dollars.

Unpenned swine must have constituted a definite hazard to agriculture since their rooting habits could easily undo the hard labor of months. Therefore, the owner of a plantation was entitled to keep a pig caught trespassing on his property or to collect damages from its owner if he had actually caught the animal *flagrante delicto*.

The law regulating education has already been given in full.

A number of laws were grouped together under "miscellaneous." They ruled that an islander desiring to cultivate any lands had to give proper notice of such intention. To prevent waste the wood left over after completion of a house had to be turned over to the next man who began a similar undertaking. The cutting of timber was so carefully controlled that people had to get permission to fell trees on their own property. The slaughter of "white birds" was punished by the fine of one dollar for each bird killed. Birds killed to provide delicacies for the sick were excepted.

The malicious, if there were any, were severely fined on Pitcairn. "There shall be no bringing up things that are past to criminate others, with a view to prevent justice with the case before the magistrate," runs the law.

Reckless cutting of the *miro* and the *purau*, the principal timber on the island, had already so decimated the supply that special steps were taken to protect these trees from further wasteful destruction. Accordingly, it was forbidden to cut the *miro* or the *purau* except for building purposes. Nor could the more cunning attempt to circumvent this regulation or seek to lay up a supply against a future shortage, for the law expressly provided that on the third year from the time a person began to cut wood for a house, he had to build it. But if the house is not begun, then the authorities may confiscate it for the benefit of the next builder.

Landmarks are important in defining the boundaries of private property, and on Pitcairn the magistrate was instructed to inspect them at least once a year, replacing all those destroyed.

Frequent reference has been made in this book to the lively intercourse with whaling ships in the middle decades of the last century. Although the simplicity and kindness of the Pitcairners were completely disarming and the crews on the vast majority of these vessels behaved towards the islanders with respect and affection, nevertheless it was necessary to regulate the mutual relationships. The sale of spirits was absolutely forbidden ashore, and no one was permitted to bring any on land except for medicinal purposes. Women were not to go aboard on any occasion except with the permission of the magistrate who had to watch over them if he were to be aboard himself. In his absence aboard, he was to appoint four men to protect them.

The value placed on the *Bounty's* anvil is stressed by the special law framed for its protection. If anyone, taking the public anvil or the public sledge hammer from the smithy, should lose it, he was to get another and, in addition, pay a fine of four shillings. This fine apparently has never been imposed, and the original anvil is still in its place.

In addition to these formally recognized laws there were, according to Brodie, a number that were unwritten but none the less effective. They were concerned with trespassing fowl, pigs, and other livestock, and with the regulation of fishing for squid or fish from certain rocks, the fishing rights of which were held as private property in certain families. "Carving upon trees is forbidden," ruled another commandment. Apparently the cutting of initials and true-lover's knots on tree trunks was considered an insidious custom, and parents, regarding such pledges as dangerous, actively discouraged their continuance. A practice long established among the Pitcairn Islanders was the appeal to the commanding officers of British men-of-war for final adjudication in disputes they were unable to arrange themselves.

Although many of these laws are still in force, others have become dead letters. The actual machinery of government has undergone a series of further modifications and changes which, however, have not affected the simple democratic character of the administration of public affairs. Alterations in the customs of the islanders have made these changes necessary. The additional laws, adopted since 1850, reflect this change in manners. Breaches of behavior, once too rare to merit specific control, are now covered by legal regulation and reprimand.

Most of my information on the present form of Pitcairn government is derived from the *Book of Records of Pitcairn Island,* which is worth a short digression before returning to the subject of modern government on Pitcairn. This volume is the lineal descendant of the famous record that preceded it: *The Pitcairn Island Register.* The Society for Promoting Christian Knowledge has performed a service to Pitcairn enthusiasts by publishing the complete *Register* which previously had been known only from inadequate quotations by Brodie and others. Started by John Buffett soon after his arrival in 1823 and continued by Nobbs, the *Register* contains the annals of the colony from the arrival of the *Bounty*, in 1790, to 1854. It was fortunate that Adams was still living when Buffett arrived, for the latter was thereby able to secure first-hand information about the happenings on the island previous to his own arrival. If for no other reason, we must at least be grateful to John Buffett because he preserved an invaluable record.

The book of records now maintained on Pitcairn contains the laws and regulations by which the islanders are governed; sections devoted to the registry of births, marriages, and deaths; lists of brands and other marks of ownership; and a roster of the British warships which have visited the island since 1860. Unfortunately the expansive style of Nobbs was not maintained, and thus the record is mainly one of fertility without the relief of such incidents as lent color to the old *Register*. The present *Book of Records* was begun soon after the return to Pitcairn and has been kept faithfully ever since, each chief magistrate being responsible for its maintenance during his tenure of office.

To return to the government of Pitcairn, the *Register* reveals that on January 1, 1893, after a conference of the principal men with Captain Rookes of H.M.S. *Champion* in October, 1892, the assembled community decided to adopt a modified system of self-rule. Conceiving that certain unnamed abuses might be corrected if a larger number of islanders were directly responsible for the welfare of the colony, they adopted a new plan that provided for a parliament of seven empowered "to legislate, to plan for the public good, to execute all decisions of the court, and to see that all public demands are attended to without unnecessary delay." In addition there were a president as the chief executive officer, a vice president, a secretary, and a judge from whose decisions one might appeal to the parliament. The complete code of laws will be found in Appendix A.

The new laws in the code of 1850 reflect the changes

in insular behavior. These additional regulations lead us to conclude that illicit sex relations have increased noticeably since that former era of innocence. There are legal provisions for illegitimacy, penalties for fornication and adultery, fines for peeping. Unhappily, we find that libel, slander, theft, wife-beating, assault, and carrying of weapons required specific enactments. It would, perhaps, be overweighting these regulations to conclude that the islanders had reverted to the practices of their mutineer ancestors. That was not the case, but I think it does suggest that the idyllic days of sweetness and light were slightly overcast by a cloud of human nature.

The marriage laws of the island also were put under the control of the parliament whose permission henceforth was needed by those wishing to marry. No legal provision was made for divorce.

The parliamentary system endured for a decade, and then in 1904 the machinery was again overhauled. There have been no major changes since. The president, vice president, and parliament were scrapped, and their places were taken by a chief magistrate, a council, two assessors, and two committees, one for internal and one for external affairs. The chief magistrate is not to hold office in the church during his term. As highest authority on the island, he is to be aided by a council composed of the two assessors and the chairman of the committees for internal and external affairs. The committee for internal affairs consists of a chairman elected annually by the people and of two members designated by the chief magistrate. The companion committee for external affairs was similarly constituted, but the body languished for want of function and was later dropped. The assessors' chief duty was to preside together with the chief magistrate at all litigations involving more than £5. Smaller sums were dealt with by the magistrate alone or at his invitation with an assessor. The office of secretary, provided by the previous system, was maintained. The details of these various offices may be found *in extenso* in Appendix A.

The laws revised at this date were similar to those pre-

viously described, with, in some cases, further provisions
to cover the greater variety of misdemeanors developed
since 1893. Abortion, for example, is officially recognized
for the first time as a crime and anyone guilty of inducing
it was liable to imprisonment. Quarantine laws were also
enacted, for Pitcairn not being a recognized port of call
had no way of dealing with visiting ships.

To provide for the imprisonment of those convicted of
serious crimes, the community has built a prison. Fortunately, it remains untenanted most of the time, although
during my visit it had one occupant who was being held
for trial on a charge of wife-beating. However, the carefully itemized regulations for the treatment of prisoners
seemed to have been in abeyance, for the man was a
prisoner only in the loosest sense of the term.

One of the duties of the committee for internal affairs
is the direction of the public work. Pitcairn Islanders are
fortunate in that they pay no taxes in the form of money.
In lieu of taxes, seven days of labor is exacted yearly
from every man over eighteen and under sixty. These
days are devoted to road-making, repair of public buildings, work on the boats, and other tasks for the common
good.

The committee also has jurisdiction over brands. With
goats grazing at will and chickens wandering about the
village it is necessary to have marks to distinguish mine
from thine. This is accomplished by branding. Each family has its special brand which is registered in the *Pitcairn Island Book of Records.** I counted 63 goat brands,
which usually are various forms of ear-slitting; 90 for
chickens, mostly different combinations of toe-cutting;
and 127 letters and combinations of letters for marking
trees. Linens are sometimes lettered with the indelible
juice of the alligator-pear seed. The corner to be marked
is held tightly over the seed and a needle or pin is stuck
through into the seed. The juice stains the cloth in the
desired pattern.

* See Appendix B.

9

"ANOTHER LANGUAGE"

Among themselves the Pitcairn Islanders speak a dialect incomprehensible to English or Polynesian ears. In conversation, however, with English or American visitors they use a familiar English spoken with a peculiar accent. Some of the men who have been to New Zealand or Australia have brought back a slightly British intonation as well as a few of the slang phrases common in that part of the Empire. But the stay-at-homes who are linguistically less stylish enunciate with a softness and a slur that is rather more pleasing than the recently imported variety of intonation.

All this goes to show that language is as much a cultural phenomenon as the construction of a house or the manufacture of *tapa*. It may be modified by cultural contact or borrowed or dropped just like any other item in the culture equipment. And in this instance, were the history of Pitcairn's settlement unknown, it might reveal the diverse origins of the community. It is a matter for regret that no previous visitor left any accurate notes on Pitcairnese, to distinguish it from its mother tongues, or bothered to record their impressions of its character. Such data would have been invaluable for comparison with the present-day dialect.

To understand the genesis of the Pitcairn dialect, we must return once more to the beginnings of the colony, to a group of men speaking no Tahitian and to a group of women speaking no English. No doubt the mutineers, like modern travelers in Tahiti, picked up a handful of native words such as *maitai, tamaa,* and *pape* (or its classical predecessor, *vai*), and imagined that they knew the language. And no doubt the Tahitian ladies in their innocence accepted such words as "goddam," and others less printable, as English fit for their use. But no one knows exactly in which medium—English or Tahitian—the mutineers and their ladies communicated: perhaps they developed a bastard language. My own guess is that the women spoke much more English than the mutineers did Tahitian, especially if we remember that the English, despite Norman Douglas, are proverbially bad linguists, and have, according to the French, forced the world to speak their language by their inability to use another.

Certainly, the tenacious loyalty of the English to their native language may be inferred from the fact that, despite the elimination of all the men save Adams, the children grew up speaking English. We have on record the astonishment of Folger, Shillibeer, Staines, and Pipon at the excellent English in which they were addressed by the Pitcairn youths who came out to greet their ships. It would be strange, however, if nothing remained of the Tahitian tongue, considering the eight or nine women who survived with Adams. They surely must have lapsed into the more familiar Tahitian when talking to their children. Nevertheless, I am aware of only one passing literary reference to the general use of Tahitian by the islanders. This suppression of Tahitian seems to me a reversal of expectation. Not only do we usually think of mothers as teaching their offspring the rudiments of language, but where the women so outnumbered the one surviving man who had no English companion to exercise and to keep agile his mother tongue, we might logically expect the natural influence of the maternal language would have predominated. But the fact remains that English was spoken by the Pitcairn children, and spoken well; and that Tahitian, if spoken at all, was so little in evidence that most of the visitors fail even to mention its use.

I first discovered that a dialect was in use among the descendants of the mutineers when I found that traces of it were still preserved on Norfolk Island among the older inhabitants. But I could recover only very little of it there. On Pitcairn, where the community has been much more isolated, Pitcairnese still flourishes, the children hardly speaking any other form of English than this to which they are bred, and the adults frequently lapse into it when they are not on their company manners. After the ear becomes accustomed to the intonation and the type of vocal changes characteristic of the speech, it becomes easy to leap to the meanings behind the queer distortions of common English words.

In many ways the dialect seems as if it had its origin in the efforts of the mutineers to teach the Tahitians the English language. The grammatical breakdown suggests this, as well as the elisions of sounds. I find that it is a common tendency for most of us when confronted with a foreigner, who has little understanding of English, to shout a horribly debased kind of English, as though bad grammar and a loud voice could render the language intelligible. (Listen to a customer in a Chinese laundry.) But whatever its precise origin, the Pitcairn dialect today consists of mispronounced English and Tahitian words with a spattering of coined words, the whole employed in a degenerate English syntax.

I append here a list of common words and expressions. Not having special linguistic knowledge, I was unable to record what I heard in the approved phonetic symbols. The list is not very ample, but I gathered what I could during intervals between other more pressing work.

PITCAIRN WORD LIST

solen: the last; *es (a) solen,* it is finished, there is no more. This word is probably derived from "sole one."

a little sullen: a little child.

illi-illi: used to describe a rough sea. The derivation is obviously from hilly, and the intensifying reduplication is a common usage in Tahitian and Polynesian in general.

tai-tai: Tahitian word meaning tasteless and, by transference, without charm when applied to people. This word also survives among the Norfolk Islanders, but it has vanished from modern Tahitian.

boney-boney: very thin. This is a nice example of Pitcairn adaptations: an English word reduplicated in Polynesian fashion with a distinction all its own.

I kawa: I don't know. *Kauaka = Kauraka,* meaning do not, occur in Tahitian. The loss of the second *k,* a phenomenon common in Polynesian, would produce a word like *kawa.* Another Tahitian word: *Kaore,* a negative adverb, also suggests *kawa.*

plān: banana, plantain. Apparently a contraction of plantain.

Es stolly: It's a story, or in more brutal manner, it's a lie. *You tallin' stolly* is a similar usage.

(a)bout you bin: Where have you been? I assume that this is descended from "whereabouts have you been?"

(a)bout you gwan: I sometimes seemed to hear this as *"bout you gowin?"* "Whereabouts are you going?"

almos' daid for tired: This needs no explanation.

lebby: Leave it alone; let it be, which can easily become *lebby* if repeated frequently without knowledge of the words in the phrase.

(d)ā: the definite article the, or sometimes the demonstrative that. For example, *gen a bed,* would mean alongside the (that) bed.

not sah: It is not so.

what a way to maik it: How do you do (make) it? This, too, can be traced simply to "what's the way to make it?"

cah fetch: can't be done.

no fet: used of things that don't fit.

huppa: bad or inefficient.

I starten: I'm starting or I'm going.

I nor believe: I don't think so.

mono-mono: very good. Here again is an example of re-duplication. *Mona* means sweet in Tahitian and in the related Tuamotuan.

soffa: softer.

fwhut you ally come yah: Why do you come here? Such a phrase recalls a dialect rather familiar to us.

fut you ally comey diffy and do daffy: Why do you come and behave that way? I think the reader can easily reconstruct "do this way and do that way" from *diffy and do daffy.*

I see yawl-ey scows segoin' out (d)a big ship: I see your boats going out to the big ship (the *Zaca* in this case).

See (d)a ship come to een: See the ship come close to land.

su'pa fai: all broken up. *Pofa'i* in Tahitian signifies to break off.

fut: What?

morga: thin.

hem: them, those as in *"hem orange on ā tree segrowin' big."*

naaway: to bathe or swim. *By you gwin naaway:* where are you going to swim? *Naue* is a Tahitian word meaning to leap or dive into water.

Los' bawl: lost ball, also used for a ship which passes by without stopping.

Thems aketch plenteh gott: They have caught many goats.

cocknut: cocoanut.

I'sa roll: I've fallen.

side: place; for example: *Up a side, Pugy'sa roll,* which would signify, Up at that place, Pugy fell down.

gingsa: ginger.

walley: valley.

Yousa heway me: You have heaved me away.

I'sa dona school: I've finished school.

Eeno: no.

You loy: You lie.

Wha you pick up ā, boy: Where did you learn that, child?

Stay-well-out: Remain where you are.

I tella you: I'm telling you.

ruma in the night: torch fishing. In Tahitian *rama* means to fish by torch light.

tolly: a kind of wood or tree.

boat of lanterns: used to describe boat-racing crews because the men's faces, covered with perspiration, shine like lanterns.

Tomolla ha tudder one: day after tomorrow.

Tomolla ha tudder one ha tudder one: second day after tomorrow.

Ā two junk torch: two-cell electric torch.

Bin tak hold: wrestled.

Aint account un: doesn't count.

Want a beak for eat it: You need a beak to eat it, therefore used for something unpalatable.

Want a tongs for eat it: has same significance as the above.

Es important es: One is assuming airs.

Dunt climb hem tree, bair you fall off: Don't climb that tree, lest you fall off.

Fus': first.

I don't know, too, myself: I don't know either.

O'er yanna: over yonder.

Come yare: Come here.

maolo: to break.

I'sa frettin': I'm fretting.

Foo you want da: Why do you want that?

Ka 'bout: I don't know where. Compare with *I kawa*.

What thing you want: What do you want?

From der way: from that way.

Nautical words and phrases are frequently employed.

"All hands," "grub," "sing out," "pull away," are among those in more common use. I overheard one sentence that was a puzzle until the light was furnished by one of the islanders. "*See ā twiss horn billeh foh pugy's*," meant nothing to me at first except that someone's attention was being directed to some object. On inquiry I discovered that the literal translation is, "See that twisted horned billy goat of Pugy" (nickname for Edwin Christian). Other sentences after the adjustment is made to the Pitcairn accent were less difficult. "*You'sa daid*," "*You'sa dirty dawg*," "*You'sa daid as a hatchet, growin' fahs*," need no commentary.

One of the peculiarities of the Pitcairn speech is the elision of the letter *r*. Even where I have written it in, I have done so not because the sound was distinct but because doing so suggested the English word more easily.

I wish it were possible to indicate the drawl and the rhythm of Pitcairn speech. It is these that give it a special character, and transmute the caricatured words into a cadence.

IV. BIOLOGICAL

10

ANGLO-POLYNESIAN

The biological experiment that blind circumstances have created on Pitcairn offers a rare opportunity for the investigation of the laws of heredity. Accident, that arbiter of events, deposited on deserted and almost unknown Pitcairn men of one race and women of another, and there accident yielded to nature. The forces thus joined were allowed to resolve themselves as surely as though they had been active chemicals in a test tube. Isolation has preserved the results.

In most communities of racially mixed origin there are usually to be discovered serious obstacles, often veritable barriers, in the path of the inquiring seeker after the laws of heredity. For example, the mixture may be so ancient that its exact composition is lost in the fogs of antiquity, and the investigator can merely prove what is already known: that race mixture has occurred. Or the social *mores* of the contracting parties may be such that parentage is systematically concealed. Or again, the half-caste population may take no interest in genealogical pursuits, and the history of their blood lines thus may be lost. These are some of the conditions which combine to give a genealogical blank. For the geneticist it is of prime importance to know precisely what elements have entered into the making of a given hybrid, when it occurred in terms of generations, what crossbreeding has occurred since the original cross, and, finally, the matings in each generation. Otherwise the conclusions derived from such studies become circular, and the investigator returns to the point from which he started.

But knowledge of the family tree is not the only desideratum, nor is its absence the only drawback. Such studies are facilitated if the parental groups are sufficiently distinctive to present clear-cut differences which may then be followed in the progeny with greater ease. Miscegenation between closely allied stocks produces complex and blurred results by virtue of overlapping characters and genetic similarities. Greater differences, therefore, between the parents clarify the consequences of mixture in the offspring.

In addition to genealogical *lacunae* and the confusion of genetic similarities, another factor frequently mars the perfection of most mixed groups as subjects for research. In the crossings of races that show marked physical differences or in cases where deep prejudice exists the partners of such unions are often unrepresentative or socially inferior members of one or both groups. It would, of course, be naive to assume that this is always the case. Where slave populations exist or where native mistresses have a recognized position, the reverse does occur, but the fact remains that the evils which are popularly assigned to the mingling of blood may with greater justice be attributed to the quality of the blood which produced the hybrid. It stacks the cards, to say the least, against the half-caste to attribute any defect in his heritage to the irregularity of his breeding.

But the social matrix of the problem has wider implications, important as these are. The social, economic, and, therefore, environmental background of the half-caste is almost always inferior to the best in the possession of one of his ancestral stocks, and frequently it is worse than the average to be found in both. The social stigmata attached to those unfortunates of mixed blood are often almost insupportable and may engender at their worst unfortunate physical and psychological consequences.

On Pitcairn none of these handicaps to the study of race mixture exist. The genealogical history of the islanders is well known from the mutineers and their consorts to the present generation. When new blood has been added, as it has been at various times, that too was recorded. Fortunately Buffett began, and Nobbs preserved, the *Register* in which, from the beginning of the colony, every birth, marriage, and death was entered. But with all this official recording, the question naturally arises whether illegitimacy may not be present here as elsewhere and thereby vitiate the results based on the official pedigrees. No doubt that little monkey running up and down the branches of a family tree can do considerable damage.

I frankly admit that this is something to give one pause. However, we can do some checking, the more tactful, perhaps, the better. I already had in my records of the Pitcairn Islanders several cases of illegitimacy. And during my visit I was able to secure considerably more information on the subject. Several of the islanders, wishing to keep the record straight, and appreciating my reasons for inquiries of so intimate a nature, gave me valuable information which coincided not only with each other's but with the official record book. I am unwilling to boast that I have detected every case of illegitimacy which has ever occurred on Pitcairn, but I feel confident that very few have escaped me. The credit goes not to me but to my informants who, moved by a sense of duty and honesty, confided in me only after the greatest internal struggles. I should add that in a settlement as intimate as Pitcairn, instances of irregularity had only to exist to be known.

Nor can the quality of the ancestry of the Pitcairn Islanders be questioned. Christian came from an ancient, respected, and influential Manx family. Edward Young was the nephew of a baronet. Quintal, McCoy, Adams, and Mills, the other four mutineers who founded families, were ordinary seamen of the working class. They were stout, hearty sailors, fit enough to endure the rough life of the sea. Their record as mutineers certainly is not above reproach, but neither were they without provocation. Their faults may have been serious, but they were, at least, positive and aggressive ones. It is recorded that the men of the *Bounty* were a superior lot, hand-picked for the job. I would rate the men as a good average lot, with a touch of the gentry thrown in. The other white men who joined the colony and commingled their blood with that of the mutineers, were likewise men of simple but sound origins. Nobbs, if the tradition is to be trusted, even laid claims to a left-handed aristocratic lineage. I emphasize these social criteria, not from any profound conviction that the best blood is concentrated in the upper classes, but to show that on the European side the ancestry of the Pitcairn Islanders is not derived from a degenerate or a depressed class.

Of the Tahitian women little is known. One or two had excellent connections, and all of them were raised in favorable conditions and belonged to a stock famous for its physical beauty. The fact that these women readily formed liaisons with the *Bounty's* crew does not argue their depravity or socially inferior status. The more than liberal ideas of the Tahitians and the almost divine repute of the white man were sufficient to account for the ease with which the sailors established these connections.

Finally, the Pitcairn Islanders, unlike other half-caste populations, have never had to eat the bitter bread of social or economic prejudice. Isolated on their fertile island, they are free of the usual disabilities under which half-castes ordinarily labor. They have an abundance of food, nutritious and varied. They are inferior to no one. In other words, they have been allowed to develop in an environment that is wholesome and in a manner dictated by their innate capabilities.

In the remainder of this chapter I shall describe some of the physical characteristics of the Pitcairn Islanders in terms of their ancestral stocks. I have followed the usual statistical procedures and have calculated the average or mean for each measurement. There were sixty-two adult men and sixty-two adult women in my total series of islanders, but in the following the males only are considered, since the comparative data for males are better. It must be kept in mind that these means represent a hypothetical Pitcairn Islander. No one individual would conform in all respects to these averages. But, on the other hand, the mean does indicate the value that covers the greatest number of cases.

Stature is a measurement subject to certain fluctuations directly correlated with environmental conditions. It has been found, other things being equal, that stature increases with improved economic status, the general assumption being that nutrition, among other factors, is mainly responsible for this phenomenon. Eschewing, therefore, the elevated statures of the English upper classes and the depressed ones of the population at the other end of the socio-economic scale, we may take 172 cm. as representative of the average Englishman. Somewhat less than this was the mean stature of the six mutineers who left progeny on Pitcairn. Taking their individual heights from the Admiralty records, I obtained an average of 170.6 cm. Tahitians are also of good stature, the men averaging about 171.4 cm. There is, therefore, but little difference in stature between the English and Tahitians. This would lead us to expect among the Pitcairn Islanders an average stature in close agreement with those of their parent stocks. If we contrast the descendants of the mutineers and the Tahitian women with the racial stocks from which they have sprung, we discover that they are taller. The male descendants of the mutineers living on Norfolk have an average height of 174.0 cm., the Pitcairn men of 173.0 cm. Moreover, this excess, though small, was once much greater. In 1825 the children of the first generation born on Pitcairn were measured by Beechey's surgeon who obtained an average of 177.8 cm., the tallest man being six feet one-quarter inch, and the shortest five feet nine and one-eighth inches.

In animal and plant experimental genetics the production of hybrids often leads to an increase in size and vigor. Such a phenomenon is technically called heterosis or hybrid vigor, and it is used extensively in the cultivation of seed corn for commercial purposes. On Pitcairn we find a human analogy to the lower forms in the increased size of the hybrid islanders. Some diminution in stature, it is true, may be noted in the present generation—the fourth, fifth, and sixth from the original cross, but it still remains greater than that of either English or Tahitian.

In the dimensions of the vault of the head there is a marked difference between the two branches of the colony. The Norfolk Island males have longer and wider heads than their relatives on Pitcairn. It must be remembered, however, that the two colonies have had a separate existence for about seventy-five years and that little of the Nobbs-Buffett-Evans heritage is represented on Pitcairn. Moreover, considerable new blood has been added to the Norfolk strain since the 1860's. Pitcairn, on the other hand, has received Warren, Coffin, and Clark.

Since I have already dealt with the Norfolk Islanders in another place, I shall confine my remarks to the Pitcairn Islanders. Their average head length of 189.6 mm. is almost identical with the head lengths of the Tahitians —188.01—and is very much smaller than English averages which range from 193 to 198, according to the group. We may conclude, therefore, that in the length of head the Tahitian heritage is dominant. The reverse is true for the head width. For this trait we find that the Pitcairn mean of 152.04 mm. falls into English group range—150 to 155—and far below the Tahitian average of 159.6 mm. The resulting cephalic index, the percentage of head width in relation to head length, of the Pitcairn Island men is intermediate between English and Tahitian.

The minimum frontal diameter is a measurement taken on the forehead. It is the minimum distance between the bony ridges which, rising from the outer corners of the eyebrows, pass upwards and backwards along the margins of the forehead. One of the most characteristic features in the architecture of the Tahitian face is the constriction of the brow, as defined above, in relation to the face width which is very great.

Let us compare the Pitcairn Island men with their ancestral stocks for this trait. The minimum frontal diameter is only 100 mm. in width which is even narrower than the equivalent feature among the Tahitians, who average 104.0 mm. Compared to the English, the gulf is even wider, for their mean is well over 106.0 mm. The face width, on the contrary, reveals a different line-up. Compared with the Tahitians the English have narrow slab-sided faces. For the latter the average is about 138–139 mm., for the former 145.7 mm. The Pitcairn Islanders, with a face width of 138.5 mm., are identical with the English. Thus the English width of face is dominant. But the minimum frontal diameter of the Pitcairners offers a puzzle, since it is unlike either parent stock, being much narrower even than that of the Tahitians. The anomaly may be explained in this wise. The proportions between the face and brow width among the Pitcairn Islanders are distinctly characteristic of Tahitians—that is, a brow relatively narrow compared with the face width. But since they have inherited a narrow face from their English ancestors, the brow, in maintaining the proportions of the Tahitian type, has had to remain much narrower than either racial average.

In height of nose, measured from the nasal root to the juncture of the nasal septum and the lip, there does not appear to be any difference between the ancestral stocks. The slight differences which exist are not great enough to exceed the large personal error involved in taking this difficult measurement. In the nose width, however, there is a definite contrast between the broadish Tahitian nose and the narrow English one. The width of the former is 43.4 mm. compared to 35–36 mm. among the English. The Pitcairn mean of 38.5 mm. is roughly intermediate. Its somewhat closer approximation to the English average may well be the effect of the additional Anglo-American blood which has reached the island since its settlement.

These few measurable features are enough to illustrate the general character of the Pitcairn heredity. The others exhibit a similar pattern. The Pitcairn Islanders reveal in their sum total a mosaic of characters, some borrowing their colors from Tahiti, others from England, with an occasional patch where the colors have run to produce a blend.

If we examine the less tangible characteristics of the Pitcairn inhabitants, we find a different pattern. I shall treat here only skin color, eye color, distribution and color of hair, nasal bridge and profile, and lip thickness.

The skin color we see in the people about us is the resultant of a number of factors: the actual amount of pigment matter in the dermis, the thickness of the epidermis, the vascularity of the skin, and the surface quality of the tissue. The precise effects of these various factors are not known nor can we, by present methods, measure them in any satisfactory and objective fashion. In lieu, therefore, of any dependable quantitative analysis of the complex phenomenon of skin color, we must, until better methods are devised, content ourselves with a rough approximation by using a color scale which gives us a rating in a graduated series. To secure the most reliable rating it is customary to observe an unexposed part of the skin, usually the inner side of the upper arm. Among the Pitcairn Islanders the determinations of skin color for this area are as follows:

VON LUSCHAN SKIN COLOR SCALE	MALES		FEMALES	
	No.	Per cent	No.	Per cent
3	7	11.29	5	8.06
7	14	22.58	14	22.58
8	7	11.29	4	6.45
9	10	16.13	5	8.06
10	12	19.35	22	35.48
11	3	4.84	4	6.45
12	5	8.06	7	11.29
13	1	1.61		
14	1	1.61		
17	1	1.61	1	1.61
18	1	1.61		

Numbers 3, 7, and 8 correspond to skin colors most frequent among north Europeans. Tahitians, however, range from numbers 10 to 22, with most of them clustering around 10 and 16–18. The Pitcairn Islanders overlap both English and Tahitian. None are as dark as the darker Tahitians and relatively few are as fair as the fair English. This kind of distribution is typical when a character is the resultant of a number of genetic factors. It is sometimes called, erroneously, blending inheritance.

Pitcairn men are somewhat lighter in hair color than the women. The males have 68.5 per cent with black hair, 29.6 per cent with dark brown, and 1.9 per cent with light brown. The females fall into the same categories, but with 78.6 per cent having black hair, 19.6 per cent dark brown, and 1.8 per cent light brown. One adult individual had blonde hair, but unfortunately he was not available for inclusion in this series. A number of the children were fair-haired, but since we are dealing only with mature subjects they must be omitted, for hair color being correlated with age darkens on maturity. Evidently the factors producing blonde hair are present among the Pitcairn Islanders but their heritage from Tahiti, where the hair is predominantly black, is sufficiently prepotent to prevent any widespread appearance of blondness.

Hair color among the English varies widely in the different districts of the British Isles, but on the whole the majority have brown hair of various shades. Compared to the English, the Pitcairn Islanders are much darker. Whereas the English have only about 5 per cent with black hair the Pitcairn Islanders of both sexes have 73.5 per cent. The Tahitians, whom the Pitcairners resemble more closely in this respect, are 80–90 per cent black-headed.

The eye color of the Pitcairn Islanders is of particular interest because of the patent contrast between the parental stocks. Tahitians are without exception brown-eyed. A small minority of them, about 15 per cent, have what might be described as light brown eyes; the remainder have deep brown. No unmixed blue eyes occur in pure-blooded Tahitians, except in an occasional albino. The English, on the contrary, are endowed with a large share of the genes which produce blue or mixed blue eyes. The percentage of blue eyes, however, varies in the different areas, but in all the blue-eyed factor or factors is generally distributed. The following table presents the average percentages of the various eye colors among British and Americans of British origin.

	LIGHT	INTERMEDIATE	BROWN
Old Americans ♂	23.8	59.7	16.5
Old Americans ♀	20.0	60.0	20.0
England, Scotland, and Wales	53.3	15.2	31.5

The "lights" include only blue or gray eyes, the "intermediates" hazel, blue-brown, or gray-brown eyes, and the "browns" only pure light or dark brown eyes. Remembering that the Tahitians are 100 per cent brown, let us examine the distribution of eye color among the Pitcairn Islanders.

	LIGHT	INTERMEDIATE	BROWN
Pitcairn men	6.45	64.51	29.03
Pitcairn women	4.84	37.09	58.06

We note first of all that the women of Pitcairn are darker-eyed than the men; 58 per cent have brown eyes compared with only 29 per cent among the males. It is tempting to link up this sex difference with the fact that the women by virtue of their sex resemble their Tahitian ancestresses more closely than their English sires. This is technically known as sex-linked inheritance. Unfortunately we cannot, on the basis of Pitcairn material, draw such a conclusion. In a perfect experiment, we might have crossed not only Englishmen and Tahitian women but also have reversed the sexes to mate English women with Tahitian men. The progenies of such matings properly controlled would have yielded data designed to answer queries whose solution must wait on other data. Nevertheless, the Pitcairn array of eye colors and their frequencies do illustrate in human heredity several well-known principles of genetics. If we allow DR or intermediate to represent the gene pattern among the Englishmen, and DD or pure brown the genetic formula for the Tahitian women, the expectations after several generations of unselected matings would be these:

	LIGHT	INTERMEDIATE	BROWN
Theoretical expectations	6.25	37.50	56.25
Actual distributions:			
Pitcairn males	6.45	64.51	29.03
Pitcairn females	4.84	37.09	58.06

We see in this table that the Pitcairn women fit the theoretical expectations as perfectly as one might expect in a small sample of sixty-two women. The men also agree with the expectation for "light" but have a very much higher proportion among the intermediates and a much smaller among the browns. The eye color among the women therefore shows a dominance of the brown over the blue, whereas for the men there appears to be an additional factor operating to modify the expected dominance of brown pigment.

Another phenomenon of considerable importance is also illustrated by these figures. It is sometimes termed the conservation of the genes. The genes are minute protein molecules which bear the substance of heredity from one generation to another. Both male and female sex cells carry approximately equivalent arrays of genes that unite on fertilization. If the genes for a specific character differ, one or the other may "dominate." This does not mean that this "recessive" gene is lost. It will reappear in later generations. Blue eyes in this case, although generally a recessive character, have once more recurred in a proportion determined by the concentration of genes for blue eyes in the population.

The nose contributes a very special character to the face. This feature among Tahitians is, as we have remarked previously, moderately wide. It is also predominantly straight in profile, 83 per cent being so classified, with 11 per cent having concave profiles and 6 per cent convex. In spite of its tendency to breadth and fleshiness the Tahitian nose is not low at the bridge like the African. As a matter of fact 76 per cent have noses of medium height; only 19 per cent have low-bridged noses, while 5 per cent have high noses. The effect of a low-spreading nose is created, however, by the great width of the bony bridge which conceals its moderate elevation.

The English nose, unfortunately, has never been described to my knowledge in comparable terms. We are all familiar, however, with the narrow, constricted, and high-bridged nose common among the British. Both convex and straight profiles are numerous, but concave outlines appear less frequently.

In comparing the Pitcairn nose with the English, it is necessary to rely on data obtained from an Old American series, since they are absent for the English themselves.

Of the Pitcairn Islanders 66 per cent have convex nasal profiles, 31 per cent straight, and 3 per cent concave. This is a distribution quite different from the Tahitian and, judged by Old American standards, very close to the English. The following table confirms this.

	CON-VEX	CONCAVO-CONVEX	STRAIGHT	CON-CAVE
Old American ♂	42.0	27.3	22.0	8.7
♂ Pitcairn	66.13		30.65	3.23
♂ Tahitian	6.1		82.93	10.97

Without quoting the actual figures, I may add that the Pitcairn women, like the men, resemble the English in this feature.

Unfortunately, information on the elevation of the nasal bridge is not even available for Old Americans. But a comparison of the Pitcairn Islanders with Tahitians shows that the former are definitely divergent in their greater elevation of the bony nasal ridge. Only 8 per cent of the men have low bridges and 47 per cent have high ones, whereas among Tahitians as many as 19 per cent have low bridges and only 5 per cent high.

For the thickness of the lips, likewise, no adequate English data exist. The Tahitian series of males provides only 1 per cent with thin lips, 88.0 per cent with medium, and 11.0 per cent with thick. The Pitcairn men equal and even surpass their Tahitian relatives in the number having thick lips—15.7 per cent. And at the same time 43 per cent of the Pitcairn men show thin lips, a percentage far in excess of the Tahitian. It is obvious, therefore, that in lip thickness the contributions of both stocks are well represented and neither dominates. However, a contributory factor to the refinement of the lip demands mention. The general loss of teeth so prevalent among the Pitcairn Islanders has caused, by the removal of the supporting structure, the lips to collapse, with a consequent appearance of a greater thinness than they might otherwise manifest.

The Pitcairn Islanders are dental unfortunates. Not one adult woman out of sixty examined had a complete set of teeth, and nineteen had all the teeth missing. Thirty-seven, or roughly 61 per cent, had lost ten or more teeth. The men are somewhat better off. I actually found five men out of sixty who still had full dentures. Eight had become edentulous and thirty-one, or about 52 per cent, had lost ten or more teeth. It is difficult to account for this dental condition. The diet appears to be adequate, although no investigation of the chemistry of the food was undertaken. The same situation prevails on Norfolk where more meat and fish are consumed. It is true that the English have notoriously bad teeth which may be an important factor in the shocking dental degeneracy on Pitcairn. Its English origin is supported by the case of Edward Young, one of the mutineers, who had already lost his incisor teeth at the age of twenty-four. Since the incisors are ordinarily among the most resistant teeth, Young's loss suggests either fisticuffs or a congenital defect. If the latter hypothesis is true, it is not difficult to see that the close inbreeding practised on Pitcairn might spread and intensify the defect among all the population.

We may sum up the heredity of the Pitcairn Islanders by saying that they show in their traits evidence of both their English and Tahitian ancestry. Some of them are, in their physical expression, more influenced by the English heritage, some more by the Tahitian, and others appear to be intermediate. Each one is a varying mixture of both. It is true that on the whole the features of the islanders are definitely English, but familiarity reveals a number of individuals who favor the Tahitian side.

During the course of my investigations I made a subjective rating of a number of men and women, according to their general appearance and, I quickly add, not one was sufficiently Tahitian in appearance to be able to pass as such, whereas a number of the islanders might readily escape detection in an English community. Of course, this preponderance of the English type is natural, for all the new additions to the colony have been of English stock. But to return to my ratings, each individual was classified as strongly, moderately, slightly English; or intermediate; or slightly, moderately, strongly Tahitian. Here are the results for fifty men and fifty-one women.

	MALES	FEMALES
Strongly English	12	6
Moderately English	8	5
Slightly English	13	8
Intermediate	11	14
Slightly Tahitian	3	13
Moderately Tahitian	3	5
Strongly Tahitian	0	2

I have already mentioned the darker complexions of the Pitcairn women. Perhaps this fact influenced me in recording a stronger Tahitian trend among the women, even though I tried to preserve a balanced judgment based on all the traits.

In a mixed population such as the Pitcairn Islanders, one might normally expect to find an increased variability. The potentialities contributed by both ancestral stocks should expand the range of the various characters among the hybrids. Actually the Pitcairn Islanders show no evidence of such a phenomenon. The statistical expression of the variability inherent in a series is measured by the standard deviation. The standard deviations of the Pitcairn Islanders are in some cases smaller than those of the English or Tahitians, in many they are the same, and in only one or two are they significantly greater. I can offer in explanation of this reversal of expectation only the suggestion that the inbreeding which has occurred among the Pitcairn Islanders has led to a greater homogeneity than exists in most mixed groups. The extent of inbreeding will be discussed in the next chapter.

11

BREEDING AND INBREEDING

Vital statistics are the bookkeeping of a population. They reveal the present state of affairs, uncover past trends, and cast up a balance, favorable or otherwise. And in this instance they provide invaluable data pertinent to the problems of race mixture.

The population figures relating to the Pitcairn Islanders presented in the following pages were derived from the previously mentioned *Book of Records of Pitcairn Island* where each birth, death, and marriage occurring on Pitcairn is entered or is supposed to have been entered. I have actually found remarkably few discrepancies or omissions. From internal evidence I have, however, been forced to assume that some of the births and deaths in the first years after the return to Pitcairn were omitted either inadvertently or because the infant died soon after birth, and the recorder, not foreseeing the needs of a future investigator, felt no compulsion to register such ephemeral additions to the colony. It is my belief that the register is sufficiently complete to yield trustworthy results. It also agrees very closely with the genealogical tables drawn up from independent sources.

One of the most remarkable facts about the population of Pitcairn is its prodigiously rapid increase. The following table illustrates this growth up to 1856, when the entire community was transported to Norfolk Island.

YEAR	TOTAL	MALES	FEMALES
1808	35		
1814	40		
1825	66	36	30
1839	106	53	53
1840	108	53	55
1841	111	54	57
1842	112	53	59
1843	119	59	60
1844	121	60	61
1845	127	65	62
1846	134	69	65
1847	140	72	68
1848	146	74	72
1849	155	76	79
1852	170		
1853	172	85	87
1855	187	92	95
1856	193	94	99

In 1858 sixteen returned to Pitcairn. In 1864 twenty-six more joined the previous lot who meanwhile had increased somewhat. There were, therefore, in 1864 about forty-five souls on Pitcairn. Seventy years later, in 1934, I found the colony increased to about two hundred, and to more than two hundred and twenty-five, including those who had emigrated to foreign lands. In these seventy years the population has multiplied itself by at least five times. Meanwhile on Norfolk the population had grown so rapidly that by 1924 there were over six hundred inhabitants. Unfortunately, the census of Norfolk includes the foreign residents, so that the actual number of descendants of the mutineers can be less exactly determined than is the case on Pitcairn. Thus in the course of one hundred and forty-five years the six mutineers who lived long enough to produce offspring have a living progeny well exceeding eight hundred on Norfolk and Pitcairn and which might easily number one thousand if all the wanderers were included. A prodigious spectacle of human breeding!

The present composition of the population living on the island is as follows:

	MALES	FEMALES
Under 18	36	27
18–44	44	38
45–64	18	24
65–86	3	9
Total	101	98

It is commonly observed in population analyses that females survive to greater ages than males. The Pitcairn Islanders are no exception to this rule. We find between the ages of sixty-five to eighty-six that the females outnumber the males three to one, and between the ages of forty-five to sixty-four the proportion of women to men is four to three. In the earlier ages, however, the males are more numerous than the females.

Actually, from 1865 to 1933 there have been 165 male to 139 female births, or 118.7 males to 100 females. This sex ratio at birth among the Pitcairn Islanders is much higher than is ordinarily expected. From 1841 to 1916, in England and Wales, the sex ratio at birth varied from 103.5 to 105.2. In Sweden, during the course of over one hundred and fifty years, the sex ratio at birth has been maintained at about 105 or 106. But the higher mortality among the males generally alters the ratio until, in the middle period of life and in old age, the women become more numerous than the men. This phenomenon we find repeated on Pitcairn. On Norfolk Island in 1924 I found a group of twenty-four survivors of the original migration, the youngest being sixty-five years old and the oldest ninety-five. Of these twenty-four, fifteen were females and nine males. It is sometimes offered in explanation of the preponderance of aged women that the greater hazards of male occupations take a greater toll on life, but unless these hazards are also to be blamed for weakening those males who survive it is difficult to see why the death rate should continue to be greater among males even during the decades of retirement from active life. There appears to be no escape from the conclusion that man is the weaker vessel.

The extraordinary increase in the population of Pitcairn suggests that in the not far distant future the island may again be overpopulated and that once more the compact little community may by sheer necessity be forced to cast off another daughter colony. Pitcairn is only slightly more than two miles long and a little more than one mile wide. Only a limited part of its precipitous surface is suitable for agriculture. Were the principles of Malthus known to them they would be only too real to the Pitcairn Islanders, who, however, do not appear to be disturbed excessively by the prospects of the crowded future. But before drawing too gloomy a conclusion from the past it would be wiser to inquire into the present trends of population replacements. In the following paragraphs, therefore, I shall set forth some of the results of various calculations I have computed from the vital records of the island. These, I think, may throw some light on the future of the Pitcairn population, in so far as it is possible to illuminate the future at all.

If the births and deaths are arranged by decades, they show the following results:

DECADE	BIRTHS	DEATHS	INCREASE
1864–1873	36	5	31
1874–1883	38	12	26
1884–1893	49	21	28
1894–1903	42	5	37
1904–1913	49	27	22
1914–1923	45	21	24
1924–1933	45	21	24

These figures seem to indicate that although the births have increased in number with the increase in population, the deaths have more than kept pace. This fact results in the net increase of population becoming progressively smaller. The decade 1894–1903 does show a sudden increase in population gain, but it is significant that it was not as a consequence of a more pronounced fertility but because of a temporary reduction in the number of deaths.

To demonstrate this decline in population increase in another manner, I shall give the percentages that each decade's increase represents of the total population. Unfortunately I have no official census figures for these periods, but if each decade's increase is added in turn to the preceding decade's total, a figure near to the actual population will be achieved. For example, there were about forty-five islanders in 1864. During the next decade to 1873 there were thirty-one more births than deaths, which would mean that by 1873 the population reached a total of seventy-six. This method of computation would, it is true, make the present population 237, whereas it is actually only two hundred.

The discrepancy, however, is not entirely the fault of the calculations but of emigrations that have removed some of the islanders to New Zealand, Australia, San Francisco, and Bridgeport, Connecticut. If the discrepancy were distributed evenly and subtracted from each decade's increase, the resulting figure would probably be near the truth, at least not sufficiently wide of it to alter the significance of the comparison I wish to draw. It would require much grosser errors in my figures than I believe they contain to affect materially the steady progressive decline in the rate of growth of Pitcairn's population. Here are my approximations to the successive rates of growth.

YEAR	ESTIMATED POPULATION	ACTUAL INCREASE	PER CENT INCREASE
1864	45		
1874	71	31	43.66
1884	92	26	28.26
1894	115	28	24.35
1904	147	37	25.17
1914	164	22	13.41
1924	183	24	13.11
1934	202	24	11.88

The high rate of increase in the first decade may be in part the consequence of the abnormal age composition of the little band that repopulated the island. There were very few old people, and a relatively large number of the inhabitants in their active child-bearing period. But the steady decline of the ratio of population replacement since 1884 seems to indicate a falling birth rate or an increasing death rate.

By the same method we may determine the percentage of deaths to the estimated population.

YEAR	PER CENT DEATHS
1874	7.04
1884	13.04
1894	18.26
1904	3.40
1914	16.46
1924	11.48
1934	10.40

These mortality percentages from 1874 to the present do not explain the previously noted decline in the rate of increase. It is necessary, therefore, to seek another cause for the decline in the rate of population increase. In order to test whether or not the birth rate in Pitcairn has declined, I have calculated the average number of children borne by the women who are listed according to the year of their birth. The following table includes all the women, regardless of their sex history.

BIRTH YEAR OF MOTHER	NUMBER OF WOMEN	AVERAGE NUMBER OF CHILDREN PER FEMALE
1790–1814	2	5.5
1815–1839	5	11.4
1840–1864	12	6.8
1865–1889	31	4.2
1890–1914	33	2.4

In the next table I have eliminated all the women except those who reached the age of forty-five and were married up to that age. It is needless to add that the age at marriage varied.

BIRTH YEAR OF MOTHER	NUMBER OF WOMEN	AVERAGE NUMBER OF CHILDREN PER FEMALE
1790–1814	1	6.0
1815–1839	5	11.4
1840–1864	8	8.0
1865–1889	20	5.0
1890–1914	2	2.5

A comparison of these two tables reveals that the character of the sex life of the women does play a part in their fertility. The women who have married or mated and have remained so to the end of their child-bearing period are definitely more fertile than those who have led more irregular lives. But both these tables reveal a similar trend—a decline in fertility. From the extraordinary child-bearing capacity capable of producing an average family of 11.4 the decline has been constant and definite. The rate for the last group of women is inconclusive, being based, in the first table, on women who are still in their active child-bearing period and, in the second, on only two women who had reached the age of forty-five. Nevertheless, it is unlikely that the fertility rate for the women born between 1890–1914 will equal that of the preceding group.

Some idea of the magnitude of these averages may be obtained by comparison with the figures for the population of the United States. For American women the estimated average number of offspring for completed families varies according to State from 2.33 to 4.13.

The decline in fertility among the Pitcairn Islanders has a counterpart in the fertility records of the Norfolk Islanders. In my study of the Norfolk Islanders I obtained the following figures.

	NUMBER OF MATINGS	NUMBER OF CHILDREN PER MATING
Original cross	6	4.17
First generation	9	7.44
Second generation	38	9.10
Third generation	77	5.39
Fourth generation	26	2.96

In the next table the average ages of the females are given at the time of their first marriage.

YEAR OF BIRTH	NUMBER	AVERAGE AGE AT FIRST MARRIAGE
1815–1839	3	15 years 3 months
1840–1864	11	21 years 10 months
1865–1889	27	22 years 11 months
1890–1914	24	20 years 3 months

The numbers are few, but as far as they are reliable the generation of women who had the magnificent child-bearing proclivities capable of producing an average of 11.4 children also appear to have married at an earlier age than their descendants. The averages for the succeeding generations are all considerably greater, and show only slight differences from 1840 on. The explanation may be that the fewer possible mates in the earlier days resulted in all the girls being rushed into matrimony as soon as it was decently possible. No later bride equaled the record of one girl born in the 1815–1839 generation. She married at the age of 14 years and 2 months. Even more remarkable was her contemporary, Maria Christian, whose record belongs with Norfolk Island statistics. Maria Christian was born in 1815, married at fourteen years of age, produced twenty-five children including twins, and survived three husbands! Such was the stuff of that fabulous generation.

The figures of the preceding table should be compared with those below which record the average age of the women at the birth of their first child.

YEAR OF BIRTH	NUMBER	AVERAGE AGE AT BIRTH OF FIRST CHILD
1815–1839	4	17 years 1 month
1840–1864	12	22 years 9 months
1865–1889	29	20 years 10 months
1890–1914	26	19 years 9 months

This table includes all the women who have given birth to a child whether with benefit of clergy or without. These averages, therefore, compared with those for age at marriage, reveal that the morality of the islanders as well as the birth rate has undergone changes. Apparently girls born after 1865 were rather impatient.

Although the famous generation of 1815–1839 leads its successors, nevertheless we find that the later generations, from 1865 on, show a secondary tendency towards a younger age at the commencement of child-bearing. If we take the age at first childbirth as an index of fertility it would appear that the latest generation has suffered no recent decline. Even though such an assumption might be tenable, there are too many other factors involved to make this as natural a conclusion as it might seem at first glance. The recent tendency toward earlier age at the birth of the first child may well be the consequence of a relaxation in sex *mores*.

This difficult question of fertility can be approached

in still another way. For the following table I have calculated the average age for the women at the birth of the last child. It is, of course, to be understood that only those women are included who enjoyed a married life up to at least the age of forty-five. Practically all, however, lived in a connubial state to a greater age than this.

YEAR OF BIRTH	NUMBER OF WOMEN	AVERAGE AGE AT FINAL PARTURITION
1790–1814	1	45 years
1815–1839	4	42 years 5 months
1840–1864	8	36 years 6 months
1865–1889	19	34 years 10 months

Taking these figures at their face value, it is clear that the period of fecundity was not only of longer duration in the earlier generations, but that it ceased sooner in the more recent generations. It is true that the numbers for the first two generations are very scanty indeed, but it may be pointed out that of the five women included in the first two generations the youngest was thirty-nine at the birth of her last child and the oldest forty-five years and five months. Three of these five had children when past the age of forty-four. Contrast this with the fact that in succeeding generations not a single woman whose record I have been able to find had a child after her forty-fourth birthday. Actually the oldest was forty-three years and six months. Most of the women in the last two generations ceased their child-bearing during or before their thirties.

I have been discussing the women without any reference to the men in this important phenomenon of child production. In the following table I have analyzed the data for the Pitcairn males from the standpoint of the age at birth of first child, regardless of marital state.

YEAR OF BIRTH	NUMBER	AVERAGE AGE AT BIRTH OF FIRST CHILD
1815–1839	4	20 years 8 months
1840–1864	12	22 years 10 months
1865–1889	24	22 years ½ month
1890–1914	23	25 years

The men show a progressive and uninterrupted increase in age before assuming their procreative functions. This is quite unlike the situation among the females who, in the more recent generations, tended to start child-bearing at an early age.

I intended tabulating the males by age at the birth of the last child in order to provide comparable data with those for the females, but I soon had confirmed what I suspected might be the truth. The age of the men at the birth of their last child was conditioned by the age of their wives. This was made all the clearer by several instances in which philandering men whose wives had long ceased to bear children were able at rather advanced ages to produce illegitimate offspring by younger women. It did not, therefore, appear to be a safe procedure to estimate the duration of the procreative powers of the men by examining their ages at the birth of their final offspring.

This discussion of the birth rates and the child-bearing ages of the Pitcairn Islanders leads to the conclusion that the rate of population increase has declined. Not only do the women produce fewer children but they now cease to bear them at all at a younger age than they formerly did. It is impossible to predict how far this drying up of fertility will continue, but it is at least clear that the island will not become overpopulated in the immediate future. In fact, the present birth rate hardly suffices to maintain the existing population and any further drop would lead to a decline. Such a prediction might come as a shock to the Pitcairn Islanders, who are accustomed to believe that their island is headed for serious overpopulation. So potent, indeed, is this belief that, aside from a natural reluctance to seeing strangers settle among them, they have always resisted the invasion of eager would-be immigrants on the ground that the island is hardly spacious enough to accommodate their own future requirements.

It is tempting to speculate on the cause of the decline in the birth rate of the Pitcairn Islanders. There are at least three obvious explanations which will occur to the reader, according to his training or bias. It is possible to argue that the high birth rate of the first generations was a perfect illustration of the hybrid vigor which is released when genetic lines are crossed, and that the subsequent decline in physiological vigor is the result of inbreeding and the exhaustion of the forces of hybrid vigor. There is much to be said for this view. Among another hybrid group, the Rehobother Bastards of South Africa, who were carefully studied by Eugen Fischer, there was no discernible diminution of a marked fertility even after five or six generations. Inbreeding, however, has been a relatively rare factor in the marriages of the Rehobother Bastards.

But the situation is rather more complex than at first appears. For example, it is conceivable that medical reasons may be causing the decline in birth rate on Pitcairn. Unfortunately no opportunity was available to determine the extent of gonorrhea or other venereal diseases among the population, for it is well known that gonorrhea is important among the causes of infertility. And it might be pointed out that the beginning of a marked decline in birth rate coincides with the breaking down of sex morality. During the second half of the last century the islanders began to find the old rigidity of conduct irksome. Under such circumstances it does not take many infections from the maritime world to spread its poison throughout a tiny population. Anyone familiar with the tobogganlike decline of the birth rate among Polynesians knows how significant the introduction of venereal disease can be—a fact that was brought forcefully to my attention on many occasions. And I have also been able to record the extraordinary improvement in the birth rate of Nuku Hiva when enlightened efforts were made to combat gonorrhea.

Finally, there is a less probable explanation but one that cannot be entirely overlooked. It is obvious that the contraceptive devices and techniques known and employed in Europe and America are not readily available to the Pitcairn Islanders, but some information may well have seeped through into the island.

From 1858 to 1934 three hundred and twenty births occurred on Pitcairn. Of this total nine were twins, giving a proportion of 1 to 35.6. The frequency of twin to normal births is usually around 1 to 80, although this proportion has been found to fluctuate among various peoples from 1:60 to 1:250. But I know of no population where the frequency of twins is as high as here. I am not acquainted with any reliable data on the phenomenon among Tahitians, but my observations do not lead me to believe that twinning is more frequent among them than among the English. It is not inconceivable that inbreeding has increased the chances for multiple births among the Pitcairn Islanders.

During the period from 1864 to 1934 inclusive there were recorded in the *Book of Records* the deaths of 114 native islanders. The following list gives the various causes assigned for the deaths and the frequency under each category.

Accident 19
Lockjaw 4
Internal injury and old age ... 1
Spinal injury 1
Consumption 12
Pneumonia 2
"Flu" and old age 1
Typhus 12
Old age 7
Paralytic stroke and old age ... 1
Dysentery 5
Heart trouble 3
Dropsy 3
Asthma and dropsy 1
Fever 3
Childbirth 3
Convulsions 2
Whooping cough 2
Stomach and intestinal trouble 1
"Disease through whole body" 1
Amenorrhea 1
Craniotomy 1
Stillborn 2
"Inherited fever" 1
Not stated .... $\left\{\begin{array}{l} 16 \text{ adults} \\ 9 \text{ infants} \end{array}\right.$

TOTAL 114

It hardly needs mentioning that the above causes of death possess doubtful value; nevertheless, the list does provide several facts of great interest. The number of deaths by accident is relatively large, comprising 16.7 per cent of the total. And if to these nineteen cases of death by accident we add the deaths by internal injury, by spinal injury, and by lockjaw (two of these were specifically stated to have acquired lockjaw from a splinter), the total of twenty-five would amount to 21.9 per cent of all deaths.

Whatever doubt may surround the other attributed causes of death, there can be no question of those by accident. They include many who were washed from rocks, some who fell from cliffs, others accidentally shot, two who were crushed by a boat, and similar victims of work and play. This large total speaks volumes for the hazards of life on Pitcairn.

Tragedy rates but a few lines in the records. On March 28, 1898, Andrew Stevens Christian, son of Francis and Eunice Christian, aged ten years and two months, was sent by his mother to climb a banana tree and gather its fruit. "He remained longer than he should," runs the account, "and, failing to answer his mother's repeated calls, she sent two of his young sisters to look and see what was the matter. Arriving at the place, they found him dead, with the banana tree lying across his body."

The twelve deaths recorded as caused by typhus occurred in 1893, "having been communicated by means of the wrecked ship *Bowdon*, lost on Oeno reef." Death by "craniotomy" was the fate of little Anderson Warner, "age about 1 hour." "Fracture of the skull due to partial craniotomy rendered necessary to save the mother's life," says the recorder. Newborn Nelly Dolly Warren died on March 26, 1911. "Cause mother being sick with fever in child birth, child also inherits the fever for few hours then died."

Among those listed under deaths were seventeen infants who died when less than one year old, and two stillborns. Not including the two stillborn infants, it appears that one in every six deaths was that of an infant less than one year old. Stated in another way, the infant mortality under one year was about fifty-six per thousand births. This is not an excessively high rate, even when compared with corresponding rates in Europe and America. In fact, it is remarkably low for a population lacking the attentions of a medical man.

If for no other reason, inbreeding among the Pitcairn Islanders would make them worthy of serious study. The limited number of families with which the colony began and the fact that only a few strangers have joined the community forced an intense form in inbreeding on passing generations. So many people believe inbreeding to be fatal to the health of families given to its practice that it has become almost an eleventh commandment: Thou shalt not marry thy cousin. Any closer blood relationship, of course, is incestuous and held in horror. Nor is this fear of inbreeding completely irrational. Numerous enough instances of cousin marriages which have led to disastrous results suggest that such a prohibition is more than an empty taboo. Inbreeding will increase very considerably the chances of the appearance of a latent defect—if there is a defect latent in the stock. But if the genetic line is sound, there should theoretically be no unpleasant consequence from cousin marriage. In fact, mice and other laboratory animals have been brother-sister mated for generations without producing an unnatural number of defectives. Moreover, there have been historic examples of brother-sister matings in Egyptian dynasties and among the Peruvian Incas which have been successful. And in many primitive societies, where cousin marriage has been a general and ancient custom, it has not inevitably led to degeneration.

The carefully preserved records of Pitcairn make it possible to draw up a family tree for each individual, and from a study of these genealogical tables we can derive an exact idea of the amount of inbreeding which has occurred in the Pitcairn ancestry of every islander. It can be easily imagined how rapidly these ancestral lines become exceedingly intricate and how difficult it would be, after five or six generations, to describe all the complicated interrelationships adequately. I have, therefore, attempted to obtain for each of my adult subjects a simple index which would express the exact degree of inbreeding. To do this I have carried each individual back to the generation of the mutineers and divided the total number of ancestors theoretically possible for that generation into the actual number found. For example, to state a case in its simplest terms, if a subject is in the fifth generation from the mutineers, he has thirty-two possible ancestors in the mutineers' generation. Now, if by actual count there are only twenty different ancestors, indicating a number of cousin marriages, then twenty divided by thirty-two gives an inbreeding index of .625 or 62.50 per cent.

Brother-sister mating in a family previously outbred would give an index of 50.00 per cent, and first-cousin marriage an index of 75.00 per cent. Previous inbreeding in such cases would, of course, lower the index. In the following table I have listed by decades the average index of inbreeding among my adult Pitcairn subjects, male and female.

	NUMBER	AVERAGE INDEX OF INBREEDING
1850–1859	4	84.38 per cent
1860–1869	7	91.07 per cent
1870–1879	15	86.67 per cent
1880–1889	22	70.87 per cent
1890–1899	26	71.36 per cent
1900–1909	26	61.96 per cent
1910–1916	23	51.53 per cent

These figures indicate a very rapid increase in inbreeding to the point where the index is practically the same as that for the offspring of a brother-sister marriage. It should, however, be noted that an index of 51.53, such as is found for the youngest subjects, is not really equivalent to an index of 50.00 for brother-sister marriage. In the former, part of the reduction comes from the doubling of ancestors five, six, or seven generations removed, while the latter reaches back only two generations. The closer to the subject's generation the doubling takes place the more intense is the inbreeding, although the index gives no measure of this. Nevertheless, it is clear that inbreeding among Pitcairn Islanders is extremely close.

One subject had an index of 25.56. In his family tree Fletcher Christian appeared seven times, Edward Young six times, John Mills three times, William McCoy three times, Matthew Quintal three times, John Adams once, and John Buffett once. This inbred young man is a healthy islander and shows no obvious stigmata of his restricted ancestry.

The rise in the average index for the decade 1860–1869 is caused by the fact that of the seven individuals born in that period four were the children of Samuel Warren, a Providence, R. I., man, who settled on Pitcairn.

It has, no doubt, occurred to the reader that the increase in inbreeding is a function both of the succession of generations and of the limitation in the numbers of the original founders. The advance of each generation doubles the possible number of ancestors for a given level. If the number of individual ancestors remains constant at that level, then the inbreeding increases proportionately to the number of generations. Unless new blood is added to the Pitcairn mixture, each successive generation will become statistically more inbred. Genetically, however, the increase in population provides an opportunity for variation and diversification of ancestral lines.

All this leads to the question whether or not the highly inbred mating of the Pitcairn Islanders has debilitated the stock. Physically, the islanders are robust and healthy. Their medical record is good, with no evidence of degenerative diseases peculiar to them. Abnormalities of physical structure are practically nonexistent on Pitcairn. As for the birth rate, it is not incontestable that inbreeding has brought about the decline I have already mentioned. Other causes might more plausibly be invoked to explain it. The only general defect I know of among the Pitcairn Islanders which may be attributed to inbreeding, is the degeneration of their dentitions.

The mental and psychological qualities of the islanders tend rather to elude exact measurement. I had no time to administer psychological tests, even if there were any adequate for the special environment in which the Pitcairners live. I have, therefore, only subjective impressions, and these are perhaps biased in favor of the islanders. Actually I knew of only two or three who were distinctly below par mentally—a small proportion in a group of two hundred. Several were dull but able to manage their affairs efficiently enough. The rest seemed to me to fit into the average range of intelligence.

As I think back to the individuals I knew on Pitcairn, I am impressed by the relatively large number of men such as Parkins Christian, Fred Christian, Edgar Christian, Norris Young, and Arthur Herbert Young and of women such as Mary Ann McCoy, Ada Christian, Margaret Lucy Christian, and Harriet Warren, who possessed qualities of leadership or traits of personality that raised them above the level of their neighbors. All in all, therefore, I can only conclude that inbreeding, as far as my evidence goes, has not caused degeneration among the Pitcairn Islanders. To that extent, this confirms the results of experimental inbreeding, that it is the presence of latent defects which makes inbreeding a dangerous thing and not any mysterious punishment consequent to the process itself.

V. DIURNAL

12

PITCAIRN DIARY: 1934-1935

This is a chapter out of a diary. At the end of each day, after hours of work, and full of fatigue, I tried to keep a record of the events of the day. They were intended merely as notes around which to fill in memories, but in the hope that they may add a significant stroke to the picture I have tried to paint of Pitcairn life I shall quote pertinent sections.

December 24. Up at 5:30. Slept rather well. After shaving, had tea and bread which were specially prepared for me, since the custom here is to breakfast at about eleven. The kindness and thoughtfulness of Eleanor and Burley are very touching. I hate upsetting their routine, but they insist they don't mind.

Kept saying "good-morning" to the numerous passers-by. The paths are close to the house so that anyone who passes by gets an intimate view of the interior and its occupants. A little after seven the bell rang to summon the men to the boats. It was the *Ruahine* arriving. The women snatched up their baskets, the men grabbed their fruit packed the night before and their wooden curios. I found myself alone in the house, even the children, excited by the event, have departed, and at last the village is quiet.

I went up to the courthouse—just in case someone left behind might come. I wrote for a while, and then a woman, lean in the Pitcairn mold and with hard round

eyes and a high-reaching curving nose, came along and
we gossiped. She spoke in a soft slurring voice. She—the
islanders in general—were glad to welcome us. They enjoyed the change. No, we were no trouble at all. It was
a pleasure. She hoped the people would come forward.
They were inclined to be a bit shy.

Then Roy Clark arrived. He came to the island in
1906 with his father, Lincoln Clark. Roy was only sixteen years old at the time. His father had been wrecked
on Oeno years before, together with Philip Coffin, a Nantucket sailmaker. Coffin married a Warren girl on Pitcairn and remained, but Clark returned to his home in
California. He was a mere boy at that time—I think he
was cabin boy. Years later, after his wife's death in California, he decided to return to the island with his son,
Roy. Lincoln died a few years ago, leaving a Pitcairn
family, and Roy has become one of the islanders. He is
a leader in the church and teaches school for which services he receives £3 per quarter. Has married a daughter
of Philip Coffin, but is childless. Showed me his house,
the oldest of the island, formerly the home of Thursday
October Christian. Part of the frame is original and
nearly a hundred years old, but the interior has been extensively altered. It was interesting to see the old-type
construction, with the sliding shutters, the wall boards
set horizontally, edge to edge, in slots. The great squared
uprights are exposed and the planks fitted between them.
Roy has promised to add to my Pitcairn word list.

Later I returned again to the courthouse. George arrived from the *Zaca* on his way to visit the Miss Ross
who is ill. T. C. came ashore also and is collecting in-
sects. I had breakfast at eleven o'clock and then returned
to the laboratory-courthouse, taking Burley with me. I
commenced my examinations with him and, having
made a beginning, worked steadily until almost five,
seeing, in all, seventeen of the islanders. Had only one
interruption when the bell rang to call the people for
the division of biscuits and flour which had been pre-

sented to them on the *Ruahine*. Each family representative brought a tin, a pail, or some other container, deposited it on the veranda of the courthouse, and then retired to the community bench to await the just apportionment. A couple of men, appointed by the council and chief magistrate, distributed into equal shares the ship's biscuits and flour so that each family received its proper share. Each family, regardless of its size, gets the same amount.

A "missionary" meeting is held every Monday night, but I wasn't able to attend.

December 25. Christmas Day! and up at 5:30 with the dawn. Very tired after a tumultuous evening. It was well after eleven before I got to bed. After supper last night we watched the rockets sent up from the *Zaca* in honor of the occasion. We stood at the windows looking across the tree-tufted slope falling below us sharply into the sea. The air was purplish blue and soft. The children enjoyed the display and the grown-ups, too. Then David Young, Eleanor's father, came in to visit. We all sat around the rough homemade table, covered with a white cloth. I had a chair but the others sat on benches. David's face was beautifully illuminated by the lamp. He has a face like Lincoln's—craggy and hollow—and the bony elevations, picked out by the light, cast heavy shadows in the deep excavations of his face. His eyes appeared to be looking out of deep caverns. I began asking him about land, government, fishing, and other Pitcairn matters. Parkins came in and joined us. I had just begun to get some interesting dope from them both when we noticed through the window that someone was approaching with a lantern. It was Parkins' wife. She wouldn't come in, but insisted that Parkins come out to her. After a minute, he politely excused himself and disappeared. We were all a bit apprehensive, for Mrs. Christian's voice sounded decidedly disturbed. I knew that my presence had caused her guarded manner.

About ten minutes later, the calm induced by a dull

lamp and a dark night was shattered into bits by the clang of the bell giving the call to man the boats. Burley, Eleanor, and I ran out into the night. I was terrified for fear that some dire thing had happened to the *Zaca* and that they had signaled for a boat. It was pitch dark —black—and I couldn't see but could only hear figures scurrying about. Electric torches began flashing like fireflies and excited voices increasing like a dread chorus. The feeling became very tense. Little groups became distinguishable as my eyes grew accustomed to the dark. I asked what the matter was. I discovered that a woman had been so seriously beaten by her husband that she was unconscious. They wanted to send a boat for Dr. Lyman.

Some of the men started for the landing place. Burley and I followed, my feet stumbling over the indistinct, rutted lane. Half way to the descent, we suddenly stopped. The men stood around indecisively—some local difficulty I couldn't fathom. Burley seemed reluctant to be mixed up in the affair. Nothing was done and after about ten minutes Burley and I returned. I hesitated about offering my services lest the islanders be embarrassed at my knowing more than was necessary concerning something of which they were rather ashamed. Everyone seemed very distraught, and Burley kept muttering "oughter kick his arse," evidently referring to the wife-beater. It was then about 9:40 and I turned in since apparently I could do nothing.

About an hour later I was wakened out of a sound sleep by George Lyman, Parkins, and Burley. Parkins had gone out after all and brought George ashore. I got up and hurriedly dressed. George and I started off for the injured woman's house. We stumbled along in the dark tortuous paths, chasing the long legs of Parkins. We found a crowd around the house and the living room full of people—like mourners at a funeral. The poor woman was in the bedroom, her mother and son hovering over her. She was unable to speak, was suffering intensely, and was almost unconscious except for the agony twitching the muscles of her face. She had stiffened into an unconscious state some time earlier and had been out for over half an hour. George examined her and found that she was suffering from some cerebral pressure. She was made as comfortable as possible. When I could be of no more assistance to George, I returned once more to Burley's and back to bed.

Early this morning George appeared for a cup of tea. The patient is a bit better. At 6:30 I was up to the courthouse ready for work, but the annual election was going on. It seems as though all the island group activities are concentrated disastrously for my work. Men and women were everywhere scribbling on ballots which consist of bits of paper. Both sexes over eighteen vote on Pitcairn. The votes were being counted by two men seated at a table on the veranda of the courthouse.

In spite of the turmoil occasioned by the balloting I was able to get under way with Mr. Cooze, who kindly volunteered to act as my assistant and secretary. Examined thirteen. Knocked off at eleven for breakfast and shortly after noon was back at work again. Meanwhile I had secured a list of twenty men who hadn't appeared and I asked Parkins to round them up. He was kind enough to do so and until nearly five o'clock I continued without interruption, adding thirteen more to the total.

I went aboard the *Zaca* for Christmas dinner. Sea was rougher, and we found it a bit hazardous clambering aboard as the boat bobbed up and down in the swell. The islanders who had come out sat around on the deck, and we played the victrola to amuse them. They asked if we had any religious music. Unfortunately, or perhaps fortunately, we had none. Then they offered to sing to us, which they did—hymns—in great vibrant voices that went out in rolling waves of sound. After they had returned to their boats, they sang again, before casting off, a song entitled "Goodbye," which Parkins boomed out was a Pitcairn song.

It was interesting to watch their faces while they were on board. Parkins with his dark skin, tall, hard, lean figure—very distinguished, masterful, and slow-speakin', but with a humorous twinkle that lights up his face so reminiscent of Tahiti. Arthur Young, shorter, with a high, beaked, red-tipped nose, a small chin, and a high bony head. He looks like an old-time professor caught out on the farm. Some of the others are like old New England tars. Still others like cockneys and a few like half-castes. Most of the men are lean and wiry, with big knobby feet and bony toes, thin hard legs, and great hairy chests. Heavy face hair is common. A recurrent type has a high, curving nose with a very small chin, even further reduced by the early loss of teeth. Exaggerated specimens of the type are Charles Young and his brother, Edwin.

The women, also, are apt to become bony and withered in middle age. There is only one who might be called the "village idiot," but he is quite able to take care of himself. In fact, he displays occasional amusing insight. A few others are not very bright, but it is difficult to make just estimates. There are shyness before strangers, a feeling of awkwardness in the presence of yachting magnificence, diffidence towards the confident, and lack of education. In spite of these handicaps it is wonderful that fine, self-possessed, and poised personalities like Parkins Christian, Arthur Young, David Young, Edgar Christian, Norris Christian, Harriet Warren, Louisa Christian, and Edith Young develop. The newer blood has not added anything noticeably superior to the population. In fact, the finest individuals appear to be those from the purest Pitcairn strains. It is regrettable that the original population were not kept unadulterated.

After our visitors left, we sat down to a grand Christmas dinner. A huge turkey and all the additions, concluding with a real plum pudding. Florence Jaques had remembered way back in September to purchase a set of little novelty figures, one for each of us. I received a nice, friendly radio greeting from Dick back in New York. The Stock Exchange seems another world from here. Mr. Cooze gave George, Templeton Crocker, and me each an ancient stone adze as Christmas presents. They were all turned over to me as the anthropologist. These relics of a former population are occasionally discovered. In the course of many years a large number have been found, but most of them have disappeared again as gifts to passing friends. Kenneth has written an interesting paper on the evidences of a former Polynesian settlement. Stone adzes and chisels in great number all show clear relationships with standard Polynesian types. The mutineers discovered a ruined *marae* (sacred enclosure) and a *tiki* on Pitcairn. Perhaps these extinct Polynesians were an offshoot from Mangareva which, after all, is only about 300 miles distant—a mere nothing to Polynesians who never flinched at 1000-mile-long voyages.

December 26. The late Christmas dinner made it impossible to go ashore last night to my discomfort, for I got little sleep on account of the roll. It was not until about nine o'clock this morning that a boat finally came out from shore to fetch me. James, George, and I, besides some of the crew, went ashore in the first boat. It seems peculiar getting into open boats as big as these. They are about thirty-seven feet long with a nine-foot beam and are manned by fourteen oars. The seats are so wide that two oarsmen and a couple besides can sit on each one without undue crowding. The old *Mahina-i-te-Pua* that Kenneth, Ua, and I sailed about 2500 miles in the Tuamotus five years ago was only twenty-five feet long, and she was decked in and had a cabin containing four bunks and the engine.

When the boats come alongside, the islanders all turn their faces up eagerly, and looking down on them from the deck is as though one were gazing down into a sea of supplicants.

Arrived at Burley's to find "breakfast" being prepared.

Although we had already eaten, it was necessary to do so again. Before eating, however, T. C. and I went off to find the Pitcairn register. I had arranged to make use of it to copy the data I need in analyzing the vital records. T. C. has kindly volunteered to lighten my chores, by copying the register for me. After breakfast, I commenced work, and from 10:30 in the morning until after five in the afternoon, had no let-up. I examined and measured twenty-four.

Toshio set up his camera and photographed all comers. I am anxious to get as complete a photographic record of the island and its inhabitants as possible. Toshio has agreed to relieve me of the burden of photography so that I may devote myself uninterruptedly to my job.

The blood groupings have not yet been started, but we hope to get that organized a little later.

Supper tonight consisted of cow peas, chicken stuffed with pieces of potato and beef, gruelly soup made of rice and macaroni, tomatoes, cucumbers, *pillihai, kumara,* tea, and bread. After supper David Young, his sister Edith, and a number of others came in and talked until 8:30. They have gone now and it is very still and peaceful as I write. Burley is sitting on the chest and the calm of fatigue has settled on him. Eleanor is plaiting a basket for me to take as a souvenir. One of the boys is watching me very studiously, while the other two are fooling on the settee in the corner.

December 27. Not much to relate for today. Merely another full day of work. I only moved from the courthouse for meals. The day began at 5:30—I'm amazed at my unwonted early rising—and work ceased with the daylight at 6 p.m. I had breakfast today at Parkins' and a good one it was. There was square pumpkin pie, but its shape detracted no whit from its goodness. Cow peas, salad, sliced tomatoes, cucumbers, potatoes, and chicken. No tea or coffee served in that house! The chicken was for my benefit, for Parkins and his family are all strict vegetarians. Parkins was characteristic. I never tire of watching him. He is very deliberate as he shifts his bulk slowly. Sprawling or towering over the table, he naturally focused all attention, as he told in his slow drawling bass voice of his experiences on Tahitian schooners.

Parkins and Arthur Young were shipmates in their youth on Tahitian trading schooners. Quite a number of the older men have served aboard ships in their younger days and are familiar with the remote coral atolls in the Tuamotus. Parkins told a long yarn about an adventure on one of the schooners in a storm, during which he defied the captain's authority and saved the schooner. He narrated a number of other stories about his sailing days on the trading schooners. Has no respect for the "drunken pigs" who captain them.

Parkins' humor is rather naive. When the first mate of the *Zaca* came in, Parkins offered him some oranges. John took one. Then very seriously and with effort Parkins drawled, "Ah wou'd'n eat that one." John replied, "Well if you wouldn't maybe I shouldn't," and was about to return the fruit. Parkins, still very serious, "No, I wou'd'n eat that one, but maybe I would eat one like it," and with that chuckled as he took one for himself. The other day when Chapin, who was botanizing, said, "That's a funny flower," Parkins asked, "What, did it laugh?"

Examined thirty-three today—a record. There are only about thirty or so adults now left to do. I have arranged with Roy Clark to have all the school children assembled one morning.

After supper tonight, went with Burley and Eleanor to the school tea which is given for the children in celebration of the close of school and the beginning of vacation. All day as I worked I watched the activity around the courthouse. Long planks set on barrels and boxes to be used as tables were erected in the open square between the church and the courthouse. When we arrived on the scene, after our supper, about thirty-odd children and assorted adults were sitting at the tables, wandering about and eating out of nondescript plates and tins. Great piles of light brown buns and thick crumbly slices of bread were stacked at intervals along the board. Huge tin sugar-basins, tureens of soup, etc. The women moving around to see that everyone was amply served, themselves munching a bun. I was invited to join the feast.

After everyone had eaten his fill, the tea things were removed and the tables dismantled and put out of the way. The adults all retired to the long bench facing the square and the children, under the direction of Roy and his assistant teachers, were lined up by sex and by size. They looked like children on exhibition day at school. The lamps and lanterns which were now lit, made the littlest tots seem very wistful. They sang a number of songs, then deployed into drill formation and executed various exercises at which one or two seemed a bit uncertain. I liked the informality and the enthusiasm of the adults who were enjoying it all very much, helping the songs a little by humming softly. But it was a funny and touching scene. A kind of brave attempt. This little human striving suddenly finding expression on a tiny speck of land with countless miles of ocean all around it. It suddenly became incredibly fragile and as defenseless as an ant hill.

The formal exercises over, the hurly-burly of the released children drowned everything else. The children, in various kinds of garments, were yelling and playing in the light provided by lanterns, open kerosene flares, and electric torches. A wandering spear of light from a torch would pick out for a moment some wildly excited child playing with all its heart. The grown-ups remained seated on the bench, talking and watching the children. It was not really very romantic, but it was pleasant as a household of playing children can sometimes be—vigorously domestic. But up above on the terracelike bank tenuous cocoanut palms, leaning gracefully, made a singularly entrancing pattern against a misty night-blue sky.

There is perhaps too much of a suggestion of shanty white about these islanders—the not quite neatly built houses, the cast-off clothing, the necessarily makeshift furniture, the air of utilizing the junk shop—which makes them too close to our seamy side to be truly romantic. One has constantly to be whipping the imagination with scenes from the *Bounty* or with glamorous names like John Adams or story-book ones like Thursday October Christian to keep from forgetting that these are Pitcairn Islanders. And yet their kindness is very touching. And I have a great affection for inarticulate Burley and Eleanor. And the clean brown paths carefully besomed each Friday, the terraced village, the cocoanut-bole-lined roads do make a nice picture. The fault lies with civilization. We have taken away their fresh, crackling *tapa* and offer only discarded clothing in its stead, we have shown them the uses of tin and destroyed the beauty of thatch, we have sent them our broken-down furniture and displaced their simple benches.

December 28. Did twenty more today. Most of the afternoon I spent with Mary Ann McCoy, a gentle old maid who was in the lot that went to Norfolk and with the first of the pilgrims who came back to the sacred island. I met her the first day. She held my hand in her quavering, feeble fingers and with an aged voice that seemed about to break into tears spoke of her pleasure in welcoming us. She is blind and moves about slowly and cautiously; her face lit with a smile is held slightly forward; and her manner is one of faith in those around her. I gave her the book that Norman Hall had entrusted to me and she was very pleased to receive it, though she sadly remarked that she could never read it herself. She is the old lady that Norman Hall quotes, but her promise is perhaps too ambitious, for she doesn't remember all the genealogies—that is too much to expect. But it is phenomenal what she does recall. I rarely found her mistaken. Her memory, as in many old people, has to run on its own way without too much interference, for then she loses the thread and must retrace. Therefore I had to listen to all her anecdotes about missionaries, etc., to cull the facts that I needed. We started by listing the first families to return and tied them on to the genealogies I had collected on Norfolk in 1923–24. The effort after a while was tiring for Aunt Ann, and I decided to adjourn the session for another time.

Today being Friday, the day before the Pitcairn Sabbath, it is called "preparation day." Food is gathered and cooked for tomorrow, the village paths are swept clean, the fallen leaves and refuse are burned, and all the necessary cleaning and scrubbing are done, for on Sabbath no one must labor. Everywhere I saw the women sweeping the paths and making great piles for burning, and indoors I found Eleanor too busy cooking to be bothered by anything else.

During dinner tonight as Burley, Eleanor, the three boys, and I all sat eating, there came the faint sound of singing. Burley recognized the direction and decided that it was coming from the throats of the island men on the *Zaca*. It sounded well coming over the blue Pacific and up the green slope of the hill. We could distinguish the words, "When twilight comes stealing over the sea." The other day when I was aboard, they had sung in great lusty and heavy voices that vibrated like organs.

Figured out today that there are exactly thirteen foreigners resident on Pitcairn. Six in the Cooze family: Mr. and Mrs. Cooze, three children, and Mr. Cooze's father, all New Zealanders; Dick Fairclough and his sister Jessie Westall who are from Birmingham, England; the Misses Aggie and Harriet Ross, retired spinsters from New Zealand; Roy Clark from California, and married to a Pitcairn girl; Adella (Schmidt) Young, the daughter of a Danish father and a Chilean mother. Old Mr. Schmidt had sent Adella to Pitcairn from Mangareva when she was little in order that she might go to school and learn English. When she grew up, Adella married Arthur Young, a *Bounty* descendant. Finally, there is a very recent and, to my knowledge, the only Polynesian addition since the original cross. This is a young Mangarevan girl, Aunoa, whom Andy married while visiting Mangareva, where he had gone with Norman Hall on the ill-fated *Pro Patria*. Thus of all these only three have added new blood to the permanent population. The known additions since the original cross are the following: Evans, Buffett, Nobbs, Warren, Coffin, Butler, Clark, Adella Schmidt, and the recent Mangarevan girl. Besides these, there has been some miscegenation not officially recognized, and several others took their wives and families when they left the island.

After dinner tonight we followed the usual Friday-night custom of Burley and of Eleanor. We joined Eleanor's family at her brother Andrew's. Andrew is the wireless operator. He has constructed a wireless set by following a book of instructions, and, having taught himself the code, is now able to pick up messages within a radius of fifty miles and can prepare the islanders for the arrival of steamers.

There gathered at Andrew's his father David and his mother Kitty, his aunt Edith and her husband and two sons, his brother and sister-in-law, his wife and three children, besides ourselves. Aunt Ann also came down from her little house, blindly tapping her way and carefully shuffling her feet encased in outsize men's shoes. We all sat around the room, some on goatskins on the floor, others on chairs and benches. We were twelve adults and eight children, gathered for family prayers. We began with a hymn. Then Andrew read a passage from the Old Testament, followed by an eloquent prayer couched by Edith in fine Biblical style. This was succeeded by the singing of hymns again—about half a dozen old favorites were sung. A particular favorite would be called for by someone and the whole party would oblige. Aunt Ann sat through it all with a beatific expression which became even more ecstatic when a hymn she had requested was sung. During these services various people slipped in for a few minutes and as quietly out again.

When the sound of our singing ceased, we could hear similar hymns from other houses where identical family groups were gathered.

Had a talk with Aunt Ann after the singing. She told me that originally all the houses were built of the wood, called *miro* on Pitcairn. It is a very hard, resistant wood and still sound in the houses, even in those parts of them that date back to the earliest days of the community. During the absence of the people on Norfolk, Captain Knowles, who had been shipwrecked on Oeno, that graveyard for ships, landed on Pitcairn. To secure timber he tore down most of the old houses and with the planks built a cutter which he sailed to Tahiti. Aunt Ann remembered that when the first lot returned to Pitcairn they found the scribblings of the sailors on their slates left behind in the schoolhouse. There was one name that seemed to have remained imbedded in her memory—John Armitage. She also informed me that Peter Butler was shipwrecked in the *Khandeish* on Oeno. Peter left twin daughters, one of whom is now the wife of Parkins Christian. Coffin and Clark were wrecked in 1881 on Henderson Island. Coffin remained, but Clark returned to California, but in 1906 came back to the island with his son, Roy. The latter is now married to Hyacinth May, the daughter of his father's old shipmate.

December 29. Up later than usual this morning— 6 a.m. But I was ready for Sabbath school when the bell rang at 7:30. I decided to sit through all the services in order to be able to observe the manner with which they are conducted on the island.

There are two assembly rooms in the church, one on the ground floor and another identical in size and similar in decoration on the floor above. The Sabbath school service began as a general meeting held downstairs. The church was crowded. Practically every able-bodied man, woman, and child attended. The service commenced with hymns. A prayer was offered by Fred Christian, assistant elder. Fred is a Titan, with a voice which seems to well up from the bottom of his entire six feet six inches. In vibrant 'cello tones he uttered his prayer in the ever-moving and hypnotic words of the Old Testament. Then followed a reading by Fred from some Seventh Day Adventist missionary literature. It contained an appeal for funds to help build a boat for the missionaries laboring in Melanesia. This being the thirteenth Sabbath since the last missionary drive, he collected the sum of £8 10s for this "thirteenth Sabbath offering." I was astounded that a congregation of only about 178 poor islanders were able to roll up such a figure. It made me rather hot to think of dragging the few hard-earned pence from these people to aid in work of doubtful efficacy. While the collection was being taken, the congregation sang a tune with the *andante* words "dropping, dropping, hear the pennies dropping," and ending with "every one for Jesus." I should like to believe that.

After the collection had been taken, the congregation divided itself into five classes, each of which retired to its own accustomed place. Several gathered in opposite corners of the upstairs meeting room. One went outdoors for its lessons. Leaving the Sabbath school to its various preceptors and preceptresses I departed to call on old Vieder Young whom I had been too busy heretofore to visit, and who, being incapacitated by a gangrenous foot, could not come to see me. Vieder was born in 1850 and has a fair memory of his visit to Norfolk. He was six at the time. He said that he didn't want to quit Norfolk, and he tried to run away as his family was about to depart. Poor youngster, he was caught on the road and carried back to his anxious parents. I was struck by the strong resemblance between Vieder and his sons Charles and Edwin. The two latter, however, are like feebler copies of the old man. They are smaller and their faces are more whittled. Vieder and his second wife, Louisa, and I worked together checking some of the genealogical data that I had arranged.

Early breakfast today in order to be ready for the eleven o'clock services. The bell rang out imperatively just as we had finished our pre-prepared meal. This time the services were in the upstairs room and were principally attended by adults, though there was a good sprinkling of children. As before, the meeting began with hymns, then a passage was read from the Scriptures. After Roy had finished his reading he called on five of us, among them myself, to rise and read designated verses. When Roy called out my name I was completely surprised and rose to read, fumbling for the chapter and verse. I felt as I did years ago when I read in class. My sensations when I had finished, a mixture of relief and desire to do it over again better, were the same as then.

Roy, being the elected elder, now proceeded to deliver his text and his sermon, based on the significance of the communion which was about to be taken. The lack of professionalism lent an air of sincerity and devotion to the preacher who acquitted himself acceptably. After the services two young men went forward to receive trays of biscuits which were passed around, then a native wine poured into tiny glasses was distributed. Burley took his wine eagerly, picking a brimming glass. Leaning towards me, he whispered with an implied smacking of lips, "It's goo-od wine." It was really terrible stuff.

After finishing the rite of communion, the men all rose and retired to the anteroom, closing the doors after them. I followed in mystification. As I stepped into the anteroom, which is really the platform at the head of the stairs, I saw a pile of white enameled basins and pitchers and a stack of hand towels. The men divided into two equal groups, the members of the one providing themselves with towels, basins, and pitchers of water; those in the other group removing their shoes and rolling up their trouser legs. The former, pairing off with the latter group, proceeded to wash the feet of their partners.

After the feet had been washed and dried, the men reversed positions and repeated the performance. This was the foot washing ceremony—the symbol of humility. It was done in utmost seriousness. It was deeply impressive.

Then back again to another prayer, more hymns, and dismissal. I was feeling rather warm by that time and glad to get out into the open.

In the afternoon Cooze came to call and I listened to an exposition of Seventh Day Adventism. The chief tenets of the faith appear to be the celebration of the Sabbath on Saturday, the belief in the imminent second coming of Christ, and the observance of dietary laws that forbid pork and scaleless fish and recommend a strictly vegetarian regimen. This all sounds remarkably like the beliefs of the Jews. Cooze takes his Bible literally. He argued the superiority of a vegetable diet by citing that the ancient Hebraic patriarchs lived immeasurably longer lives before they ate from the fleshpots of Egypt. I did not point out that in all likelihood the ancient patriarchs ate plenty of flesh as do most nomadic herders, or that "fleshpots" sometimes referred to other forms of sustenance, or that in agricultural Egypt vegetables perhaps were more abundant than they were in Judaea.

Tiring of this theological monologue, I suggested visiting John Adams' grave, which Aunt Ann told me is near the site of Adams' house. Therefore the grave must also be near where the original village stood. We found the grave on the further outskirts of the present village. It is marked by a simple headstone on which is inscribed:

SACRED

TO THE MEMORY OF

MR. JOHN ADAMS

WHO DIED MARCH 5TH 1829

AGED 65 YEARS.

IN HOPE

Three other graves alongside Adams' are marked by anonymous boulders and are the resting places of some

of the women in Adams' family. All around is a thick
mass of lantana and various brambles which makes it
impossible to explore the terrain. All one could see was
that it was flat land and rather extensive.

At 3:30 in the afternoon there was another service—
the young people's—which was a repetition of the earlier
ones.

Had supper this evening at David Young's. Family
prayers followed. It was while we were sitting in the living room comfortably talking that the bell rang again—
7:30 and time to attend the church business meeting.
There is such a meeting every quarter, but this, it being
the last quarter of the year, was the most important. As
usual the session opened with the singing of a hymn. No
gathering of Pitcairners is decent without the chanting
of a hymn. The next item was the reading of the various
committee reports. As each committee was called, the
chairman rose, walked to the front of the congregation,
and delivered his or her report, reading from manuscript.
There were reports on the distribution of missionary literature to passengers and crew of passing steamers, reports on church attendance, on the Sabbath school, on
the young people's society, etc., etc. But one that interested me very much was concerned with the tithes. The
tithes committee listed an extraordinary amount of food-
stuff turned in for the benefit of the church. Each householder is conscientious in this duty. There is a special
tithe house for the storage of the fruit of the land, but
being able to sell only very small quantities to occasional
ships, a vast amount of the stuff rots and is thrown away.
Nevertheless, no one thinks of reducing the tithes to a
smaller fraction.

Another report that I found full of interest was the
statement of the financial affairs of the church. During
the preceding year the sum of £240 odd was collected
from this tiny community. It seems extraordinary to me.
The only apparent source of money income is from the
sale of curios and small quantities of fruit to the steamers.

Edith told me that one-tenth of this goes for the support of the church, aside from good-will, freewill, and thank offerings. Some individuals gave as much as £6 and £8. Most of this money is sent to the church in New Zealand for the support of the faith. It astonishes me that the population gives so lavishly. It is sincere giving, for they deprive themselves of many necessities in order to swell the fund. Of course, there is a strong pride in their record, and the letters of praise from their church, no doubt, supply a recompense.

All the reports were accepted by vote. Then Fred Christian rose to propose changing the hour of Sabbath school from 7:30 a.m. to 10:00 a.m. Fred, his six feet six rising to its full height and his deep bass filling every cranny of the room, argued that the later hour would allow the people more time in which to prepare their lessons. This proposal seemed to start a mild tempest. Excited figures kept popping up on all sides. Each in turn argued pro or con. Arthur Young heartily seconded the idea because his digestion had suffered as a result of the disruption of his meal times caused by the inconvenient hour. Others preferred the earlier hour for the sake of the children. It was cooler in the early morning. Those who spoke did so with admirable poise and brevity. A vote favored the present hour of 7:30.

After the business meeting Parkins brought up the question of the luncheon which the islanders were giving the *Zaca's* party on the morrow. Details were discussed. As gently as he could, he asked the parents to keep their children within bounds. Seizing the opportunity to speak to the entire adult population, I asked permission to address them. It was granted, and I spoke briefly for myself and the others on the *Zaca*, thanking them all for the hearty and affectionate welcome they had offered us.

After meeting, Arthur asked me to breakfast at his home on the next day. I accepted with pleasure. On arriving home again, we received some visitors. Edith and her family dropped in. Again I got busy with my word

list. Edith was less shy than the others about giving me
real Pitcairn words and expressions. I found Eleanor
more reticent from a feeling of shyness and of reluctance
to inspire mirth or contempt for their dialect. When she
saw that my interest was real and not designed for humor she became more communicative.

Edith is very keen and has a fine sense of humor. She
has derived considerable amusement from the passengers
on the steamers. Invariably when she goes out and
speaks to them, they look on her as a strange kind of
creature. She said she felt as though she were being in-
spected very carefully. From the tag ends of their memories the passengers seem to recall that Pitcairn is the
island whose people were regenerated after a sinful conception, that the Pitcairners are the pattern of virtue and
godliness. But their impertinence is truly extraordinary.
Edith said that these ten-minute acquaintances asked the
most intimate questions which they themselves would
deeply resent from another. Most frequently the tourist
ladies wished to know "if the people on Pitcairn *really*
live without sin." To this inquisition Edith usually responded with infinite good nature that the Pitcairn people are merely human like other folks. I've never been
able to determine exactly why quite decent people automatically become insufferable the moment they start
traveling. Perhaps it is because subconsciously they
metamorphose the new and the strange into the inferior
and, as a corollary, a note of condescension creeps in.

December 30. Have been here a week today. Roy
Clark was as good as his word, for this morning at six
the school bell rang to assemble all the scholars. I hastened over to the schoolhouse. The forty-odd children of
school age were outdoors in the yard playing. They
ranged from little tots about six to almost grown-up boys
and girls. And a fine lot of children. I worked hard and
steadily for about three hours, seeing each child in turn.
It was an enormous help to have the routine organized

this way. As I finished with one, Roy would have another ready to step forward so that no time was lost.

After my school work, I called on Vieder again, both to add him to my series, thus completing it, and to dredge more genealogical minutiae from his memory. Chatted with Vieder until I saw the *Zaca* crowd appearing on the road below the porch. When I saw their familiar faces, I had a curious feeling as though I had been away on a visit all this time.

T. C. went off to copy from the *Register,* George to see his various patients, and the others to their special occupations. At ten I hied me to Arthur Young's to breakfast. The women were still occupied in its preparation when I arrived, so I waited in the living room talking to young Ray, Arthur's son. The house is very neat and clean and better furnished than most. The walls are painted a pleasant blue. There was a victrola which Ray was operating to produce dreadful music from ancient, scratched discs. The rest of the furniture consisted of a native-made but nicely polished table, a sofa, and several sturdy, simple chairs. A number of family photographs and decorative pictures on the walls. We ate a very nice breakfast out of doors, served by Arthur's handsome daughter.

From Arthur's I went to Edgar Christian's to relieve T. C. on the copying. At 12:30 I returned to meet George. By one o'clock we had our apparatus set up for blood-grouping and ready for finger-sticking.

Outside in the square there was a hammering and a pounding. Tables were being set up for the dinner in our honor. At the inner side of the square under an overhanging bank the men had started fires on which the food was cooking. The entire business seemed to be in the custody of the males. Above the tables an awning of sail-cloth was stretched. A constant stream of people bearing bread, pies, roast chicken, and other edibles. This great concourse of the inhabitants enabled us to gather sixty-five subjects on short order. The first few were dubious about having their fingers pricked. But that wore off when they discovered that it didn't hurt. They were all very curious to see their blood under the microscope.

At four o'clock we all sat down to the dinner. All of the *Zaca's* crew that could be spared were on hand. The central table was reserved for us. T. C. sat at the head and Parkins on his right. Several men and women hovered at our backs, leaning over our shoulders to brush off the flies with leafy twigs. It reminded me of Beechey's account of the fly-brushing activity of Pitcairn ladies of over a century ago. The usual blessing was sung instead of spoken. The food was very abundant and good. Potatoes, chicken, fish, roast goat, salad with cocoanut-milk dressing, pineapple, sweet potatoes, *pillihai*. I recognized Mrs. Parkins Christian's contribution by the square shape of the delicious pumpkin pie. After the meal was over the islanders gave three cheers for the *Zaca*, a compliment which we of the *Zaca* returned. It all ended with a graceful speech by T. C. and the singing of the "Star Spangled Banner" and "God Save the King."

December 31. Had a final session with Aunt Ann Mc-Coy today. The dear old lady was in her bedroom when I arrived, and she asked me to wait in her minute sitting room while she changed her dress. During the process, I could observe her quarters. It is a tiny one-story house divided into two halves, one of which is a sitting room, the other subdivided into a bedroom and a kind of storeroom. The sitting room contains a table, an easy chair on one side of it, a couple of other chairs, a chest of drawers, and a sea chest—all scrupulously neat and clean.

Aunt Ann deprecated the behavior of the younger generation. She felt that they had lost the moral fiber of their ancestors. "Since the *Acadia* was wrecked here," she informed me, "the young people have changed." "If only the parents would train their children in the way they should go," she lamented. And she added, referring to the parental attitude towards the sins of their children,

"But they make light of it." "Loose conversation leads to sinful behavior" was another of her comments.

The Polynesian inheritance cannot be blamed for this "sinful behavior," for among the worst offenders are those with the most European blood.

Aunt Ann and I went over long charts which I had constructed and checked all the names I had recorded. It was a tedious job, and I was glad when it was completed. As I was about to leave, Aunt Ann produced a basket and a string of seed beads as a gift to me. I was extremely touched.

After leaving Aunt Ann's I sketched and photographed Norris Young's house, since it shows along its façade and on one side the old type of construction. The heavy, sinuous logs of *miro* are still sound. Unfortunately the interior has been entirely altered. A kind of match boarding now covers the inner walls.

At eleven o'clock, had another session with the register, copying until one o'clock by which time my hand had succumbed to writer's cramp. I had arranged to meet George at 1:30 at the courthouse where we again set up a laboratory for blood-groupings.* We made good progress, raising our samples from sixty-five to eighty-two. During a lull when the supply of subjects was temporarily exhausted, I started down the road to get blood samples from Aunt Ann and Vieder Young who were unable to get up to the courthouse. As I left Aunt Ann's holding a test tube containing a few drops of blood in a saline solution, I met Eldon Coffin running hard down the lane, his face and arms glistening with sweat, yelling as he ran, "Ray's a hit. Ray's a hit." He was leaving a wake of excited women drawn to the lane by his shouts. Ray is the seventeen-year-old son of Arthur Young. Apparently from Eldon's hurried account he and Ray were out hunting goats near Tautama on the other

*The results of our examination of the blood groups will appear later in a technical report on the Pitcairn Islanders.

side of the island. One of the shots from Eldon's gun had ricocheted from the bole of a tree and hit Ray. Some of the women immediately recalled that Adella, Ray's mother, hadn't wished him to go off hunting that morning. And an unexpressed but pregnant moral was implied. A group of men had already started on the run to fetch Ray back to his home. Along the village lane little groups of excited women were discussing the accident and anxiously awaiting Ray's arrival. George had been informed and his reassuring presence was the subject of much congratulation.

About a quarter of an hour after Eldon's frantic announcement, Ray appeared leaning on a couple of men, but walking. He had started to crawl toward the village as soon as Eldon had left him, and the rescue party found him well on the way home. I saw him stretched out on the floor of his home. He had been hit by a .22 long shot, the bullet having lodged in his right buttock. George, having prepared him for the ordeal, began probing for the bullet with no success at first. It was necessary to make an incision and a local anaesthetic and additional instruments had to be sent for aboard the *Zaca*. During the wait, Ray was moved to the sofa and made comfortable. When the necessities arrived, George continued his search and finally found the bullet close to the skin but about eight or ten inches from its point of entry. It was a nice operation.

The circumstances under which it was imperative to work were most primitive. A crowd of the islanders gathered around to watch, and another larger one sat outside waiting for the removal of the shot which was then passed eagerly from hand to hand.

We had planned to board the *Zaca* at five in the afternoon in order to sail early in the morning, but the accident interfered with these plans. Ray wasn't finally sewn up until about 7:30. George and I had to spend the night ashore since it was too late to go out to the *Zaca*, and moreover George wished to see his patient once more before departing.

January 1, 1935. My day commenced when George came in at 5:15 and woke me up. It was as lovely a day as have been all the others since our arrival. This perfect weather makes for easy landing and has been a never-failing topic of conversation. Ours has been the longest visit by a ship in the memory of the present inhabitants.

While George went off to make his rounds, I remained behind to do a bit of writing and to take a few photographs. On his return we both went to see how Ray was progressing. We found him in excellent condition. Arthur gave George and myself canes as presents. Later Edith arrived with another. George has been loaded down with gifts from grateful patients who have no other means of showing appreciation.

At Burley's until 8:15 waiting for the men to start down to the boats. Most of the men and some of the women were preparing to go out to the *Zaca.* The women are very excited about the visit to the yacht since they haven't been out since our arrival. On the way down we bade those who were remaining a fond good-bye. Met old Frank Christian who was waiting at the edge of the cliff to give me a couple of pairs of island canvas slippers. He also lent me an ancient photograph of his father, Thursday October Christian. Those who were not coming along remained on the cliff to watch our descent and to wave farewell.

The launching of the boats was uneventful. It was a wrench to watch the island recede. I had had ten happy busy days. The islanders had taken us to their hearts so completely that it was easy to become somewhat sentimental about parting.

More than seventy islanders, men and women, came out to the *Zaca* in two whale boats and in two canoes, or scows as they are called. They filled the decks and sat about everywhere. We took parties of them in relays to inspect belowships.

Burley and Eleanor clung to me and I showed them my cabin where we sat for a while. Burley gave me a beautifully inlaid collar box, a puzzle box, a cigarette box, and a basket of fruit. Eleanor had two baskets for me. We said our private good-byes, Eleanor silently weeping and Burley gripping my hand and his voice husky. My own voice and eyes were in a similar condition.

We then went back on deck where the ship's victrola was being played. But the islanders preferred to make their own music, singing "Happy New Year" and a number of other songs.

It is customary to have an annual boat race on New Year's, but our visit had upset their plans. But when the men discovered that we would have enjoyed watching a boat race, they quickly organized an impromptu affair. The two boats were quickly filled with the rowers. The race was from the shore to the *Zaca*. It was exciting and well done.

After the rowers were back on board again and had regained their breath, they once more broke into song. This time they started with "We Shall Meet by the River" and continued to sing hymn after hymn until all the general favorites had been exhausted. Parkins finally gave the word, and the departure began. The anchors of the *Zaca* were hauled aboard, and the engines began to throb and black clouds to pour out of the exhaust pipes. Then as the *Zaca* and the boats drew apart, the islanders once more lifted up their voices in song. Our parting view was of boat-loads of natives standing up to pour their voices into the air.

VI. POSTSCRIPT

13

PRESENT AND FUTURE

It is now more than a generation ago since I last saw Pitcairn Island. For some years I kept in fairly close touch with its affairs, for the islanders are excellent correspondents and write to a wide circle of friends. The war broke this connection, but nevertheless news trickled out and I would hear from time to time of the course of events.

The war years were hard on the islanders, not that they were in want or hunger, but because they were cut off from their friends and from the supplies that they had come to depend upon. Such things as glass for windows, sheets of corrugated metal for roofs, nails, needles, clothing were unobtainable. One does not realize how important these things become until one has to find substitutes for them.

The war also brought a profound effect on the size of the population. The need for labor in New Zealand created opportunities that appealed to some of the island families who migrated chiefly to Auckland, where a small colony was settled. This was brought to my attention by Mr. H. E. Maude, who through his official duties in Fiji had developed an interest in the history of Pitcairn and knew of mine. Although I had planned to visit this tiny outpost of Pitcairn during my visit to New Zealand in 1949, the affairs of the scientific meeting I was attending interfered and I did not see any of my old friends.

It was not until 1958 that I again saw one of the islanders. Parkins Christian, whom I have already described in some detail, suddenly arrived in New York as a delegate to an International Congress held by the Seventh Day Adventists. Before he left for Ohio where the Congress was to be held, I managed to see him and catch up on news of the island. He was much amused by the newspaper reporters who, he said, seemed to think he had never worn shoes and were disappointed that he remained self-possessed among the wonders of New York. It would have perhaps startled his interviewers to know that he had traveled more widely than some of them and had visited the cities of New Zealand and Australia. I discovered from Parkins and again from a fellow islander who visited New York still more recently that the emigration begun during the war has continued and that the population on Pitcairn is now down to less than 150. The educational opportunities for their children to be found in New Zealand, aside from obvious economic advantages, attract some of the families; and now that a tiny beachhead is established there the chances are that a certain proportion of the population will continue to be drawn off in the future. The fears of overpopulation under these circumstances need not trouble them any longer.

Whether this interesting people will survive as a distinct population either on Pitcairn or elsewhere is open to question. It is highly probable that the New Zealand branch will continue to siphon off more of the islanders who, inevitably, it seems to me, will become absorbed into the New Zealand population.

Even if some islanders remain on Pitcairn, their chances of survival become increasingly precarious as they are reduced in number, for the hazards to the survival of a small isolated population become proportionately great.

APPENDIX A

LAWS AND REGULATIONS
OF THE PITCAIRN ISLANDERS

From the *Book of Records* of Pitcairn Island*

*Form of oath to be administered to witnesses in court,
by the Judge.*

(*The witness, standing before the judge, is told by the
judge to lift up his right hand and take the oath. The
judge then administers the following oath.*)
"You (*here the judge mentions the full name of the
witness*) do hereby solemnly swear before God, that
in the case now before the court, you will tell the
truth, the whole truth, and nothing but the truth."
"Do you thus swear?"
(*Witness answers, "I do"*).
(*Judge says, "So help you God"*).
On the arrival of H.B.M.S. "Champion," October 3,
1892, Capt. Rookes, her commander, at a meeting with
the principal members of the community suggested some
changes in the form of government, to what had, until
then, been followed.

* Words within double parentheses (( )) were crossed
out in original records.

His suggestion was thankfully received and heartily adopted, and accordingly, on January 1, 1893, the voters assembled, and the suggestion was carried into effect, seven members being nominated to form a parliament, and from among those seven, the following officers were elected, viz. a president, a vice-president, two judges and a secretary.

RESOLUTION.

Whereas, We have witnessed in the past, that, thro' lack of strength and firmness, on the part of the government officers, some evil has resulted, and,

Whereas, we believe that a larger number of officers would tend to make a stronger government, and that plans for the public welfare would be executed with better success, therefore,

Resolved, That we heartily endorse the plan of having a government consisting of a parliament of seven, with power to legislate, to plan for the public good, to execute all decisions of the court, and to see that all public demands are attended to without unnecessary delay.

DUTIES OF THE OFFICERS.

The President.

1st. It shall be the duty of the president to preside at all sessions of the parliament, and at all assemblies of the regular voters.

2nd. To order and to see that all acts of the parliament, and all laws, are properly executed.

Vice President.

The duty of the vice president shall be to perform the duties of the president in his absence.

Secretary.

The secretary shall be charged with the custody of all papers, and documents of every description belonging to the parliament, and shall, at each meeting, make a true record of all the actions of the said parliament. Beside this, he shall act as treasurer, to hold all public funds subject to the order of the parliament.

Judge.

The judge shall preside at all sittings of the court, and shall decide cases brought before the court, according to the letter of the law, and to appoint all sessions of the court, and its adjournment.

Court of Appeals.

Should either party in a case before the court be dissatisfied with the decision of the judge, said party may appeal to the parliament, a legal quorum of which shall constitute a final court of appeals. The parliament, however, may refuse a case tried by the judge, if, in their estimation, the case has been fairly tried and justly decided.

Notice.

1. All fines are so decided according to the discretion of the court.
2. Any fine, a draft of the same, when paid in work, shall be eight hours a day.
3. All fines paid in cash, must be in either English or American coin.

Laws and Regulations.

Law One.

No one shall be allowed to assemble the court without a good evidence or satisfactory proof against an opposing party or parties, without laying himself open to punishment. Anyone so offending shall be fined sixpence an hour for that time.

Law Two.

Refusal to obey any of the lawful orders of the court shall be punishable by a fine of from one to five pounds sterling.

Insulting the court will be regarded as a grave offence.

Law Three.

No one shall call in question any preceding case that has passed the investigation of the court to prevent the course of justice.

Anyone so offending shall pay a fine within £1 to £4 sterling.

Law Four.

Any two persons convicted of the crime of fornication shall pay a fine of within £4 to £20. Should said crime result in offspring, the father shall support the child as long as it lives. ["Needs supporting," the original wording.]

Further, anything coming from the father to support his illegitimate child, as long as it lives with the mother, shall be sent to the mother thro' the hands of the parliament.

Law Five.

Any persons convicted of the crime of adultery, shall be punished by paying a fine within £10 to £25.

Law Six.

If two persons of the opposite sex, one, or both of whom, at the time shall be legally married, shall associate together in secluded places or otherwise, on terms of intimacy not consistent with his, or her, marriage vows, or in a manner to cause separation from his, or her,

husband or wife, they shall on conviction be fined within
£2 to £10.

Any person or persons aiding or abetting them in this
crime shall pay the same amount.

It shall be lawful for the court to punish the crime of
adultery ((by banishment)) from the island as well as
fining the parties.

Law Seven.

It shall be unlawful for two persons of the opposite
sex to associate together at such times and in such places
as shall tend to create scandal, or to endanger the morals
of the rising generation by their evil example. Further,

It shall be unlawful for any householder to allow any
such persons who may have thus offended, to meet at
his, or her, house, or premises, to further their evil designs without fear of discovery. Fine from £1 to £3
sterling.

Law Eight.

It shall be unlawful for anyone of the opposite sex to
intentionally remain near the place where the women
and girls do their washing.

Anyone so offending, shall pay a fine of from £2 to
£4.

Law Nine.

It shall be unlawful for any persons to raise a fake report against his neighbor out of malice or revenge.

Whoever is convicted of such offence, shall pay a fine
of, from 10 to 20 shillings.

Law Ten.

Whoever is convicted of stealing, shall be fined within
£1 to £10. The stolen property also shall be made
good.

Law Eleven.

Parents shall be responsible for property stolen by their children, (for the purpose of supporting their families, or otherwise) from the age of 16 years and under.

Law Twelve.

Should any person or persons bring forward any charges against anyone, said charge or charges having a month previous to the time of its being made known to the parliament, and produced for the sake of malice or revenge, such person or persons must be punished as the case is determined upon by the court.

Law Thirteen.

Any man who shall beat, or in any way abuse his wife, shall pay a fine of within £1 to £15.

Law Fourteen.

Any person, in a quarrel, striking his opponent with the fist, or with any kind of weapon, shall pay a fine of from £1 to £6.

Should the blow be returned, save in a case of self-defence, both parties shall pay the same fine. Any one is at liberty to defend himself.

Law Fifteen.

It shall be unlawful for any person to carry concealed weapons, or to appear before the court or parliament with deadly weapons on their person.

The fine for this law is £1 to £10.

Law Sixteen.

Any person or persons after this date, 24 September 1884, maliciously wounding, or causing the death of a cat, without permission, will be liable to such punishment as the court will inflict. Further, Any person, or persons aiding, or abetting in the aforesaid misdemeanor, will also be convicted under the same indictment. Should any dog, going out with his master, fall in with a cat, and chase him, and no effort be made to save the cat, the dog must be killed for the first offence. Fine 10 shillings.

Cats in any part of the island doing anyone damage, must be killed in the presence of one of the members of parliament.

Law Seventeen.

It shall be unlawful for any person or persons to treat cruelly, or to beat in an unmerciful manner, their fellow beings, or animals of whatever kind, to injure them or in any way to inflict pain. First violation of the law punishable by reprimand of the court. Subsequent violations by fine of from 12 to 40 shillings.

Law Eighteen.

Should any man's fowls do damage to his neighbor's property, the owner of the fowls must take them away. The owner of the plantation must first notify his neighbor concerning his chickens and if he refuse to remove them, the owner of said plantation shall be at liberty to shoot them.

Law Nineteen.

Any person or persons going after fowls in any part of the island, must call one or more of the other parties who have chickens in the same direction. Should any of the parties refuse to go, they must bear whatever damage may be done.

Anyone found going without consulting any of the said parties, is amenable to a fine of from 4 to 20 shillings.

Law Twenty.

Should any dog be found killing fowls or eating eggs, he is to be killed for the first offence.

Law Twenty-one.

Shooting goats from the bend of the ridge at White Cow's Pen inland toward Ante Valley, and following the same line up to William's Block, and across to the head of McCoy's Valley, Taro Ground and so on throughout the entire boundary line for goats, is strictly prohibited.

Fowls may be killed with bullets if found in the place allotted to goats.

Discharging of bullets from firearms anywhere within the village, is not allowed, except it be into the air, or into the sea. First offence reprimand. Second offence eight shillings.

Law Twenty-two.

Threatening the life of any person or persons will be regarded a great crime. Any such threats will be punishable by the decision of the court.

Law Twenty-three.

It shall be unlawful for any one to land from ships, drugs of any kind without first getting permission from the president. Anyone found doing so shall be punished. Further,

It may be lawful for parents to treat their own children in case of sickness with any kind of medicine that may alleviate their pain, or give relief. But no one will understand that he is at liberty to treat, or give any dose of medicine, unless it be one of his own family, without first getting license from the president. If anyone be found so doing, he shall be severely punished, as the court shall decide.

Law Twenty-four.

Any person or persons going to the sugar mill, and eating the sugar cane which belongs to another after it has been cut and brought there, and that without the permission of the owner of said sugar cane, shall be submitted to whatever punishment or fine the judge may see fit to impose upon him.

Law Twenty-five.

From henceforth (April 6, 1896) no person or persons are allowed to bring cocoanut or cocoanuts from 'TOtherside unless accompanied by one or more of the members of parliament, on the first week of every month, on Sundays, (unless otherwise arranged thro' unforeseen circumstances) and, further,—

No one, while at the above named place will be permitted to use cocoanuts from other persons trees, without first obtaining permission from the owner or owners, thereof.

All cocoanuts needed for cooking while stopping at 'TOtherside must be gathered in the presence of one of the members of parliament.

Law Twenty-six.

All the men, and the boys from the age of 14 years and upward, to whatever age the parliament may think proper to limit, are to be employed in the public work on the island, whenever their services are required.

Law Twenty-seven.

Any person, or persons, calling at, or passing by, places where public work is being done, or where persons are filling appointments made by the judge, president, or parliament, staying around, meddling, or interfering with them in their business, and thus hindering work, or in any way causing trouble, must be submitted to whatever penalty the judge may think fit to impose.

Law Twenty-eight.

No one is allowed to pay *gratis*, without first consulting with the court in regard to the matter.

Law Twenty-nine.

Whoever shall do any action which, though it has not been mentioned above,—is contrary to the decency, peace and good order of the Island, shall be punished by a fine not exceeding ——

Law Thirty.

Reports from children under the age of 14, will be noticed. Also, offenders under that age, when found guilty of glaring misdemeanors, will have punishment meted out to them by the parliament.

Law Thirty-one.

The use of bows and arrows, rifles, revolvers, or firearms of any description, by children under the age of 14 years, is strictly prohibited.

Marriage Laws.

ARTICLE 1. The solemnization of marriage shall be wholly under the direction of the parliament.

ARTICLE 2. The president of the parliament shall, by virtue of his office, be authorized to perform the marriage ceremony. In his absence, the acting vice-president shall have the same authority.

ARTICLE 3. Any ordained minister of the Gospel or an ordained local church elder, may perform the marriage ceremony when authorized to do so by the parliament.

LAWS AS REVISED IN 1904

Administration as laid down by His Majesty's Deputy Commissioner B. F. Simons.

The chief magistrate (who must not be a church officer) as the representative of the people will be elected by them annually.

He will be the chief official authority on the island and as such, will take general cognizance (knowledge of judicial notice) of the affairs of the island in the manner herein provided for. He will preside over and be assisted by a council composed of two assessors and the chairman of the committee for dealing with the Internal and External affairs of the Island hereinafter mentioned. This council, presided over by the chief magistrate, will deal with, and decide upon any question or any differences of opinion that may arise in connection with, or between, the committee((s)) above mentioned, or in any other matters affecting the well being or the welfare of the community.

Should it at any time be necessary, this council is authorized through the Chief Magistrate to submit to the Deputy Commissioner for the consideration of His Majesty's High Commissioner for the Western Pacific, any suggestions or questions affecting the local laws or regulations—either in regard to their amendment, their execution, their extension or otherwise; but no such suggestions or amendments can be carried into effect pending the written authority of the Deputy Commissioner.

A committee composed of a chairman elected annually by the people and of two members elected annually by the Magistrate in council, will be charged with the Internal and External affairs of the Island—such as cultivation, branding and care of animals, poultry and matters of a like nature. This committee is empowered to draw up local regulations for the furtherance of their duties which will become law on being approved and promulgated by the Chief Magistrate in Council.

The deliberations of this committee will be entered into a book kept by the Government Secretary which must be submitted to the Chief Magistrate once a month for his approval and signature.

A similar committee appointed and composed in the manner mentioned in the preceding paragraph will be charged with the External affairs of the Island, such as the disposal and shipment of produce, the working of vessels owned by the Islanders etc. etc. This committee will deliberate (weigh in the mind) on the question of produce suitable for export, the rearing of pigs and other animals for commercial purposes etc. and will submit its views for the consideration of the officers charged with the Internal affairs of the Island. The proceedings of this committee will be entered into a book kept by the Government Secretary which must be submitted to the Chief Magistrate once a month for his approval and signature.

Local Registrar and Government Secretary.

A capable Government Secretary must be elected annually by the people. This officer will keep a record of all cases tried in the Local Court of Justice. He will see that proper minutes of the deliberations (act of weighing in the mind) of the Chief Magistrate in Council are kept. He will also record the proceedings of the Committees charged with the Internal ((and External)) affairs of the Island and submit them from time to time to the Chief Magistrate as provided for. He will undertake the official correspondence of the Chief Magistrate and see that copies of the same are kept and properly filed in the archives of the Island. This officer will further deal as directed by the Chief Magistrate with the communications of the Deputy Commissioner and see that they are correctly filed for easy reference together with any documents affecting the public affairs of the Island.

The Government Secretary will also act under the direction of the Chief Magistrate, as Government Treasurer. In this capacity he will be responsible for the disbursement (pay out) of Public Funds and will see that correct a/cs with vouchers (a paper that concerns a receipt) and receipts are carefully kept.

The Government Secretary will each half year, prepare returns of cases tried before the Court, of the deliberations of the Chief Magistrate in council and of the proceedings of the Committee((s)) for Internal ((and External)) affairs for transmission to the Deputy Commissioner for the consideration of the High Commissioner for the Western Pacific.

In the event of the death of the Chief Magistrate during his term of office, a person to fill the vacancy for the rest of the term may be elected by the council. A vacancy in the Council may be filled on the nomination of the Chief Magistrate.

Judicial.

The Chief Magistrate who is the chief judicial authority will impartially and strictly enforce the local laws and regulations in force. In both civil and criminal matters in which justice can be met by a fine not exceeding £5, or by imprisonment not exceeding one week, the Chief Magistrate will act alone. In all other cases he will be assisted by two Assessors, members of his council, elected annually for the purpose.

In cases tried before the Chief Magistrate with Assessors, in the event of a difference of opinion between them, the combined voices of the Assessors will prevail, but the punishment to be awarded will be determined by the Chief Magistrate alone.

Civil and criminal matters of a serious character for which punishment is not provided for in the local laws and regulations must be dealt with by His Majesty's High Commissioner's Court for the Western Pacific at Pitcairn Island.

Local Court of Justice at Pitcairn Island.

The court will be opened for the administration of Justice on the Monday of the second and fourth weeks of each month and will be presided over by the Chief Magistrate with or without Assessors as may be necessary.

LOCAL LAWS AND REGULATIONS AT PITCAIRN ISLAND.

1. Summons and orders of the Court are to be obeyed immediately. Any infringement of this regulation will be deemed Contempt of Court and will be punished accordingly, either by imprisonment for 24 hrs. or by a fine of 20/ according to the decision of the Court.

2. Any person convicted of seducing a girl under the age of 14 yrs. will be liable to a fine of £20, with or without imprisonment, not to exceed one month. Any person convicted of being the father of an illegitimate child will be fined £5 and will be called upon to pay 2/ per week for the maintenance of the child until it arrives at the age of 14 yrs.

3. The question of Adultery and Rape (Violation by force) cannot be dealt with by the local Court. Such matters must be referred to the High Commissioner's Court for the Western Pacific.

4. If two persons of opposite sex one or both of whom are legally married to other persons shall be found in adultery or shall associate together in secluded places for the purpose of acting in a manner not consistent with his or her married vows, or for the purpose of committing carnal offenses, they shall on conviction be fined from £5 to £10 each, independent of any action which may be taken subsequently under paragraph 3. Any persons aiding or abetting in the offence referred to above are subject to like penalties on conviction.

5. Unmarried persons of either sex congregating together in such a manner as to cause scandal or to endanger the morals of the younger members of the com-

munity, will upon conviction be fined from £2 to £5. Further any householder or other person conniving (to wink at) at the offence mentioned in this paragraph will upon conviction be liable to similar penalties.

6. Any male person intentionally loitering about the places where the women do their washing will upon conviction be fined from 10/ to 40/.

7. Any person ((defaming)) slandering another in a spirit of malice or revenge, will, on conviction, be fined from 10/ to 20/. In cases of a gross or serious character recourse (application as for help) may be had to the High Commissioner's Court for the Western Pacific.

8. Any person over the age of 14 yrs. convicted of theft will be punished by either a fine not exceeding £20, or imprisonment not exceeding one month, or both, and the stolen goods must be returned or made good. Offences under this paragraph, which, either on account of the value of the property involved, or the gravity and circumstances of the case, cannot be dealt with locally, will be tried in the High Commissioner's Court for the Western Pacific.

9. Parents instigating their children under the age of 14 yrs. to steal produce or other goods, will on conviction, be dealt with under the provisions of paragraph 8; the children so offending will be admonished by the Chief Magistrate on the first offence; for the second or subsequent offence they will receive from 3 to 12 strokes with a cane, according to the age and health of the child and to other circumstances. Children under the age of 14 yrs. convicted of theft under circumstances other than those above mentioned, will, for the first offence, receive from 3 to 12 strokes of cane. For a second or Subsequent offence, they will be imprisoned from 3 to 7 days. In both instances the parents or guardians of the child so offending will be called upon to return the goods stolen or to pay the value of the same to the owners.

10. Any person committing a breach of the peace, such as striking or abusing his wife, striking any person either

with his fist or with any weapon, save in self defence, and all other offences not provided for that may disturb the peace of the community, shall on conviction be fined from 10/ to £5, according to the gravity (seriousness) of the offence. An habitual disturber of the peace may be dealt with in the High Commissioner's Court for the Western Pacific.

11. Firearms, or other weapons may not be carried by any person under the age of 14 years. Persons over that age will be permitted to carry firearms for shooting purposes on obtaining a license from the Chief Magistrate, the charge for which will be for three months 2d, for six months 3d, for one year 6d. Licenses may not be transferable. Any person convicted of carrying firearms, concealed or otherwise, without a license will be fined £2.

Any person coming into Courthouse while the Court is sitting with arms on his person will be fined £1 for contempt of Court.

12. All regulations promulgated by the Chief Magistrate, on the recommendation of the Committees charged with the Internal ((and External)) affairs of the Island, relating to the preservation of cats, cruelty to animals etc. depredation (to destroy) caused by fowls and dogs, the shooting of goats and chickens and matters of a similar nature, are to be strictly adhered to. Any infringment of these regulations ((both)) as regarding Internal ((and External)) affairs will be punished by a fine of from 5/ to £1 at the discretion of the Court.

13. Firearms must not be discharged within the precincts of the village except as authorized under the provisions of the preceeding paragraph.

14. Threats against the life of any person or persons will be dealt with under paragraph 10 and are subject to like penalties. All persons meddling, interfering or hindering other persons in their employment will be charged with committing a breach of the peace and will also be dealt with under the provision of paragraph 10.

15. Abortion is a serious crime and is punishable by a

lengthy term of imprisonment. Any such cases occuring on Pitcairn Island must be brought to the notice of the Deputy Commissioner who will deal with them under the provisions of His Majesty's Order in Council. The Chief Magistrate will not fail to keep himself informed of any such cases or suspected cases, and will immediately act as directed above. Further, in order to prevent the misuse of imported drugs, the Chief Magistrate will, alone, authorize a competent person to import ordinary and simple medicines for the use of the Islanders. The person selected for this duty will exercise his discretion in the issue of such drugs, bearing in mind that any misuse of the privilege accorded to him will be severely dealt with by His Majesty's High Commissioner's Court for the Western Pacific.

16. All men and boys over the age of 14 years are renumeration (reward & recompense) when required, should circumstances permit. It is to be clearly understood, however, that if in the opinion of the Committee((s)) charged with the Internal affairs of the Island, the crops or produce will suffer by the employment of the men as above mentioned, that their services are to be dispensed with until a more fitting occasion.

It could be arranged, however, that such men willing to carry on the Public Work of the Island should be permitted to do so by the said Committee provided that the interests of their respective plantations do not suffer in the meanwhile. In any case it will be the duty of the Chief Magistrate to support the Internal interests of the Community equally with those appertaining to Public Work. Prisoners may be employed on Public Work.

17. The evidence of children may be accepted provided that such children are of a sufficient age to understand the nature of an oath or the nature of the deposition (act of determining) they are called upon to make.

18. All fines and penalties levied (collected) in cash are to be held at the disposal of His Majesty's High Commissioner for the Western Pacific.

Persons unable to pay cash fines or penalties may be permitted to work out the same in the service of the Public departments at the rate of 5/ per day, provided that outside of the Sabbath day, the said person is allowed one day per week for the care of his own plantation or interests.

19. Foreigners, should they visit and reside on Pitcairn Island at any time, should be made acquainted with the laws and regulations governing the Island. No one except His Majesty's High Commissioner for the Western Pacific, or, under certain circumstances, the Deputy Commissioner is legally empowered to deport a person from the Island.

20. No alcoholic liquors are to be imported into the island by the islanders except such as may be required for medical purposes and then only under the written permission of the Chief Magistrate. Other residents and foreigners may from time to time import sufficient for their personal use with the written sanction of the Chief Magistrate. These persons, however, are prohibited from selling or disposing of the same, or any portion of the same, to the natives of the Island under the penalty of a fine not exceeding £ 10 for the first offence, and a similar fine with imprisonment not exceeding one month for a second or subsequent offence. Smuggling will be punished by similar penalties and the liquors confiscated.

21. In the event of the death of a person under suspicious circumstances, the Chief Magistrate assisted by his council, will enquire into the matter, examine witnesses and take down evidences and submit the same, together with his covering report, for the consideration of the Deputy Commissioner.

22. No punishments, pains, or penalties, other than those above provided for can be imposed by the Chief Magistrate. Cases of a grave and serious character will be dealt with by His Majesty's High Commissioner's court for the Western Pacific at Pitcairn Island.

23. These Laws and Regulations will come into force on

and from Thursday the 19th day of May 1904 but are subject to the concurrence and revision of His Majesty's High Commissioner for the Western Pacific.

Read at the close of law 16.

Prisoners may be employed on Public Work.
No. 24 and 25 of the Local Laws are found on page 93 of this book.

REGULATIONS MADE BY CAPT. GARNIT, APPROVED BY R. T. SIMONS.

Constant disputes having arisen as to the control of the boats, in the future the boats are to be under the control of the committee for Internal ((External)) affairs who will not only require the men for manning them, but will requisition men for keeping them in order, a certain number of hours each week.

24. It having been brought to the notace of the Deputy Commissioner that theft accompaned by burglary is a frequent occurance on Pitcairn Island, it is hereby enacted that when there is a suspicion that goods stol-((l))en are secre((c))ted in one or other of the islanders houses a written warrant may be issued by the Chief Magistrate for the ((serch)) search of the said houses by the court policeman, and cases are to be tried in the High Commissioner's court for the Western Pacific.

25. No Pitcairn Islander shall board a passing ship untill it has been definitley ascertained that no sickness of any kind exist on board.

INSTRUCTIONS IN REGARD TO THE YEARLY ELECTION OF GOVERNMENT OFFICIALS.

a. Every native born inhabitant of the island who has attained the age of eighteen years shall be qualified to vote at the election of government officers. Foreigners may take part in election and local affairs provided that the community is willing.

The Chief Magistrate and the two assessors must always be natives of Pitcairn Island.

b. Within the first five day after the twentieth of December in each year the Chief Magistrate and Government Secretary shall prepare a register of all persons qualified to vote at the election of government officers.

This register shall be signed by the Chief Magistrate and committed to the care of the Government Secretary.

c. The register so prepared shall be called the Register of voters and shall be used at the election of government officers and shall continue to be used untill superseded by a revised registere. And no person shall be entitled to vote at any election whose name is not upon the register of voters. Candidates for the ((office)) post of Government officers shall be nominated in public meeting by the community. Such nomination shall be publicalty notified not less than four days before the day fixed for the election.

d. On a day within 5 days after the 25 of December of each year and at a place and hour of which forty eight hours public notace shall be given by the Chief Magistrate the persons desirous of voting at the election shall repair to the place so notified for the holding thereof and ((and)) there severally (each by itself or taken singly) tender their names to the Recorder (that is the government secretary), who shall be appointed (approved by the Deputy Commissioner) by the Deputy Commissioner to be recorded in favour of the particulars candidate for the posts of Government officers for whom they shall severally (separatly) desire to vote.

e. The Recorder shall be provided with a book in which he shall before the election is held enter each in a separate column the names of the candidates for election. And the particular post for which each has been nominated. And upon a vote being tendered him he shall then and there record the name in the sight of the person who tender it.

f. At nine oclock in the forenoon of the day of election the votes when given shall be counted by the person appointed to receive and record them and the names of the successful candidate by him publically notified.

g. All government officers for the year shall be elected at one and the same time.

Local Laws no 24 and 25 continued from page 90.

Local Laws 24. It having been brought to the notice of the Deputy Commissioner that theft accompanied by burglary is a frequent occurence on Pitcairn Island it is hereby enacted that when there is suspicion that goods stolen are secreted in one or other of the Islanders houses, a written warrant may be issued by the Chief Magistrate for the search of the houses by the Court Police man. such cases are to by tried in the High commissioners court for the W.P.

25. No Pitcairn Islander should board a passing ship until it has been definitly ascertained that no sickness of any kind excists on board.

R. T. SIMON's
*H.M.S. Deputy Commissioner
for Pitcairn Island*
12 of June 1903
Pitcairn Island

REGARDING PROSECUTION IN POLICE CASES.

In the case of a criminal action where there is no prosecutor and it is necessary for the public morals that the case should come into court, the Chief Magistrate should detail the constable or some one outside the case altogether to prosecute in court.

The Chief Magistrate should not prosecute himself as he is judging the case.

Payment for fines may be received in arrowroot or

fungers at the discretion of the Chief Magistrate when the culprit states he is not able to pay in money.

VAUGAN LEWIS
Captain. R.N.
A Deputy Commissioner for the Western Pacific.

Pitcairn Island
7th July. 1909.

Prison Rules.

1. Prisoners are not allowed to communicate with any one outside the prison. And no communication is to take place between prisoners, whilst in their cells.
2. Nothing whatever is allowed to be passed in or out of the prison without permission of the jailer.
3. No food is allowed between meal hours.
4. Prisoners are to keep clean the inside of the prison, and outside near the prison under the supervision of the jailer.
5. No visitors are allowed to visit prisoners without a written permit from the Chief Magistrate and that visit to take place between 4 and 6 P.M. on —— of each week, the visit not to extend beyond 30 minutes. Bible workers may visit at any time providing they have their permit from the Chief Magistrate.
6. Prisoners are not allowed to write letters and no writing material is to be passed in or out of the prison without having been read by the jailer.
7. No one is allowed near the prison unless on business.
8. Prisoners misbehaving themself will be liable to extra imprisonment or loss of food as the court may decide.

VAUGAN LEWIS
Captain R.N.
Deputy commissioner for the Western Pacific.

Prison Routine

hours

6.0   A.M.   Rise—clean out cells, and wash.

6.30 ⎫
to   ⎬ //   Walking exercises—20 paces up and down
7.30 ⎭   with an interval of 4 paces between each prisoner.

7.30.   //   Return to large room.

8.30   //   Breakfast (clean large room)

9.15   //   Muster for labour. Road making & stone breaking, wood cutting, digging, etc.

Noon.   Return to large room.

1.00   P.M.   Muster for labour.

4.0   //   Return to large room and wash.

4.30   //   Tea, clear up large room and remain there.

7.50   //   Prepare bedding and return to their cells.

8.0   //   Lock up cells.

VAUGAN LEWIS
Captain R.N.
Deputy commissioner for the Western Pacific
7th July 1909.

March 15th 1915.

Extract from the Deputy commissioner at
Papeette, Tahitei, last communication for 1913.

It is suggested that before any outside person should be allowed to come and reside on Pitcairn Island that he should have the permission of the Deputy commissioner to come. And also that before coming he should deposit with the Deputy commissioner a sum of money, the money to be forfeited should he have an illegitimate child while resident in Pitcairn. If he should marry the money to be returned to him.

H. A. RICHARD. *Deputy Commissioner*
Papeette.
Tahiti.

no.2. It having been pointed out to me that there is no authority for the detention of an accused persons in serious cases which have to be reported to the High Commissioner's Court it is my direction the Chief Magistrate and assessors is authorized to ensure the necessary confinement.

E. S. S GAUNT
21 July. 1906
Captain and senior Naval Officer

no. 3. Minutes of council of 22nd February 1905, show that it was decided to ask the Deputy Commissioner to extend no. 16, of the local laws so as to allow of the women being employed roofing public buildings.

I am in favour of this, exempting women three month's gone with child, but it is not a matter of urgency and can await the decision of the Deputy Commissioner.

Internal
((Ex))ternal Committe's Regulations

1. The boat and boat house and public trading will be under the control of the ((external)) internal committee who will require men for manning as well as for keeping them in order. ((from the Internal Committee)) [Note: The next sentence is marked "Left Out."] The committee will deal with all affairs from boathouse to ship and ship to boathouse.
2. Suitable men will be appointed ((yearly)) by the committee to act as traders ((and tally)).
3. Public interest will be given preference over private, an exception being made in regard to tithe produce.
4. Goods obtained from passing vessels &c. will be retained for the use of public departments if so needed.
5. a. To Captains
Feb 16th 1917 Should the acting committee consider it best for no women passengers to be in the boats when working for their purpose the coxswain or whoever in

charge of such boats are to submit to the acting committee.

b. That in the matter of overloading and in regard to the carrying or not of any person other than the actual members of the crew, and the Com. representative you are being responsible, in the case of accident, you* shall have full authority whenever the necessity exist, such as bad weather, leaky boats, &c. But in all ordinary circumstances the arrangement of the ((Ex))ternal [Note: Changed to Internal] Committee shall stand, and whenever possible as many as two places are to be available for ((surf)) ship missionaries should such wish for passage.

c. You shall receive a list of public stuff in your boat and you will be responsible for the same until handed over to the committee's representatives. All stuff is in your charge as long as it is in your boat.

d. If on board ship you consider it unsafe to remain longer, the committee's representative and passangers will always be ready to leave at your request; your crew being always subject to your instruction.

In case of emergency, and in cases in which it is not possible to consult a member of the committee for whose purpose the boats are being used ((you)) any capable man [Note:† the words "any capable man" are inserted later in pencil] will act as seem best under the circumstances.

On Sabbath days one boat only will go off to calling ships in the following order—Ella May Longboat, Adelia May clew boat, Surprise Life boat [Note‡: The proper names are inserted later] Any member or crew wishing to be excused from conscientous reasons can make arrangements with the captain of his boat.

[NOTE: The following two sentences are marked "Left

* ("You" is inserted in pencil later.)
† Erasure and last three words inserted later in pencil.
‡ The names inserted later.

out."] No public trading will be conducted by the committee on such dys.

Repairs and alterations to the boats will be effected by the ((Ex))ternal Committee.

It will be the duty of the captains to report to the committee whenever his boat need attention. Captains of boats will have the right to work with the boat builders on their own boats. Small jobs such as repairing of clits, leathering oars etc. will be attended to by the captain and crew.

6 a. To coxswains: Boat's cargoes will be discharged by the watches of the boats in turn under the instruction of the coxswain.

b. The care of the boats when laying along side vessels will devolve upon the crew who will perform this duty in turns under the instruction of the coxswain.

No one who has been left in charge or partial charge of a boat will leave such boat without the sanction of the coxswain.

7. Any person stealing or inciting others to steal or committing any other misdemeanor on board passing ships will be prosecuted before the Local Court by the ((External)) Internal Committee. [Note: The word anyone is later inserted before the word Internal. viz. "by the anyone Internal Committee."]

INTERNAL COMMITTEE REGULATIONS

1. a. All persons liable for public work shall assemble at the Court house within 15 minutes after the ringing of the bell.

b. Men unable from sickness or other reasons to answer the call to public work shall send written notace to the Chairman of the Internal Committee.

c. Any neglect of public work authorized by the Committee; such as sweeping of the road, or neglect to render prompt obediance to lawful demand of overseer will be deemed an offence against these Regulations.

2. a. Any persons using public property shall sweep and

put in order the buildinds and return tools etc. to their appointed places in good order.

b. Refuse from the mill house must be carried beyond the first row of cocoanut tree.

c. The throwing of rubish such as cane or arrowroot refuse ect. in any of the public roads is prohibited.

d. Firewood may be split on public roads when necessary, but persons so doing must clean up the roads after they have finish.

3. a. Any person destroying or interfearing with public property will be prosecuted.

b. Suitable men will be appointed by the Committee to keep the water works in good order and to advise the Committee of any work necessary not within their line of duty.

4. a. No sea bathing will be allowed within the village unless bathers are clothed from neck to knee. Village limits mean from Rocks to Landing inclusive.

b. Bathers in any other parts of the Island must be similarly clothed where there are the two sexes. Cases of immergences are excusable.

5. a. Cruelty, birds ect. is forbidden. The word cruelty means the giving of unnecessary pain or torment.

b. No wild cats, or sparrow are to be destroy except as the Committee may direct.

c. The Noddy may be killed from ((Dec.)) Feb 1 to July 31 and the White birds from Jan 1 to July 31 only.

6. a. ((Goats)), Pigs, horses ((or cows)) will not be allowed to run loose. Any of the above mentioned animals found straying may be driven to the Magerstraits house where the owner shall pay the sum of 1/ before receiving his animal. Half of the above amount is to be given as a reward to the person secureing the straying animal.

7. Any animal or bird, except ((goats)), horses, ((cows)), committing a second depredation the owner having been warned of the first offence may be destroyed. ((Goats)), ((cows)) or horses, committing a

second depredation the owner thereof shall be fined from 5/ to £1 in addition to making good the damage to the one despoiled.

[Note: The two following rules regarding dogs are marked Ammended].

Dogs chasing goats may be killed for the first offence, in the act anywhere. Dogs destroying chickens without their masters must be killed for the first offence.

8. a. The shooting of goats will be allowed outside the following boundaries only: From the bend of the ridge at White Cow pen inland, toward Outer Valley following the same line to William's Block, across the head of Mc-Coys Valley and Taro Ground, from thence along the ridge to the head of Paavala Valley, Itie and Mr. Nobbs cocoanuts. No one is allowed to shoot goats anytime and anywhere on the island for shot.

b. That outside these boundaries bullets may be fired into the air sea and earth only.

c. Persons carlessly shooting with fire arms bows and arrows or throwing stones across the public roads will be prosecuted.

9. a. The committee will appoint suitable men to act as goat masters. One of whom, or of the committee, must either brand or witness the branding of all kids and goats. [Note: The entire last sentence is marked Left out].

b. No one shall chase or catch kids or goats without the sanction of one of the goat masters.

c. No one shall kill kids or goats unless accompanied by two other men. [Note: This sentence is marked Left out].

d. The ears of kids and goats killed must be shown to one of the committee, or goat masters, and to the Gov.-Sec. to be recorded. [Note: This sentence is marked Left out].

10. a. Each family on the Island shall not keep more than ((six)) four breeding nanies.

b. This Reg. was changed by R. T. Simons Dep. Commissioner in the year 1907.

[Note: Original version—]: Families not residing on the Island but expecting to return may have not more than three breeding nannies kept for them the committee being informed of the caretaker's name.

[Note: Altered version—]: Families not residing on the Island have the same privelage to keep four breeding nannies just the same as those on the Island the committee being informed of the caretaker's name.

c. Goats suffering from "Big Bubby" must be either isolated or killed unless heavy with kid; when the goat masters may allow it to remain untill after kiding.

11. a. Persons intending to kill fowls outside village limits shall first give notice to those owning fowls in the same vacinety.

b. [Note: Marked Left out]: Persons killing, selling or in any manner despose of fowls or turkey must present the legs to some one of the members of the government.

12. No one shall plant or erect buildings within one yard of the boundaries of their lands without the written consent of the owner of the adjoinin lands.

13. a. Children under 14 years of age are forbidden to light fires on land except under the supervision of an adult.

b. Any persons lighting fires on lands within five yards of the bounderies without permission of the owner of the adjoining lands; or leaving the fire before it is out, will be held responsible for any damage done by the fire.

14. a. Cocoanuts at Tedside will be gathered under the supervision of one of the committee on such days only as the committee shall appoint.

b. In case of necessity cocoanuts may be picked anytime for drinking purposes.

c. Cocoanuts elsewhere may be picked anytime in company with ((two)) three owners of the same patch.

d. From this date the 4th of May 1914 the gathering of Fungers will be considered as a regulation of the Internal committee, the chopping of sticks bearing fungers for firewood is also prohibited.

Amendment

9. Any person or persons wanting to catch goats must give notice to the Committee and the Committee are to see to the catching of said goats, as decided by the committee.

Amendment

Reg. no 11. Any person or persons killing chickens, if they eat it, they must let the owners or the Chief Magistrate know about it, if they take it in payment for their property.

Amendment

Reg. No 7 Dogs Apr. 1st 1924.

Dogs destroying chickens or goats, the owner of such dogs pay damage for first offence, for second offence the dog or dogs are to be killed. Dogs biting any person without cause are to be killed for first offence.

APPENDIX B

From the *Book of Records* of Pitcairn Island

FAMILY BRANDS IN GOATS
[Note: Selected at random]

THURSDAY CHRISTIAN. Right ear forked. Left ear split.

WM. G. CHRISTIAN. Right ear forked. Two slits in left.

JAMES CHRISTIAN. Both ears split. Back piece on right cut off.

EDWARD CHRISTIAN. Both ears split. Both pieces behind cut off.

PHILIP C. COFFIN. Both ears split. Front piece on left and back piece on right cut off.

VIEDER YOUNG. Right ear cut off. Left ear forked (*nannie*).

Split both ears (*wether*).

[Note: In all about 63 goat brands are recorded]

FAMILY BRANDS IN CHICKENS
[Note: Selected at random]

ROBERT BUFFETT. Right short toe behind, left short toe
inward.
FREDDIE WARREN. Left long toe.
BURLEY WARREN. Two behind toes inside on left leg.
BENJAMIN YOUNG. Inward and long toes on right.
    About 90 chicken brands are recorded.

FAMILY BRANDS IN TREES
[Note: Selected at random]

ALICE BUTLER.	AY
THURSDAY O. CHRISTIAN.	IX
MABEL WARREN.	XII
JAMES WARREN.	XV
ALPHONSO CHRISTIAN.	A+
GERARD CHRISTIAN.	AN
FRED CHRISTIAN.	HM
VIOLA YOUNG.	▷◁
ANDY WARREN.	EN.

    Over 125 tree brands are recorded.

PUBLISHED SOURCES

The following list is appended for those readers who wish to explore the principal sources of information concerning the *Bounty* and the colony on Pitcairn.

BARROW, SIR JOHN. *The Eventful History of the Mutiny and Piratical Seizure of H. M. S. Bounty.* London: 1831. Also in reprints.

BEECHEY, CAPT. F. W. *Narrative of a Voyage to the Pacific and Bering Strait.* London: 1831.

BELCHER, LADY. *The Mutineers of the* Bounty *and Their Descendants in Pitcairn and Norfolk Islands.* London: 1870.

BLIGH, LIEUT. WILLIAM. *A Narrative of the Mutiny on H. M. S. Bounty.* London: 1790.
A Voyage to the South Sea. London: 1792.

BRODIE, WALTER. *Pitcairn Island and the Islanders in 1850.* London: 1851.

FRYER, JOHN. *Journal* (with Bligh, W. *Voyage of the* Bounty's *Launch*). London: 1934.

LUCAS, SIR CHARLES. *The Pitcairn Island Register Book.* London: 1929.

MOERENHOUT, J. A. *Voyages aux Îles du Grand Ocean.* Paris: 1837.

MORRISON, J. *Journal of James Morrison,* boatswain's mate of the *Bounty.* London: 1935.

MURRAY, REV. T. B. *Pitcairn: The Island, the People, and*

the Pastor. First published in 1853 and repeatedly republished.

RUTTER, OWEN. *The Court-Martials of the* Bounty *Mutineers.* Edinburgh: 1931.

SHAPIRO, H. L. *Descendants of the Mutineers of the* Bounty. Bishop Museum, Honolulu: 1929.

SHILLIBEER, LIEUT. J. *A Narrative of the* Briton's *Voyage to Pitcairn Island.* London: 1818.

YOUNG, ROSALIND AMELIA. *Mutiny of the* Bounty *and Story of Pitcairn Island, 1790–1894.* Oakland, California: 1894.

INDEX

ABOUT THE AUTHOR

HARRY L. SHAPIRO is Chairman of the Department of Anthropology and Curator of Physical Anthropology at The American Museum of Natural History. He is also Adjunct Professor of Anthropology at Columbia University. Born in Boston, Massachusetts, in 1902, he graduated *magna cum laude* in 1923 from Harvard University, where he also received his A.M. and Ph.D.

Dr. Shapiro's major research has been in the fields of physical anthropology, human biology, and the study of race mixture and population. He has been particularly interested in the South Pacific, having conducted studies in Norfolk Island, Tahiti, the Marquesas, and Hawaii. The Hall of the Biology of Man, which opened at The American Museum of Natural History in 1961, was conceived and supervised by Dr. Shapiro.

A Thaw Fellow and Tutor in Anthropology at Harvard from 1924 to 1926, he was appointed Research Professor at the University of Hawaii from 1930 to 1935, began teaching at Columbia University in 1938, and has been professor there since 1942.

A Fellow of the National Academy of Sciences, Dr. Shapiro is also a member of the American Anthropological Association (of which he was president in 1948), the American Association of Physical Anthropology, the American Eugenics Society (of which he is president), and the American Ethnological Society. He was formerly chairman of the Anthropology Section of the New York Academy of Sciences.

Dr. Shapiro's books include: *The Heritage of the Bounty* (1936), *Migration and Environment* (1939), *Race Mixture* (published by UNESCO in 1953), *Aspects of Culture* (1957), and *The Jewish People, A Biological History* (1961); he has edited *Man, Culture, and Society* (1956).